Strategic Human Resources Management in Schools

Strategic Human Resources Management in Schools provides a new approach to human resources management, grounded in the perspectives of cutting-edge practice, research, and theory. Traditional human resource (HR) practices in education have operated in an isolated and reactionary manner; this book explores an updated version of personnel administration that links strategic human resources to organizational goals, educational mission, educator well-being, and student success. Coverage includes exemplar strategic HR practices from progressive organizations and leading companies, discussion of tricky issues like discrimination and implicit bias, and developmental and humanistic support of teachers as well as support staff, including paraprofessionals, food service workers, and bus drivers. The Talent-Centered Education Leadership (TCEL) model presented in this book explores how educational leaders can create a nurturing and inclusive workplace for all educational staff, which is ultimately critical for improvement in student learning and strengthening recruitment and retention of a quality education workforce. Designed for aspiring leaders, this volume is grounded in the Professional Standards for Educational Leaders (PSEL) and National Educational Leadership Preparation (NELP) Building and District Level standards and is full of rich pedagogical features including cases, "warning boxes" to explore areas particularly thorny to navigate, questions for discussion, and various learning activities.

Henry Tran is Associate Professor of Educational Leadership at the University of South Carolina, USA and the Editor of the *Journal of Education Human Resources.*

Carolyn Kelley is the Jim and Georgia Thompson Distinguished Professor of Education at the University of Wisconsin-Madison, USA.

PSEL/NELP LEADERSHIP PREPARATION SERIES

Series Editors: Michelle Young and Rose M. Ylimaki

The New Instructional Leadership
ISLLC Standard Two
Edited by Rose M. Ylimaki

Political Contexts of Educational Leadership
ISLLC Standard Six
Edited by Jane Clark Lindle

Developing Ethical Principles for School Leadership
PSEL Standard Two
Edited by Lisa Bass, William Frick, and Michelle Young

Leading Continuous Improvement in Schools
Enacting Leadership Standards to Advance Educational Quality and Equity
By Erin Anderson, Kathleen M.W. Cunningham, and David Eddy-Spicer

Strategic Human Resources Management in Schools
Talent-Centered Education Leadership
By Henry Tran and Carolyn Kelley

For more information about this series, please visit: www.routledge.com/PSELNELP-Leadership-Preparation/book-series/PSEL

Strategic Human Resources Management in Schools

Talent-Centered Education Leadership

Henry Tran and Carolyn Kelley

NEW YORK AND LONDON

Designed cover image: © Getty Images

First published 2024
by Routledge
605 Third Avenue, New York, NY 10158

and by Routledge
4 Park Square, Milton Park, Abingdon, Oxon, OX14 4RN

Routledge is an imprint of the Taylor & Francis Group, an informa business

ISBN: 978-1-032-59974-8 (hbk)
ISBN: 978-1-032-59801-7 (pbk)
ISBN: 978-1-003-45706-0 (ebk)

DOI: 10.4324/9781003457060

Typeset in Aldus and Helvetica Neue
by Apex CoVantage, LLC

This book is a co-publication of Routledge and the University Council for Educational Administration - UCEA.

We dedicate this book to teachers and school leaders that devote themselves to making schools great.

Contents

Series Editor Introduction

The Importance of Talent-Centered Education Leadership

Over the past few decades, educational research has highlighted the crucial role of principal leadership in school improvement and has advanced our understanding of specific leadership practices that make a difference. Studies have identified common leadership domains in which principals spend their time, including administration, instructional leadership, internal and external relations, and teachers' professional development (Lee, 2021).

In November 2015, the Professional Standards for Educational Leaders (PSEL), previously known as the Interstate School Leaders Licensure Consortium (ISLLC) standards, were approved by the National Policy Board for Educational Administration (NPBEA). Grounded in current research and leadership experience, these standards outline the knowledge and skills expected of educational leaders (Canole & Young, 2013; CCSSO, 1996, 2008). The 2015 PSEL standards place a strong emphasis on students and student learning, outlining foundational principles of leadership to ensure that each child receives a high-quality education and is prepared for the 21st century (CCSSO, 2015, p. 2). These standards are student-centric, guiding educational leaders in their practice to improve student learning outcomes and promote equity (CCSSO, 2015, p. 1). The 2015 PSEL standards encompass various leadership domains, including Mission, Vision, and Improvement; Ethics and Professional Norms; Equity and Cultural Responsiveness; Curriculum, Instruction, and Assessment; Community of Care and Support for Students; Professional Capacity of School Personnel; Professional Community for Teachers and Staff; Meaningful Engagement of Families and Community; Operations and Management; and School Improvement.

As a companion to the PSEL standards, the National Educational Leadership Preparation (NELP) standards were developed to guide leadership preparation programs in designing curriculum, pedagogy, and clinical experiences that prepare aspiring leaders to effectively assume their roles (NPBEA, 2018). Educational leadership preparation programs play a critical role in equipping leaders with the necessary tools and competencies to excel in their roles. This book series, aligned with both the NELP and PSEL standards, serves as a valuable resource for educational leadership preparation faculty and students, connecting the standards to research and practice. The series highlights the specific knowledge and skills essential for effective leadership, such as working collaboratively with others, using multiple sources of data, and making informed decisions, and provides guidance on how to work effectively with others, use multiple sources of data, and make sound decisions, among other critical functions.

Throughout the books in this series, authors provide opportunities for aspiring leaders to engage in practical work and consider diverse perspectives on authentic problems of practice, including those of students, teachers, parents, administrators, and community members. Through real-world scenarios, case studies, and problem-based learning, aspiring leaders can develop their abilities in understanding and addressing complex challenges with various stakeholders.

This particular volume introduces Talent-Centered Education Leadership as a new framework for human resources in today's schools. Tran and Kelley draw on research, practice, and theory to expand our thinking about the ways in which people are managed in educational organizations.

The volume offers principles and guidance for school and system leaders that support both equitable student needs and teacher working conditions. In so doing, Tran and Kelley offer theory, research, and practical strategies to achieve school personnel goals as outlined in the Professional Standards for Educational Leadership (PSEL) and the National Educational Leadership Program (NELP) standards.

The volume is organized into ten chapters that examine the tenets of Talent-Centered Education Leadership, including working conditions for staff excellence and reducing teacher turnover, talent motivation, planning for recruitment and retention, employee hiring, teacher induction, professional development and coaching, communities of practice, performance appraisals, and teacher leadership development. Each chapter provides an overview and rationale for a particular aspect of Talent-Centered Education Leadership as well as strategies for effective implementation. Chapters provide case studies and discussion questions that can be used in courses for aspiring leaders as well as professional development.

Tran and Kelley have articulated a new and exciting framework for Talent-Centered Education Leadership with resources to address two of the most pressing issues in education today: teacher turnover and equitable student success in schools. The book is intentionally organized to provide knowledge, skills, and powerful learning strategies for effective leadership that are grounded in Talent-Centered Leadership and meet the aims of PSEL and NELP.

Rose M. Ylimaki and Michelle D. Young

REFERENCES

Canole, M., & Young, M. D. (2013). *Standards for educational leaders: An analysis.* Council of Chief State School Officers.

Council of Chief State School Officers (CCSSO). (1996). *The interstate school leaders licensure consortium: Standards for school leaders.* Author.

Council of Chief State School Officers (CCSSO). (2008). *Educational leadership policy standards: ISLLC 2008.* Author.

Council of Chief State School Officers (CCSSO). (2015). *Professional Standards for Educational Leaders* (PSEL). Author.

NPBEA. (2018). *National Educational Leadership Preparation (NELP) program recognition standards building level.* www.npbea.org

Acknowledgments

We would like to thank Drs. Rose M. Ylimaki and Michelle D. Young for their invitation to take the journey to share our work in hopes of advancing the field of education human resources management. We also thank Dr. David G. Buckman and Dr. Carmen Bartley for their research support, and especially for their contributions to Chapter 5 and Chapter 8 respectively. Finally, we would like to thank our families for their unwavering support in our lives.

CONFLICT OF INTEREST STATEMENT

Carolyn Kelley has an ownership interest in the Comprehensive Assessment of Leadership for Learning, which supports leadership development in schools.

Preface

Strategic Human Resources Management in Schools: Talent-Centered Education Leadership

BOOK PREMISE

This volume provides a new approach to strategic education human resources management that is grounded in the perspectives of cutting-edge practice, research, and theory. Traditional human resource practices in education have operated in a reactionary manner, with a focus on "putting out fires" (Weick, 1996). Under such a personnel philosophy, each human resource activity is addressed independently and in isolation (Tran, 2015). A more updated version of personnel administration focuses on strategic human resources or capital management, with human resource activities linked to organizational goals (i.e., primarily interpreted as student achievement test score gains) (Odden, 2011). Yet how this approach has been implemented has been utilitarian in nature, where members of the workforce are utilized as human *resources* in service of achieving their employer's goals, without any consideration for the employee's own goals and internal motivation. The approach instead opts to focus primarily on oversimplified "carrot-and-stick" forms of rewards and punishment to motivate teachers. Furthermore, how this approach has been implemented has resulted in an overemphasis of meeting the goal post (e.g., improvement in how the accountability metrics look) rather than goals of schooling, while promoting a simultaneous dehumanization and de-professionalization of teaching that has motivated a recent wave of massive state-level teacher walk-outs and teacher shortages across the nation (Apple, 2009; Tran & Smith, 2019, 2022).

While these corporate education reform efforts purport to encourage the adoption of business practices in schools, they rely on an outdated industrial manufacturing style model for their human resource practices (Altman, 2013). These practices espouse what has been traditionally referred to as a *Theory X* management philosophy, which emphasizes accountability and a penal model of school reform, as opposed to a *Theory Y or Theory Z* strategic HR management philosophy as practiced by most progressive "greatest place to work"[1] companies (e.g., Google, Meta, AirBnB). Modern strategic human resource practices as utilized by these companies emphasize teamwork, collaboration, employee empowerment, respect, development, and flexibility as opposed to individualism, competition, privileging, and punishment by ranking of employees. They also provide resources and effort into the intentional design of a supportive employee experience for their workforce.

Consequently, this volume promotes the Talent-Centered Education Leadership (TCEL) model (Tran, 2022), which adds value to the aforementioned models by strategically linking human resource activities to accomplish the educational mission based on the talent-driven foundational goal of creating a great workplace. Creating a great workplace for employees has implications for improving the work culture that is critical for improvement in student learning and strengthening recruitment and retention of a quality education workforce. A TCEL approach to human resources management is based on the philosophy of inclusive talent management, which recognizes that a *one-size-fits-all* perspective for dealing with employees cannot possibly be optimal for everyone and that each individual should be recognized and supported as the "whole person" they are. This is particularly critical as the workforce becomes increasingly diverse and workplace inclusion becomes a legitimate interest of employers.

Figure 0.1 provides a brief overview of the evolution of education human resources management.

Furthermore, although we are critical of how outdated industrialized manufacturing business models inspired by Henry Ford and Frederick Winslow Taylor (Altman, 2013; Au, 2011) have been applied to education, we do believe there are strategies that school districts can learn from successful and progressive noneducation organizations. These progressive organizations operate with an "employer of choice" strategy (Hinkin & Tracey, 2010) that relies on the foundation of professional respect, teamwork, employee recognition, development, and empowerment.

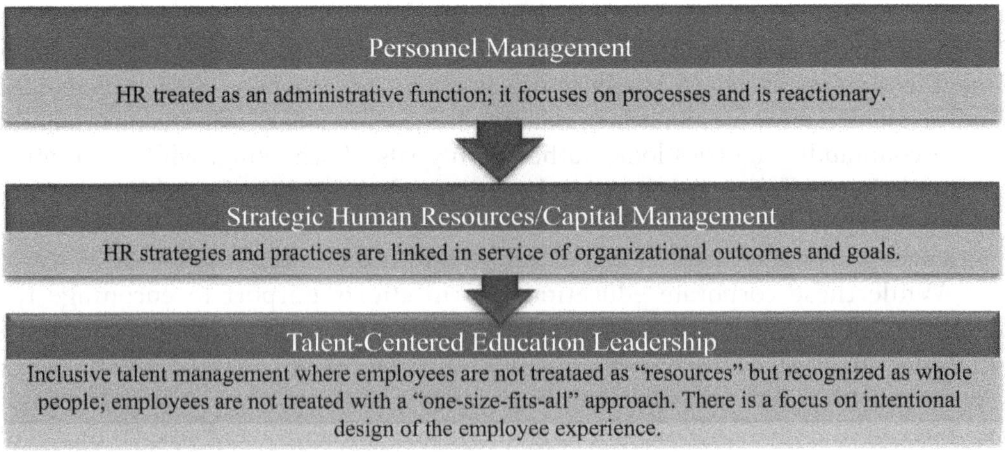

Personnel Management

HR treated as an administrative function; it focuses on processes and is reactionary.

Strategic Human Resources/Capital Management

HR strategies and practices are linked in service of organizational outcomes and goals.

Talent-Centered Education Leadership

Inclusive talent management where employees are not treataed as "resources" but recognized as whole people; employees are not treated with a "one-size-fits-all" approach. There is a focus on intentional design of the employee experience.

Figure 0.1 Evolution of Education Human Resources Management

THE IMPORTANT ROLE OF THE SCHOOL LEADER FOR TALENT-CENTERED EDUCATION LEADERSHIP

A key element of building a great workplace is talent development, and the school principal can be thought of as a human capital developer (Donaldson, 2013), supporting and building the capacity of teachers, which will, in turn, improve their confidence and, consequently, their retention and performance (as reflected in various metrics including student achievement). The principal is instrumental in helping develop a culture that is a "great place to work."

Consequently, we draw on progressive talent management questions practiced by successful businesses and noneducation organizations to put new meaning to practicing education human resources through the framework of a "business model," specifically one that moves away from a standardized product focus to one that emphasizes value and care for its employees, a humanistic framework compatible with education. This is the bedrock of TCEL.

The text is grounded across the strands of the new Professional Standards for Educational Leaders (PSEL) and National Educational Leadership Preparation (NELP) Building and District Level standards, with particular focus on PSEL Standard 6 (Professional Capacity of School Personnel), NELP Building Level Standard 7 (Building Professional Capacity) and NELP District Level Standard 6 (Operations and Management). As leadership related to human resources management affects the whole organization, the book will also address aspects of other PSEL standards, including PSEL Standards 1 (Mission, Vision and Core Values), 3 (Equity and Cultural Responsiveness), 7 (Professional Community for Teachers and Staff), 9 (Operations and Management) and 10 (School Improvement) as they relate to the strategic talent management process.

Table 0.1 provides a crosswalk aligning each chapter with the primary PSEL and NELP building- and district-level standards:

Table 0.1 Crosswalk of Chapters and PSEL and NELP Building and District Level Standards

Chapters	*Relationship to PSEL Standards*	*Relationship to NELP Building Level Standards*	*Relationship to NELP District Level Standards*
Chapter 1: Introduction to Talent-Centered Education Leadership	Standard 6	Standard 2.1 Standard 7	Standard 4.2 Standard 6.3
Chapter 2: Optimizing Working Conditions for School Staff Excellence	Standard 6h Standard 6i	Standard 7.2	Standard 2.1
Chapter 3: Talent Motivation	Standard 6f	Standard 7.2	Standard 6.1

(*Continued*)

Table 0.1 (Continued)

Chapters	*Relationship to PSEL Standards*	*Relationship to NELP Building Level Standards*	*Relationship to NELP District Level Standards*
Chapter 4: Planning for Talent Needs: Recruitment and Retention	Standard 6a Standard 6b	Standard 7.1	Standard 6.3
Chapter 5: Selection	Standard 6a	Standard 7.1	Standard 6.3
Chapter 6: Induction	Standard 6b	Standard 7.1	Standard 6.3
Chapter 7: Professional Development and Coaching	Standard 6c	Standard 7.3 Standard 7.4	Standard 4.2
Chapter 8: Communities of Practice	Standard 6d	Standard 7.2	Standard 2.1
Chapter 9: Performance Appraisal	Standard 6e	Standard 7.4	Standard 4.4
Chapter 10: Teacher Leadership Development	Standard 6g	Standard 7.3	Standard 6.3

Given that teachers and principals are inequitably distributed across school types (Fuller et al., 2017), special attention will be paid to addressing human resource barriers in impoverished rural and urban contexts to maximize the opportunities of placing effective educators in the presence of all students regardless of their geographic residence. We will consider how school leaders can create employee experience programs that are needed to motivate and engage employees in different working conditions.

Figure 0.2 displays a visual for the concept framework for the book.

The chapters are organized according to the conceptual framework as follows:

Part 1 *Setting the Stage for a Great Workplace*

Chapter 1: Introduction to Talent-Centered Education Leadership
Chapter 2: Optimizing Working Conditions for School Staff Excellence
Chapter 3: Talent Motivation

Part 2 *Getting the Right People*

Chapter 4: Planning for Talent Needs: Recruitment and Retention
Chapter 5: Selection

Figure 0.2 Framework of the Book

Part 3 *Building Human Capacity*

Chapter 6: Induction
Chapter 7: Professional Development and Coaching
Chapter 8: Communities of Practice
Chapter 9: Performance Appraisal
Chapter 10: Teacher Leadership Development

Each chapter includes:

- Definitions of relevant terms and discussion of the associated topics from a strategic talent management perspective
- Samples of exemplar strategic HR practices from progressive organizations in education and from leading companies
- Alignment of chapter topics to the relevant PSEL standards within each chapter
- A "warning box" to aspiring school leader candidates for areas particularly susceptible to implicit bias/discrimination/antithetical influence on diversity
- "Managing up" case studies that address how principals can work with the district office or impact district policy to address chapter-related issues
- "When it's not rosy" case studies with discussion questions for students to consider how to address chapter-related issues in less-than-ideal circumstances

- Additional learning activities that connect research to practice, such as case examples with discussion questions, applications, and field assignments
- Key highlights at the conclusion of each chapter

CONCLUSION

Increasingly, research has suggested that toxic workplaces can have harmful consequences for employees. For example, teacher burnout has been associated not only with student physiological stress (Oberle & Schonert-Reichl, 2016), but teachers' states of depression have also been found to be linked to student well-being (Harding et al., 2019). To what degree the teacher outcomes are negative depends on how supportive the work environment and leadership are. Specifically, poor and toxic leadership has been linked with psychological conditions like anxiety and depression (Bender & Farvolden, 2008) as well as health conditions such as serious cardiac conditions (e.g., heart attack) (Nyberg et al., 2009). Therefore, it is not surprising that the perception of poor or ineffective leadership has been identified as the strongest factor influencing to teachers' intention to leave their positions (Ladd, 2011). Teachers risk a lot to themselves by staying in a work environment that is unsupportive, unhealthy, and even toxic.

Ultimately, employers that demonstrate a TCEL approach to employee management are able to avoid many of the aforementioned negative employee consequences and outcomes. The benefits they reap include a workforce that is not only happier and healthier but also more engaged, higher performing, and more likely to stay. These employers accomplish this by demonstrating a commitment to the people and humanity of the organization. They not only avoid micromanaging their workforce, but are also proactive with attending to employee needs, empowerment, and work-life balance. Moreover, they display empathetic leadership and value each and every person in the institution. In the context of the "Great Resignation" (i.e., a labor environment experiencing recent record high rates of turnover) (Tessema et al., 2022) and massive educator staffing challenges across the nation (Tran & Smith, 2022), being Talent-Centered is no longer a luxury for employers but a necessity. This book provides the science and guidance to help leaders develop that perspective to encourage those practices.

NOTE

1 As identified by Fortune list.

REFERENCES

Altman, S. (2013). The bad business of education reform. *Edushyster.* http://edushyster.com/the-bad-business-of-education-reform/

Apple, M. W. (2009). Education, markets, and an audit culture. *Critical Quarterly, 47*(1–2), 11–29. https://onlineli brary.wiley.com/doi/abs/10.1111/j.0011- 1562.2005.00611.x

Au, W. (2011). Teaching under the new Taylorism: High-stakes testing and the standardization of the 21st century curriculum. *Journal of Curriculum Studies, 43*(1), 25–45.

Bender, A., & Farvolden, P. (2008). Depression and the workplace: A progress report. *Current Psychiatry Reports, 10*(1), 73–79.

Donaldson, M. L. (2013). Principals' approaches to cultivating teacher effectiveness constraints and opportunities in hiring, assigning, evaluating, and developing teachers. *Educational Administration Quarterly, 49*, 838–882.

Fuller, E. J., Hollingworth, L., & Pendola, A. (2017). The Every Student Succeeds Act, state efforts to improve access to effective educators, and the importance of school leadership. *Educational Administration Quarterly, 53*(5), 727–756.

Harding, S., Morris, R., Gunnell, D., Ford, T., Hollingworth, W., Tilling, K., Evans, R., Bell, S., Grey, J., Brockman, R., Campbell, R., Araya, R., Murphy, S., & Kidger, J. (2019). Is teachers' mental health and wellbeing associated with students' mental health and wellbeing? *Journal of Affective Disorders, 242*, 180–187.

Hinkin, T. R., & Tracey, J. B. (2010). What makes it so great? An analysis of human resources practices among Fortune's best companies to work for. *Cornell Hospitality Quarterly, 51*(2), 158–170.

Ladd, H. F. (2011). Teachers' perceptions of their working conditions. *Educational Evaluation and Policy Analysis, 33*(2), 235–261.

Lee, M. (2021). Principals' time use as a research area: Notes on theoretical perspectives, leadership domains, and future directions. In: Moosung Lee, Katina Polluck and Pierre Tulowitzki (Eds.), *How school principals use their time* (pp. 9–21). Routledge.

Nyberg, A., Alfredsson, L., Theorell, T., Westerlund, H., Vahtera, J., & Kivimäki, M. (2009). Managerial leadership and ischaemic heart disease among employees: The Swedish WOLF study. *Occupational and Environmental Medicine, 66*(1), 51–55.

Oberle, E., & Schonert-Reichl, K. A. (2016). Stress contagion in the classroom? The link between classroom teacher burnout and morning cortisol in elementary school students. *Social Science & Medicine, 159*, 30–37.

Odden, A. R. (2011). *Strategic management of human capital in education: Improving instructional practice and student learning in schools*. Routledge.

Tessema, M. T., Tesfom, G., Faircloth, M. A., Tesfagiorgis, M., & Teckle, P. (2022). The "great resignation": Causes, consequences, and creative HR management strategies. *Journal of Human Resource and Sustainability Studies, 10*(1), 161–178.

Tran, H. (2015). Personnel vs. strategic human resource management in public education. *Management in Education, 29*(3), 112–118.

Tran, H. (2022). Revolutionizing school HR strategies and practices to reflect talent centered education leadership. *Leadership and Policy in Schools, 21*(2), 238–252.

Tran, H., & Smith, D. (2019). Insufficient money and inadequate respect: What obstructs the recruitment of college students to teach in hard-to-staff schools. *Journal of Educational Administration, 57*(2), 152–166.

Tran, H., & Smith, D. A. (2022). *How did we get here? The decay of the teaching profession*. IAP-Information Age Publishing, Inc.

Weick, K. E. (1996). Fighting fires in educational administration. *Educational Administration Quarterly, 32*(4), 565–578.

PART 1

Setting the Stage for a Great Workplace

CHAPTER 1

Introduction to Talent-Centered Education Leadership

Chapter Summary

This chapter introduces a motivational education talent management framework known as Talent-Centered Education Leadership. The chapter draws on research, practice, and theory to both evolve thinking about the way people are managed in education and to provide guidance for aspiring and current school leaders that can be used today to enhance the academic work environment. As supplementary material, this chapter presents a case study and discussion questions for readers to consider.

Effective educational leaders develop the professional capacity and practice of school personnel to promote each student's academic success and well-being.

(PSEL Standard 6: Professional Capacity of School Personnel)

INTRODUCTION

In the past few decades, education reforms have significantly shifted school research and policy attention to student learning outcomes, typically measured by standardized test scores. In the interest of equalizing educational outcomes, teachers have been at the center of a system that expects a) all students to learn at high levels (as seen through the philosophy undergirding federal efforts such as the *No Child Left Behind* law) and b) teachers to be responsible for ensuring that students learn. Some argue that the policy changes and the way these reforms have been enacted have de-professionalized teaching and have placed

DOI: 10.4324/9781003457060-2

significant pressure on teachers, too, often without adequate support or recognition (Pawlewicz, 2020). Given the obvious importance of student learning outcomes, organizational and policymaking attention in education is usually directed at meeting student needs. Unfortunately, it is often done at the neglect of addressing the needs of teachers.

As former South Carolina educator Sariah McCall noted in her publicly shared resignation letter to the Charleston County School District (Strauss, 2019),

> I cannot set myself on fire to keep someone else warm. . . . The unrealistic demands and all-consuming nature of the [teaching] profession are not sustainable. I am still a human being. There was no time to be a functioning human being and give this job all the attention and love it deserves. This career with its never-ending list of "extra duties and responsibilities" that we are not given the resources for completing. I cannot let a career dictate and demand all of me for another minute, and I will not be bullied into continuing to do so out of misguided guilt for possibly neglecting the children. It is unrealistic to expect this much from people. We're teachers, but we're still people.

The parallel to the overemphasis on student needs to the detriment of teacher needs in the private sector would be businesses that focus the entirety or majority of their attention and efforts on external customers to the neglect of their employees. Most progressive organizations have evolved beyond that approach (Gallup, 2018), realizing that organizational performance suffers when workforce needs are not attended to. In fact, the latest trend in the broader field of human resources management has adapted design thinking and prior emphases on customer experience to introduce an employee experience (EEX) approach to talent management (Mahadevan & Schmitz, 2020). Just like companies collect data to inform their decision-making to customize experiences for their customers, the EEX approach to talent management is similarly based on iterative testing and data-informed decision-making based on employee feedback and ideas in a bottom-up process that promotes a human-centered organizational learning culture (Tran & Smith, 2020b). The field of education would do well to learn from this change, with an understanding that addressing both teacher and student needs mutually support one another (Tran, 2020). Case in point, addressing student needs (e.g., providing food for those who are hungry) removes barriers for teachers in the execution of their job duties given that students can better focus on learning in class when their basic needs are met, and addressing teacher needs similarly allows teachers to better focus on tending to their students without being concerned with dealing with outside distractions (e.g., unreasonable parental demands and criticisms, inadequate compensation to pay the rent or mortgage).

Unfortunately, instead of bridging the divide, student issues are often framed in opposition to teacher needs. For example, in 2018 and 2019, we witnessed a historic movement of teacher activism that resulted in a wave of teacher strikes that rippled across the United States (Tran & Smith, 2019). While the reasons that teachers and supporters marched varied (e.g., inadequate funding, low teacher pay, insufficient resources), the movement was undergirded by a common focus on addressing the perennial and pervasive pattern of unfavorable teacher working conditions. These conditions have contributed to what some are calling a "national teacher shortage," with recent estimates suggesting the nation was short approximately 112,000 teachers in response to labor demand, with an additional 109,000 employed individuals uncertified for their positions (Sutcher et al., 2019). The high turnover stems from poor working conditions, low pay, and a lack of support. Unfortunately, these occurrences have left scores of students in oversized classrooms, many with unqualified teachers. Instead of supporting teachers in their endeavors to improve their working conditions, opponents criticized teachers for their efforts by claiming that they were harming and betraying students by being out of the classrooms (Finne, 2018). The then U.S. secretary of education, Betsy Devos, specifically called out teachers for pursuing their own interests and neglecting student needs by being out of the classroom (Reilly, 2018). To make matters worse, teachers were also threatened with punishment and lawsuits for exercising their voices and agency in their activism (Roberts, 2018; Vyse, 2019).

The teacher versus student rhetoric persists despite consistent evidence that demonstrates that what teachers were asking for in their walkouts has direct benefits for student outcomes. Kraft and Papay (2014), for instance, found that over a ten-year time frame, schools with stronger professional work environments (those that include more support and collaboration) experienced stronger improvements (i.e., 38% increase) in their students' end-of-year math test scores than teachers in schools with weaker work environments. Similarly, school funding has been linked with student outcomes (Baker, 2012; Verstegen & King, 1998). Relatedly, low salaries have been found to be predictive of teacher turnover (Nguyen et al., 2020), which has been linked to a negative disruptive effect on student achievement (Ronfeldt et al., 2013). In sum, teachers are the core value providers of schools, and schools can only succeed if teachers are well-trained and well-supported and are viewed as critical organizational assets. This is one of the primary reasons why building leadership capacity is essential for education.

In the last few decades, American public schools have operated in an era of accountability, ushered in by the *Nation at Risk* report (1983) that publicized concerns about their performance relative to their international peers and solidified by the federal *No Child Left Behind* (2001) legislation that brought to them "high stakes" compliance-oriented work environments. This era saw the promulgation of policies and practices that relied heavily on rewards and punishments to motivate teachers towards achieving preferential outcomes, which in this case primarily took the form of raising student test scores on standardized achievement exams (Ford et al., 2018). This emphasis on hierarchical control and conformity prescribed how teachers should be teachers (in fact, there existed "teaching scripts" that were promoted to ensure teachers "stick to the script"), which usually resulted in limiting teacher creativity, autonomy, and innovation. Organizational theorists have referred to this as a Theory X management approach, which relies on external stimuli such as rewards and penalties for employee control, in contrast to a Theory Y management approach, which motivates by tapping into employee's self-interest in work and their internal desire to self-direct (McGregor, 1960). While Theory X–style management was the standard human resource management (HRM) approach for businesses in the 1950s, it has become increasingly unpopular with "most business schools normally teach[ing] a more Theory Y approach to management" (Gannon & Boguszak, 2013, p. 86).

BOX 1.1: MANAGING UP: SCHOOL AND HRM PARTNERSHIP

While a Theory Y management approach has its benefits, its emphasis is restricted to the individual manager (McGregor, 1960). Instead, TCEL is grounded in a Theory Z approach that addresses the management philosophy of the entire organization. While it demonstrates concern for organizational performance, it is also deeply attentive to the holistic (i.e., professional and personal) welfare of its workers (Ouchi & Cuchi, 1981).

Theory Z–oriented organizations show loyalty to their workers by providing them with appreciation, care, and support, and, in turn, this inspires loyalty back from employees who work hard and excel. Theory Z emphasizes a collective perspective based on organizational engagement, participation, and collaboration where employees have input towards affecting changes that will impact them, and all the organization's stakeholders work in tandem to contribute to its success.

Although influential, school leaders alone are limited in how they can affect the macro employer culture and organizational management philosophy. In that regard, district HRM can serve as a powerful ally to school administrators. It is important that district and school leaders have a strong partnership because HRM is not the sole responsibility of HRM professionals. Rather, it is most effectively conducted when HRM and line managers, such as school principals, are harmonized with respect to the organization's human resources vision (Currie & Procter, 2001). For example, district HRM can develop clear procedures and provide substantive information to school-level administrators to enhance school performance. In fact, HRM-developed detailed evaluation rubrics have served as valuable tools for principals to help them focus on what matters when conducting performance evaluations, supporting teacher development, and reducing subjectivity in the process (Neumerski et al., 2018). Working with the district, structured rubrics can be developed to enhance the predictive validity of the evaluation process towards outcomes that are valued by the school community. The district office can also train principals on how to communicate the mechanics of assessment scores so that the principals can clearly explain to teachers how their scores were calculated in order to create transparency (and therefore trust) in the process. A clear plan for how teachers should respond to the evaluation can lend itself to the provision of meaningful feedback for teachers. Even when accounting for school characteristics and teacher working conditions, teachers are more satisfied when they perceive their evaluation experiences to be more supportive (especially when they feel their evaluations have resulted in positive changes in practice) (Ford et al., 2018).

Education reformers that draw on the rhetoric of business comparisons in their support of the aforementioned accountability-oriented policies are actually not inspired by the latest HRM trends but, instead, root their efforts in an "outmoded and discredited economic model of reform" (Giroux & Saltman, 2009, p. 776). After historically creating a system where humanity was largely designed out of workplaces (e.g., through factory-style paradigms, automation, and treating employees as organizational cogs), "[t]oday organizations around the world are trying to figure out how they have to redesign themselves to focus more on people . . . more on humans" (Morgan, 2017, p. xxi). In a *Forbes* article on the future of work, Towers-Clark (2019) identified the trends of increasing organizational transparency and anti-hierarchy, and observed,

> we are seeing a greater focus on equal rights for all employees, flexible and considerate schedules and company structures, and a far greater emphasis on accountability around poor working conditions. Cut-throat business practices are becoming less and less acceptable under the vigilant eye of social media, and this can only be a good thing for workers of all descriptions.
> (para 7–8)

Yet in the last several decades, education seems to have been moving in the opposite direction. Ford et al. (2018) explain that the psychic rewards that initially attracted many to the teaching profession have been increasingly diminished by the way the work of the teaching profession changed due to external accountability pressures and the internal organizational responses to them. These changes include the lack of corresponding support for teachers to help navigate ever-increasing work demands, ongoing assault on teacher professionalism and autonomy, low respect for the profession and those in it, and insufficient relative pay when compared to those in professions with similar education and training (Tran & Smith, 2019). Uncoincidentally, most parents in the country do not want their children to become teachers and their children typically concur (Phi Delta Kappa, 2018). This negative perception of the teaching profession has been reflected in enrollment declines in teacher preparation programs and significant rates of turnover from those in the profession (Garcia & Weiss, 2019). It seems the nobility that was once associated with being a teacher has faded for many.

WHY IS A NEW APPROACH TO EDUCATION HRM NEEDED?

To understand the need for a new approach to education HRM, it is useful to revisit how HRM has evolved across occupations, and in education specifically. Morgan (2017) describes the evolution of HRM in four distinct phases. The first and earliest phase focused on utility, that is, employers provided the basic resources for employees to do the job, but there was limited attention paid to employee needs and well-being beyond that. The second phase was heavily influenced by the work of early theorists like Frederick Winslow Taylor and Henri Fayol and emphasized productivity. It treated employees with a factory assembly line approach in the pursuit of how to get employees to be the most productive possible with streamlined processes and scientific management (Taylor, 2004). In the third phase, employers realized that they could affect how employees feel about their work and those affective reactions to work mattered for organizational outcomes such as employee retention and performance. Consequently, they increased their reliance on surveys to capture employee feedback and began to prioritize employee engagement to focus more on what employees care about instead of a pure focus on employee contributions to organizational productivity. In this phase, there was increased attention paid to organizational culture, such as investing in corporate culture programs, work flexibility and perks, or other engagement initiatives to increase the appeal of the workplace. Finally, in the modern progressive phase (where some employers are beginning to head), organizations work to intentionally design an employee experience where their workers *want* to (as opposed to *need* to) engage with their work (Morgan, 2017). It is a more systemic and longer-term approach than the HRM strategies in the earlier phases. Of the four phases, education has primarily operated within the earlier two realms.

Traditional human resource (HR) practices in education have often operated in a reactionary and transactional manner, with a focus on "putting out fires" (Weick, 1996), conformity to rules, and compliance with bureaucratic policies. Under such a *personnel management* philosophy, each HR activity is typically addressed independently and in isolation (Tran, 2015). Practices such as teacher observations for evaluations were often conducted to comply with administrative mandates, rather than as a resource to identify effective and ineffective teachers, let alone to substantively improve instruction (Kraft & Gilmour, 2017).

Odden (2011) and his colleagues provided a more updated version of that philosophy that focuses on *strategic human capital management*, with HR activities linked to organizational goals (i.e., primarily student achievement test score gains) (Odden, 2011). This was an important step towards evolving HRM in education, and it aligns with HR being seen more as a "business partner" to core operations in the broader HR field (Mahadevan & Schmitz, 2020). Odden rightly recognized that HRM in education was not connected to the broader organizational goals of schools and often worked at cross-purposes with student learning and development. His efforts to think strategically about human capital management focused on recognizing the important role that teachers play and how to think across HR systems to align their goals and create clear signals to teachers about what the organization values and, by extension, how teachers should spend their time. From this second phase of education HRM thinking and advances in its related research, much more clarity was provided concerning "effective" evidence-based practices, but there were also many challenges that were unearthed during these efforts. For instance, policymakers were often overeager to push for application of *strategic human capital management*–based initiatives that were still in an experimental research stage. One example of this was the push to use value-added test scores to evaluate teachers even though the research was still in its infancy and the process was not necessarily ready for "prime time" (see Chapter 9). Despite the fact that this precondition was not yet established (i.e., the science of identifying highly effective performers consistently and validly was not yet available), reformers pushed for the implementation of performance pay systems that depended on accurate performance evaluations. Consequently, many pay systems were poorly designed and ineffective in promoting teacher excellence (see Chapter 3). They also created incentive structures that ran counter to the risk-averse culture of schools and promoted uniformity and standardization over individual merit and where teachers sometimes preferred not to be rewarded for excellence because they did not want to be part of a competitive system with winners and losers.

Furthermore, despite the intense reform efforts, there was minimal substantive change in how HR practices were handled in schools (Kraft & Gilmour, 2017). In fact, a recent national survey of education HR practices suggests that many public school districts continue to operate with outdated HR practices, such as failing to provide new teachers with substantive onboarding, mentorship for success, access to learning systems for professional growth, or an inclusive and supporting work environment for their retention (Konoske-Graf et al., 2016). In short, there were many indicators that point towards education HRM failing to address the systemic needs of teachers and administrators.

Talent-Centered Education Leadership

This volume focuses on a new approach to education HRM known as Talent-Centered Education Leadership (TCEL). Introduced by Tran (2020), this approach is grounded in the education working conditions literature as well as cutting-edge talent management (TM) theories and practices. While HRM deals with the overall employee management of the organization, TM is a subset of HRM that specifically focuses on the cultivation, engagement, motivation, development, and retention of its talent. Critical to TCEL is how "talent" is interpreted and defined. Tran explains that although TM has been defined in numerous ways, it is most commonly treated as an exclusionary HRM approach that emphasizes developmental support and attention to only a small group of "talent," in this case, the employees with the highest potential and performance in the organization (Gelens et al., 2013). In education, an exclusive TM approach has been promoted by those who advocate utilizing value-added teacher performance ratings for the purposes of workforce ranking for merit pay (Holland, 2005) or retention (Hanushek, 2011; Nitter, 2018). Cultural scholars, however, argue that this non-inclusive perspective represents an Anglo-American view that is at odds with more collective-oriented cultures (Dries et al., 2014; Festing et al., 2013; Swailes et al., 2014), including public sector organizations like public schools (Ford et al., 2010; Chun & Rainey, 2005). Consequently, a tension exists between the individualistic merit perspective, which seeks to identify and reward the "star" teacher, compared to the collaborative perspective, which promotes the idea that student success is a communal effort and that individualized identifications of "star" performers are not necessary or even appropriate (e.g., English teachers are not the only teachers that teach students how to write and read, as students also learn to write and read in history, math, and other subjects).

Relatedly, how education employers have historically defined "talent" and how they have defined "professionalism" often perpetuated inequity for traditionally marginalized groups. For example, these groups are disproportionately affected when workers are criticized or even penalized for being "unprofessional" by their employers because they dressed in nontraditional gender-conforming attire (Iskander, 2022) or styled their hair in braids or dreadlocks (Lucero, 2022). From a Talent-Centered Education Leadership perspective, this is nonsensical as these employees unfairly face unfavorable employment responses for factors that have nothing to do with their job performance. In other words, they face workplace discrimination for non-job–related reasons.

Instead of drawing on the exclusionary perspective of TM, TCEL draws on the more recently conceived *inclusive talent management* perspective that encourages organizations to view employees as having differentiated talents and recognize the potential of all their employees. The organization's role is to help employees identify and cultivate those talents. According to Downs and Swailes (2013), "[t]alent identification should encourage people to consider and to realize what matters to them in line with the interests of the organization" (p. 277). Within a TCEL framework, this does not suggest a one-size-fits-all approach, as public school personnel management is often criticized for, but rather TCEL encourages the nurturing of individual capabilities and the potential of all employees to do work that is meaningful to them while contributing to the social well-being of others (e.g., coworkers, students). In fact, the name Talent-Centered Education Leadership leads with the word *talent* because it is understood that equity and excellence are not mutually exclusive.

Like its student-based counterpart differentiated instruction (Valiandes, 2015), TCEL seeks to create a more equitable approach to TM by recognizing and acknowledging the importance of diversity and not treating everyone as having the same needs and motivations (Tran, 2020). The approach goes beyond addressing issues of diversity of representation by maintaining a work environment that cultivates a sense of belonging for all employees. This is highly relevant in the modern-day context as younger generations of workers are increasingly looking for more diverse and inclusive workspaces (Lanier, 2017). It is also a more ethical approach, treating employees not as means to an end (i.e., tools to help the organization achieve its goals) but rather as ends in themselves (Downs & Swailes, 2013; Strike et al., 2005; Tran, 2020). This point is particularly relevant in HRM given the longstanding understanding of the conflict between employee advocacy and strategic control and exploitation of employees for employer benefit (Mahadevan & Schmitz, 2020).

Talent-centered organizations that approach HRM (and subsequently TM) from the superlative employee relations approach have reaped the benefit of performance excellence (Piening et al., 2013). Social exchange theory (Blau, 1964) has been a useful framework for HR scholars to understand this relationship. It argues that when employers show goodwill to their employees through positive HRM, the employees reciprocate by becoming more committed, hardworking, and higher performing. The social exchange is most critical at two major junctures for school employee relations.

First, principals can directly provide administrative support to teachers to develop their human capital (i.e., teachers' knowledge, skills, and abilities). Principals can further leverage their own social connectivity to provide teachers with the requisite social capital (e.g., through mentorship and peer networks) to further enhance teachers' human capital, if the former is facilitated both individually and collectively within and outside schools (Tran & Smith, 2020a). The employer-employee relational bond is strengthened when employers provide the type of support that shows employees they are cared about and valued, which facilitates a more supportive relationship between the two. This has been documented to improve both employee outcomes like retention and performance outcomes like student learning gains (Jacob et al., 2015).

Given that the primary motivating factor for entry into the teaching profession is often the desire to educate and positively impact student outcomes (Shuls & Maranto, 2014), leveraging and blossoming that altruistic sentiment can yield positive dividends for effective education TM. In contrast to the earlier models of HRM, the TCEL approach presented in this volume offers education strategic TM that adds value to the aforementioned models by strategically linking HR activities to accomplish the educational mission, based on the employee-centered foundational strategy of *creating a great workplace*. Creating a great workplace for employees has implications for improving student learning and strengthening recruitment and retention of a quality education workforce. While the education literature has traditionally focused on HR practices that emphasize teachers and principals, this text broadens that emphasis to highlight the social complexities of relationships in educational organizations between school leaders, teachers, staff, and students.

Our emphasis is critical to illuminating the difference between a hyper-rationalized productivity output model, where the only measurable gains are student achievement, to a more enlightened, evidence-based recognition that the entire educational enterprise is based on relationships between people (not parts, widgets, or materials). Even though we argue that investment in people is an investment in the organization that will yield returns in the form of organizational performance, ultimately truly progressive organizations will do so because they care about their people (Tran, 2020). When education leaders focus on their faculty and staff, the faculty and staff can focus on their students. In contrast, when everybody focuses on the students, the faculty and staff are left behind and increasingly become dissatisfied and disengaged and are more likely to depart. The result is a revolving door of new faces that create barriers to the development and sustenance of the adult-student bonds and trust that are necessary for cultivating a thriving learning environment.

In response to the needs of education HRM, we believe there are strategies that education can learn from progressive organizations both in and outside of education. Progressive organizations operate with an "employer of choice" strategy (Hinkin & Tracey, 2010) that relies on the foundations of professional respect, teamwork, employee recognition, development, and empowerment. They are built from business philosophies that suggest "if you create a great place to work, great work takes place" (Rusty Lindquist, Bamboo HR, as cited in Ferguson, 2016).

We draw on research evidence, advance theory, and describe TM practices of progressive organizations to help reconceptualize what TM means in education. We encourage movement away from a standardized product focus to one that emphasizes not only performance but also value and care for employees, a humanistic framework compatible with education. Contextualized to a school setting, according to Josh Bersin (The Josh Bersin Company, 2021), founder of Bersin at Deloitte, a leading talent management, research, and advisory service company, the question for school employers should be:

> How do stakeholders [including the school principal] improve the employee experience (EEX)?

By addressing this question, we inquire: *How can we create an employee journey map that highlights all the "moments that matter" to build the ideal employee experience?* (Josh Bersin, founder of Bersin at Deloitte; The Josh Bersin Company, 2021). A key element of building a great workplace is talent development, and the school principal can be thought of as a human capital developer (Donaldson, 2013), supporting and building the capacity of teachers, which will, in turn, improve their confidence and, consequently, their retention and performance (as reflected in various metrics, including improvement in student test scores) (Tran & Smith, 2020b). For example, principals can conduct focus groups with their employees to identify and better understand important milestones that represent meaningful moments in their tenure with the organization to leverage and build on the potential of those moments. Consequently, the principal is instrumental in helping develop the work environment into a "great place to work."

Principles of Talent-Centered Education Leadership

Tran and Jenkins (2022) identify seven core research-based principles that undergird TCEL. These principles are based on the foundation of TCEL, which is to humanize the education workspace. Table 1.1 identifies each principle and its associated research base/support.

The School Principal and Education HRM

Increasing work-related demands and accountability pressures in schools can exert a physical and mental toll on teachers. For instance, work demands have been linked to teachers' work-related stress, absences for "mental health days" (Harrison et al., 2015), and desires to leave the profession (Ryan et al., 2017). Moreover, work-related stress is associated with teacher anxiety and depression (Mahan et al., 2010). When employees are not operating with a healthy and sound body and mind, their work performance and relationships undoubtedly suffer. Progressive organizations are attuned to the holistic needs of their

Table 1.1 Principles of Talent-Centered Education Leadership

Principles	*Research Base/Support*
Talent-Centered Education Employers and Leaders . . .	Based on research that has consistently supported these principles across sectors (including in business and education)
1. Recognize employees are the most important asset to the organization; Educator and student needs are not mutually exclusive.	For example, teachers have been found to be the most important school input for students' academic achievement (Hanushek, 2016; Rivkin et al., 2005).
2. Emphasize inclusive talent management; they create inclusive work environments and understand how talent is defined can marginalize or recognize the diversity of talent to leverage innovation.	For example, the presence of Black teachers has been found to be linked not only to improved student achievement for Black students but also non-Black students as well (Klopfenstein, 2005).
3. Focus on the employee experience (EEX).	For example, research has suggested teachers have different needs throughout their career span and that support should be targeted to the needs appropriate for their specific experience levels (Tran & Smith, 2020a).
4. Utilize data to inform decision-making, especially as it relates to designing positive and engaging EEX	For example, conduct working conditions surveys, analyze data, and implement policy changes to improve employee experiences (Tran & Jenkins, 2022).

(*Continued*)

Table 1.1 (Continued)

Principles	*Research Base/Support*
5. Empathize with employee needs by authentically and regularly listening to their concerns and feedback. Value employee input by authentically and regularly listening to their suggestions and ideas and by providing them workplace autonomy and flexibility.	For example, there is a body of research that has consistently identified administrative support as the most important factor influencing teacher retention. This is important for numerous reasons. Beyond the costs of teacher replacement (which are funded by tax dollars in public schools), there is also the linkage between repeated teacher turnovers and a decline in student achievement (Bartanen et al., 2019; Tran et al., 2023).
	For example, teachers who perceive their input to be valued more and have more autonomy in their workplace are less likely to want to leave their employer (Horng, 2009).
6. Focus on employee engagement as a valued organizational outcome.	For example, teacher engagement has been linked to student achievement and teacher turnover (Wang et al., 2022; Johnson, 2021).
7. Consistently show and demonstrate respect for education employees.	For example, the demonstration of respect (ranging from respect from their administration to society at large) not only has been found to be critical for teachers in the profession but the perception of the lack of respect also plays a pivotal force in dissuading college students from considering teaching as a profession (Tran et al., 2023; Tran & Smith, 2019).

workers and understand that beyond merely providing jobs, employers need to demonstrate care for their employees' well-being (Morgan, 2017). When stress is work-induced, there are often work-related solutions. For example, teacher self-efficacy has been found to partially mediate the effects of accountability pressures on teacher burnout (Yu et al., 2015; Wang et al., 2015), and school leadership can enhance teacher self-efficacy through the facilitation of administrative and peer support (Calik et al., 2012; Duyar et al., 2013).

Consequently, in what many perceive to be an inhospitable context, school leaders can play an especially critical role in buffering the external pressures and distractions faced by teachers so that they can focus on doing their jobs (Shirrell, 2016; Rutledge et al., 2009). In fact, principals have been described as the "broker of workplace conditions" in schools (Johnson, 2006, p. 15), with vast influence in shaping their teachers' work lives. For example, principals can influence how the work gets done at the school and how people feel about their work, with enhancement of working conditions improving teacher satisfaction (Cha & Cohen-Vogel, 2011). Moreover, administrative support has consistently been identified as the most salient factor influencing teacher employment decisions, such as their recruitment (Tran & Dou, 2019; Tran & Smith, 2020a) and retention (Burkhauser, 2017; Horng, 2009; Ladd, 2011). These findings corroborate the old saying that emphasizes the importance of that supervisor-employee relationship by suggesting that people don't quit their jobs, but rather they quit their bosses.

Although emphasized much less than the instructional focus in principal scholarship and preparation programs, school leaders' time spent on organizational management skills including HRM activities, such as hiring, employee management, and professional development implementation, has been found to be influential for student test score growth, teacher satisfaction, and teacher/parent assessment of school climate (Goldhaber et al. 2017; Grissom et al., 2013; Horng et al., 2010). Because leadership involves motivating people and leadership styles can influence the type and ways TM is practiced in organizations (Vermeeren et al., 2014), TM is a critical component of the principal's job.

BOX 1.2: KNOW THE RULES AND FOLLOW THEM

Schools operate in complex political, legal, and cultural environments. School leaders are responsible for navigating these environments by reading, studying, and following contract provisions and paying attention to laws and policies that have implications for leadership practice. In working to establish the conditions for success, school leaders need to know and follow the provisions of the contract/collective bargaining agreement. They need to buffer and support school personnel to effectively serve student needs and back them when they make decisions that are likely to elicit controversy. In short, the principal needs to know the rules and follow them; working within the rules, they should seek pathways that advance educational goals and promote a positive, supportive culture.

Culture and Climate

A school's culture represents the informal norms and tacit rules that are followed within the environment, including "the way people act, how they dress, what they talk about or consider taboo, whether they seek out colleagues or isolate themselves, whether they work together" (Peterson & Deal, 2011, p. 7), while climate refers to how people feel about the culture. School culture and climate are increasingly being recognized as valid indicators of school quality. Reviewing their data can unearth issues related to systemic inequities, students' socioemotional learning, and workforce morale. The *Every Student Succeeds* Act allowed for the inclusion of non-test score–based measures for school accountability, and as a result, states have moved to include school climate data in their school quality measures.

BOX 1.3: WARNING – DATA TIMELINESS

If culture and climate matter, it is important that school leaders regularly measure them within their environments. These data can help inform decisions and improve employers' understanding of employee needs, giving workers an internal platform to have a voice in providing inputs and feedback concerning what they care about and why. The truth is, employees increasingly rely on external platforms, such as social media and internet sites, to share their experiences and voice their commentary about workplace issues (Morgan, 2017). By providing an outlet, employers have a chance to learn about the issues and act in response to their employees' concerns before the reputation of the school or district is negatively affected in the eyes of the public.

According to Morgan (2017), worker-friendly organizations, like Google, increasingly rely on people analytics and draw on big data (from performance to psychological data) to better understand the needs of their employees. Fear of litigation causes many employers to be overly conservative with their HRM, encouraging them to treat everyone the same, without recognition that *equal* treatment does not necessarily mean *fair* treatment. For example, employees have different developmental needs, and mandating uniform professional development to the entire workforce can encourage employee resentment and disengagement. The use of people analytics can allow for the development of personalized coaching designed and delivered to each employee for their individual professional growth. The analysis of employees with data science has only recently been a role adopted by HR, but in occupying this role, they can provide individualized data analysis to help support manager decision-making as organizations strive to be more people-centric.

One problem with data use is when the data are untimely. The data become less useful and relevant to inform decision-making as they become dated, and episodic snapshot assessments of the school culture may not accurately reflect the day-to-day workplace environment. Morgan (2017) observes that progressive, people-oriented organizations have been moving away from the singular annual review event, to focus more on assessing the overall process in real time through tools such as intranets, apps, social media, surveys, interviews, and focus groups. Shorter weekly pulse checks can help employers better know their employees, and they can serve to either replace or supplement longer annual workplace feedback surveys. Longitudinal data allow for tracking changes in how employees feel across a given time span, which allows leaders to better assess whether workplace improvement efforts are "working," giving them an opportunity to adjust midstream if they are not. In short, it gives employers an opportunity to learn about the needs of their employees and respond quickly to them.

Principals can occupy an influential role in shaping the culture and, consequently, the climate of the school (Peterson & Deal, 2011). In fact, it has been said that "[t]here is a possibility, underemphasized in leadership research, that the only thing of real importance that leaders do is to create and manage culture and that the unique talent of leaders is their ability to work with culture" (Schein, 1992, p. 2). Through their influence on the culture and interactions with their employees, Gallup (2015) found that managers, like principals, explain 70% of their employee's engagement. When employees are engaged and convinced that they should care about what happens at work, they are not only tuned into their responsibilities, but they also exhibit discretionary efforts (e.g., helping their coworkers succeed) that benefit the organization because they *want* to as opposed to *have* to.

An important aspect of a healthy workplace culture is the extent to which the organization is perceived to be fair. Organizational justice refers to the perception of how fairly employees are treated at work, which includes dimensions such as fairness in promotional opportunities, resource allocation, and process in determining outcomes (Gelens et al., 2013). Lower perceptions of organizational justice have been linked to outcomes such as teachers' intention to quit (Basar & Sigri, 2015). In fact, lower perceptions of schools' organizational ethics (as reflected by the ethical principles by which the school operates and the decisions made by the school in response to internal or external stimuli) have been linked to various symptoms of organizational withdrawal including lateness, teacher absences, and intent to leave (Shapira-Lishchinsky & Rosenblatt, 2010; Shapira-Lishchinsky, 2012). Leaders can influence the perception of fairness in the culture by being authentic, transparent, consistent, empathetic, and dependable.

While most in supervisory positions can talk the talk and communicate the rhetoric of the importance of being fair, supportive, inclusive, and attentive to the needs of their employees, often the manager's perceptions of whether their day-to-day work environment reflects these attributes differ from their employees' perceptions (Lester et al., 2002). Perception can shape reality because even if managers believe themselves to be fair, workforce morale will still be harmed if their employees do not believe this to be the case. This is why before exercising leadership of others, it is important to be self-reflective and truly understand yourself (Morgan, 2017) and why others perceive you the way that they do. School leaders can grow through development of their empathy, emotional intelligence, and cultural responsiveness to better know themselves to understand others. This enhanced sense of self-awareness can help to reduce bias in decision-making and mitigate favoritism, thereby improving the perception of organizational fairness.

BOX 1.4: WHEN IT'S NOT ROSY: WHO IS CONSIDERED TALENT?

You are an assistant principal at Gardner Middle School and are having a lunch meeting with your principal. He tells you that the up-and-coming teacher Sam just made it to year five at the school and has shown tremendous potential for upward momentum. Therefore, your principal plans to offer Sam the vacant instructional coach position. You are a bit surprised to hear this, as you know Jennifer, a decade-long teacher at the school, has expressed an interest in the instructional coach position for the past three years. She has expressed an interest in providing less experienced or less effective teachers mentorship and support through that role. She has applied for the position twice but did not receive the job offer. You overheard that she has told her colleagues that she was not offered the position because of her race and gender and because she doesn't look or talk like the other administrators (who do not share her cultural and demographic background) in the school. You bring this to your principal's attention, but he says that Jennifer does not exhibit the traits and personality that those in leadership at the school should have. He noted that he considers the instructional coach as part of the school leadership team and said that people who complain when they do not have their way are too immature to be a part of the team. He said that team players should put their team's needs ahead of their own. The principal plans to hire Sam and not advertise the position as he feels "there is no need to."

Discussion Question: What do you feel about this decision? Should the school have any concerns? If not, why do you feel this way? If so, what are those concerns and how might the process be improved to help mitigate them? Rationalize and justify your response based on ethical, legal, professional, and/or leadership frameworks.

Learning Activities

Discussion Questions:

1. What can be done to mitigate employees' perceptions of inequality when employing a TCEL approach that differentiates employees based on their needs and competencies?
2. Does a great teacher make a great principal? What distinguishes the former from the latter?
3. Ever-growing work responsibilities, technological advances, and the aftermath of the COVID-19 pandemic have resulted in more work being "taken home," blurring the line between home and the workplace. Working within

this context, how might you as an administrator work to promote the work-life balance of your employees?

4. As a school leader, how will you show your commitment to empowering your employees, valuing communication and collaboration, and developing and maintaining trust and safety? What does it mean when an organization can show it effectively addresses these issues?
5. Would you say that your school is a desirable place to work? Why or why not? How would you enhance its desirability?

CONCLUSION

While we believe in the value of a TCEL approach to TM for organizations and the education field, we also acknowledge that it is impractical to jump from point A to point Z while skipping all the in-between. We are careful not to veer too far into the territory of utopian theory and ground ourselves and readers in working through the practical realities of the current work environment and its associated limitations. With this text, we draw on research, practice, and theory to both evolve education TM and provide guidance for aspiring and current school leaders that can be used today. However, while the scholarship lays the foundation for TCEL, we are constrained by the fact that most of the research evidence cited in this volume comes from education HRM operating within the current policy accountability context. This results in a heavy reliance on student test score growth as a proxy for performance. While this work has value, we balance it with research focusing on other important outcomes to present a more holistic representation of the value of effective HRM. In other words, while test scores are one measure of school performance, they are not the only important measure. Fortunately, the varied research with its diverse outcomes tells a consistent narrative concerning the importance of the organization showing commitment and care for its employees, which can be demonstrated through actions such as the provision of support, autonomy, and discretion for how they do their job, empowerment for innovation, workplace flexibility, appreciation and recognition for accomplishments, opportunities for growth, and a culture of safety and trust. Finally, it is also worth noting that our ability to design an effective TCEL HRM system does not rely on our inattention to student outcomes (even if they are measured partially by test scores) but that it also requires more focus on emphasizing what matters for training programs and developmental advancement of the education leadership field.

Summary of Key Points

- In recent decades, educational policy reforms have stripped teacher autonomy and increased workload and pressure, which have led to declining interest in the teaching profession and what some have called "a demoralized teacher

workforce" and a "national teacher shortage." This has set the stage for the need for a new type of education human resource management.
- This chapter introduces the concept of Talent-Centered Education Leadership (Tran, 2020), an education talent management approach that emphasizes prioritizing the needs of employees and valuing them while providing them with support and care. It strategically links HR activities to accomplish the educational mission, based on the employee-centered foundational strategy of *creating a great workplace*. The approach is grounded in the education working conditions literature and cutting-edge talent management theories and seeks to intentionally design employee experiences where their workers *want* to (as opposed to *need* to) engage with their work. Seven core research-based principles undergird TCEL.
- Talent-Centered Education Leadership is a more inclusive and ethical approach to talent management than prior models. It accomplishes this by viewing employees as having differentiated talents and recognizing the potential of *all* its employees. The organization's role is to help employees identify and cultivate those talents. TCEL encourages the nurturing of individual capabilities and the potential of all employees to do work that is meaningful to them while contributing to the well-being of others (e.g., coworkers, students). It treats employees as ends in themselves rather than simply means to an end. In the case where the talents of individuals are misaligned with the mission of the organization, then they may be counseled to grow outside of the organization.
- The school principal is critical for education human resource and talent management, and their influence is often mediated through their impact on school culture and climate. Because of their importance, school culture and climate should be regularly assessed, and school principals should work with their human resource support (e.g., district HR) to continuously improve it.

REFERENCES

Altman, S. (2013). The bad business of education reform. *Edushyster.* https://nepc.colorado.edu/blog/bad-business-education-reform

Baker, B. D. (2012). *Revisiting the age-old question: Does money matter in education?* Albert Shanker Institute.

Bartanen, B., Grissom, J. A., & Rogers, L. K. (2019). The impacts of principal turnover. *Educational Evaluation and Policy Analysis, 41*(3), 350–374.

Bartoletti, J., & Connelly, G. (2013). *Leadership matters: What the research says about the importance of principal leadership* (p. 16). National Association of Elementary School Principals. www.naesp.org/sites/default/files/LeadershipMatters.pdf

Basar, U., & Sigri, Ü. (2015). Effects of teachers' organizational justice perceptions on intention to quit: Mediation role of organizational identification. *Educational Sciences: Theory and Practice, 15*(1), 45–59.

Blau, P. M. (1964). *Exchange and power in social life* (p. 352). John Wiley & Sons.

Burkhauser, S. (2017). How much do school principals matter when it comes to teacher working conditions? *Educational Evaluation and Policy Analysis, 39*(1), 126–145.

Calik, T., Sezgin, F., Kavgaci, H., & Cagatay Kilinc, A. (2012). Examination of relationships between instructional leadership of school principals and self-efficacy of teachers and collective teacher efficacy. *Educational Sciences: Theory and Practice, 12*(4), 2498–2504.

Cha, S. H., & Cohen-Vogel, L. (2011). Why they quit: A focused look at teachers who leave for other occupations. *School Effectiveness and School Improvement, 22*(4), 371–392.

Chun, Y. H., & Rainey, H. G. (2005). Goal ambiguity in US federal agencies. *Journal of Public Administration Research and Theory, 15*(1), 1–30.

Currie, G., & Procter, S. (2001). Exploring the relationship between HR and middle managers. *Human Resource Management Journal, 11*(3), 53–69.

Donaldson, M. L. (2013). Principals' approaches to cultivating teacher effectiveness constraints and opportunities in hiring, assigning, evaluating, and developing teachers. *Educational Administration Quarterly, 49*, 838–882.

Downs, Y., & Swailes, S. (2013). A capability approach to organizational talent management. *Human Resource Development International, 16*(3), 267–281.

Dries, N., Cotton, R. D., Bagdadli, S., & de Oliveira, M. Z. (2014). HR directors' understanding of 'talent': A cross-cultural study. In A. Al Arris (Ed.), *Global talent management: Challenges, strategies, and opportunities* (pp. 15–28). Springer International Publishing.

Duyar, I., Gumus, S., & Sukru Bellibas, M. (2013). Multilevel analysis of teacher work attitudes: The influence of principal leadership and teacher collaboration. *International Journal of Educational Management, 27*(7), 700–719.

Ferguson, H. (2016). 'If you create a great place to work, great work takes place': BambooHR's Rusty Lindquist on rewards and recognition. *Recruiter.com*. https://www.recruiter.com/i/if-you-create-a-great-place-to-work-great-work-takes-place-bamboohrs-rusty-lindquist-on-rewards-and-recognition/

Festing, M., Schäfer, L., & Scullion, H. (2013). Talent management in medium-sized German companies: An explorative study and agenda for future research. *The International Journal of Human Resource Management, 24*(9), 1872–1893.

Finne, L. (2018). Teacher strikes hurt students and divide the community. *The Seattle Times*. www.seattletimes.com/opinion/teachers-please-dont-strike-again/

Ford, J., Harding, N., & Stoyanova, D. (2010). *Talent management and development – An overview of current theory and practice*. Bradford University School of Management.

Ford, T. G., Urick, A., & Wilson, A. S. (2018). Exploring the effect of supportive teacher evaluation experiences on US teachers' job satisfaction. *Education Policy Analysis Archives, 26*, 59.

Fuller, B., Waite, A., & Torres Irribarra, D. (2016). Explaining teacher turnover: School cohesion and intrinsic motivation in Los Angeles. *American Journal of Education, 122*(4), 537–567.

Gallup. (2015). *State of the American manager: Analytics and advice for leaders*. Gallup.

Gallup. (2018). State of the American workplace. https://news.gallup.com/reports/199961/7.aspx?utm_source=article&utm_content=daily-employee-engagement

Gannon, D., & Boguszak, A. (2013). Douglas McGregor's theory X and theory Y. *CRIS-Bulletin of the Centre for Research and Interdisciplinary Study, 2013*(2), 85–93.

Garcia, E., & Weiss, E. (2019). *The teacher shortage is real, large and growing, and worse than we thought*. Economic Policy Institute. www.epi.org/files/pdf/163651.pdf

Gelens, J., Dries, N., Hofmans, J., & Pepermans, R. (2013). The role of perceived organizational justice in shaping the outcomes of talent management: A research agenda. *Human Resource Management Review, 23*(4), 341–353.

Giroux, H. A., & Saltman, K. (2009). Obama's betrayal of public education? Arne Duncan and the corporate model of schooling. *Cultural Studies? Critical Methodologies, 9*(6), 772–779.

Goldhaber, D., Grout, C., & Huntington-Klein, N. (2017). Screen twice, cut once: Assessing the predictive validity of applicant selection tools. *Education Finance and Policy, 12*(2), 197–223.

Grissom, J. A., Loeb, S., & Master, B. (2013). Effective instructional time use for school leaders: Longitudinal evidence from observations of principals. *Educational Researcher, 42*(8), 433–444.

Hanushek, E. (2011). Lifting student achievement by weeding out harmful teachers. *Eduwonk.com.* www.eduwonk.com/2011/10/lifting-student-achievement-by-weeding-out-harmful-teachers.html

Hanushek, E. A. (2016). What matters for student achievement. *Education Next, 16*(2), 18–26.

Harrison, D., Labby, S., & Sullivan, S. (2015). Absent Texas teachers: Reasons and revelations. *Texas Association of Teacher Educators, 5,* 18–32.

Hinkin, T. R., & Tracey, J. B. (2010). What makes it so great? An analysis of human resources practices among Fortune's best companies to work for. *Cornell Hospitality Quarterly, 51*(2), 158–170.

Holland, R. (2005). *Merit pay for teachers: Can common sense come to public education* (p. 5). Lexington Institute. http://lexington.server278.com/docs/708.pdf

Horng, E. L. (2009). Teacher tradeoffs: Disentangling teachers' preferences for working conditions and student demographics. *American Educational Research Journal, 46*(3), 690–717.

Horng, E. L., Klasik, D., & Loeb, S. (2010). Principal's time use and school effectiveness. *American Journal of Education, 116*(4), 491–523.

Iskander, L. (2022). "I assumed it was a much safer place than it really is": Nonbinary educators' strategies for finding school jobs. *Journal of Education Human Resources, 40*(1), 114–134.

Jackson, K. M. (2012). Influence matters: The link between principal and teacher influence over school policy and teacher turnover. *Journal of School Leadership, 22*(5), 875–901.

Jacob, R., Goddard, R., Kim, M., Miller, R., & Goddard, Y. (2015). Exploring the causal impact of the McREL Balanced Leadership Program on leadership, principal efficacy, instructional climate, educator turnover, and student achievement. *Educational Evaluation and Policy Analysis, 37*(3), 314–332.

Johnson, S. M. (2006). *The workplace matters: Teacher quality, retention, and effectiveness.* www.files.eric.ed.gov/fulltext/ED495822.pdf

The Josh Bersin Company. (2021). *The definitive guide: Employee experience.* Retrieved from https://joshbersin.com/ex-definitive-guide-2021/

Johnson, D. D. (2021). Predictors of teachers' turnover and transfer intentions: A multiple mediation model of teacher engagement. *Journal of Education Human Resources, 39*(3), 322–349.

Klopfenstein, K. (2005). Beyond test scores: The impact of Black teacher role models on rigorous math taking. *Contemporary Economic Policy, 23*(3), 416–428. https://doi.org/10.1093/cep/byi031

Konoske-Graf, A., Partelow, L., & Benner, M. (2016). *To attract great teachers, school districts must improve their human capital systems* (pp. 1–30). Center for American Progress.

Kraft, M. A., & Gilmour, A. F. (2017). Revisiting the widget effect: Teacher evaluation reforms and the distribution of teacher effectiveness. *Educational Researcher, 46*(5), 234–249.

Kraft, M. A., & Papay, J. P. (2014). Can professional environments in schools promote teacher development? Explaining heterogeneity in returns to teaching experience. *Educational Evaluation and Policy Analysis, 36*(4), 476–500.

Ladd, H. F. (2011). Teachers' perceptions of their working conditions: How predictive of planned and actual teacher movement? *Educational Evaluation and Policy Analysis, 33*(2), 235–261.

Lanier, K. (2017). 5 things HR professionals need to know about generation Z: Thought leaders share their views on the HR profession and its direction for the future. *Strategic HR Review, 16*(6), 288–290.

Lester, S. W., Turnley, W. H., Bloodgood, J. M., & Bolino, M. C. (2002). Not seeing eye to eye: Differences in supervisor and subordinate perceptions of and attributions for psychological contract breach. *Journal of Organizational Behavior, 23*(1), 39–56.

Lucero, L. (2022). A maze of challenges and opportunities: An autoethnography of a queer Latinx woman and her journey in elementary education workplaces in the borderland. *Journal of Education Human Resources, 40*(3), 305–334.

Mahadevan, J., & Schmitz, A. P. (2020). HRM as an ongoing struggle for legitimacy: A critical discourse analysis of HR managers as "employee-experience designers." *Baltic Journal of Management, 15*(4), 515–532.

Mahan, P. L., Mahan, M. P., Park, N. J., Shelton, C., Brown, K. C., & Weaver, M. T. (2010). Work environment stressors, social support, anxiety, and depression among secondary school teachers. *AAOHN Journal, 58*(5), 197–205.

Mazor, A. H., Zucker, J., Sivak, M., Coombes, R., & Van Durme, Y. (2017). *Reimagine and craft the employee experience: Design thinking in action* (pp. 1–8). Deloitte Development LLC.

McGregor, D. (1960). *The human side of enterprise* (Vol. 21, pp. 166–171). McGraw Hill.

Morgan, J. (2017). *The employee experience advantage: How to win the war for talent by giving employees the workspaces they want, the tools they need, and a culture they can celebrate.* John Wiley & Sons.

National Commission on Excellence in Education. (1983). A nation at risk: The imperative for educational reform. *The Elementary School Journal, 84*(2), 113–130.

Neumerski, C. M., Grissom, J. A., Goldring, E., Rubin, M., Cannata, M., Schuermann, P., & Drake, T. A. (2018). Restructuring instructional leadership: How multiple-measure teacher evaluation systems are redefining the role of the school principal. *The Elementary School Journal, 119*(2), 270–297.

Nguyen, T. D., Pham, L. D., Crouch, M., & Springer, M. G. (2020). The correlates of teacher turnover: An updated and expanded meta-analysis of the literature. *Educational Research Review, 31*, 100355.

Nitter, K. (2018). *The use of teacher effectiveness in layoff decisions.* National Council on Teacher Quality. www.nctq.org/blog/The-use-of-teacher-effectiveness-in-layoff-decisions

Odden, A. R. (2011). *Strategic management of human capital in education: Improving instructional practice and student learning in schools.* Routledge.

Ouchi, W. G., & Cuchi, W. G. (1981). *Theory Z: How American business can meet the Japanese challenge* (Vol. 13). Addison-Wesley.

Pawlewicz, D. D. A. (2020). *Blaming teachers: Professionalization policies and the failure of reform in American history.* Rutgers University Press.

Peterson, K. D., & Deal, T. E. (2011). *The shaping school culture fieldbook.* John Wiley & Sons.

Phi Delta Kappa. (2018). *Teaching: Respect but dwindling appeal.* https://pdkpoll.org/wp-content/uploads/2020/05/pdkpoll50_2018.pdf

Piening, E. P., Baluch, A. M., & Salge, T. O. (2013). The relationship between employees' perceptions of human resource systems and organizational performance: Examining mediating mechanisms and temporal dynamics. *Journal of Applied Psychology, 98*(6), 926.

Reilly, K. (2018, September 13). I work 3 jobs and donate blood plasma to pay the bills. This is what it's like to be a teacher in America. *Time Magazine.* https://time.com/5395001/teacher-in-america

Rivkin, S. G., Hanushek, E. A., & Kain, J. F. (2005). Teachers, schools, and academic achievement. *Econometrica, 73*(2), 417–458. https://doi.org/10.1111/J.1468-0262.2005.00584.X

Roberts, L. (2018). Roberts: Arizona legislator threatens to sue over teachers' strike. But sue who? *AZ Central.* www.azcentral.com/story/opinion/op-ed/laurieroberts/2018/04/24/roberts-arizona-legislator-threatens-sue-over-teachers-strike-but-who/548103002/

Ronfeldt, M., Loeb, S., & Wyckoff, J. (2013). How teacher turnover harms student achievement. *American Educational Research Journal, 50*(1), 4–36.

Rutledge, S. A., Harris, D. N., & Ingle, W. K. (2009). How principals "bridge and buffer" the new demands of teacher quality and accountability: A mixed-methods analysis of teacher hiring. *American Journal of Education, 116*(2), 211–242.

Ryan, S. V., Nathaniel, P., Pendergast, L. L., Saeki, E., Segool, N., & Schwing, S. (2017). Leaving the teaching profession: The role of teacher stress and educational accountability policies on turnover intent. *Teaching and Teacher Education, 66,* 1–11.

Schein, E. H. (1992). *Organizational culture and leadership* (Vol. 1). John Wiley & Sons.

Shapira-Lishchinsky, O. (2012). Teachers' withdrawal behaviors: Integrating theory and findings. *Journal of Educational Administration, 50*(3), 307–326.

Shapira-Lishchinsky, O., & Rosenblatt, Z. (2010). School ethical climate and teachers' voluntary absence. *Journal of Educational Administration, 48*(2), 164–181.

Shirrell, M. (2016). New principals, accountability, and commitment in low-performing schools. *Journal of Educational Administration, 54*(5), 558–574.

Shuls, J., & Maranto, R. (2014). Show them the mission: A comparison of teacher recruitment incentives in high need communities. *Social Science Quarterly, 95*(1), 239–252.

Strauss, V. (2019, April 16). Why this South Carolina teacher quit mid-year: 'The unrealistic demands and all-consuming nature of the profession are not sustainable.' *Washington Post.* www.washingtonpost.com/education/2019/04/16/why-this-south-carolina-teacher-quit-mid-year-the-unrealistic-demands-all-consuming-nature-profession-are-not-sustainable/

Strike, K. A., Haller, E. J., & Soltis, J. F. (2005). *The ethics of school administration.* Teachers College Press.

Sutcher, L., Darling-Hammond, L., & Carver-Thomas, D. (2019). Understanding teacher shortages: An analysis of teacher supply and demand in the United States. *Education Policy Analysis Archives, 27*(35). http://dx.doi.org/10.14507/epaa.27.3696

Swailes, S., Downs, Y., & Orr, K. (2014). Conceptualising inclusive talent management: Potential, possibilities and practicalities. *Human Resource Development International, 17*(5), 529–544.

Taylor, F. W. (2004). *Scientific management.* Routledge.

Towers-Clark, C. (2019, December 11). The future of work in 2020 and beyond. *Forbes.* www.forbes.com/sites/charlestowersclark/2019/12/11/the-future-of-work-in-2020-and-beyond/

Tran, H. (2015). Personnel vs. strategic human resource management in public education. *Management in Education, 29*(3), 112–118.

Tran, H. (2020). Revolutionizing school HR strategies and practices to reflect talent centered education leadership. *Leadership and Policy in Schools,* 1–15. https://doi.org/10.1080/15700763.2020.1757725

Tran, H., & Dou, J. (2019). An exploratory examination of what types of administrative support matter for rural teacher talent management: The rural educator perspective. *Educational Leadership Review, 20*(1), 133–149. www.icpel.org/uploads/1/5/6/2/15622000/elr_volume_20_1 fall_2019.pdf

Tran, H., & Jenkins, Z. (2022). Embracing the future of education work with talent centered education leadership. *Journal of Education Human Resources, 40*(2), 266–276.

Tran, H., & Smith, D. (2019). Insufficient money and inadequate respect: What obstructs the recruitment of college students to teach in hard-to-staff schools. *Journal of Educational Administration, 57*(2), 152–166.

Tran, H., & Smith, D. A. (2020a). Designing an employee experience approach to teacher retention in hard-to-staff schools. *NASSP Bulletin, 104*(2), 85–109. https://doi.org/10.1177/0192636520927092

Tran, H., & Smith, D. A. (2020b). The strategic support to thrive beyond survival model: An administrative support framework for improving student outcomes and addressing educator staffing in rural and urban high-needs schools. *Research in Educational Administration & Leadership, 5*(3), 870–919.

Tran, H., Cunningham, K., Yelverton, V., Osworth, D., & Hardie, S. (2023). How Can School Leaders Retain Teachers? The Relative Importance of Different Administrative Supports for Teacher Retention in Different Types of Schools. *NASSP Bulletin, 107*(3), 185–217.

Valiandes, S. (2015). Evaluating the impact of differentiated instruction on literacy and reading in mixed ability classrooms: Quality and equity dimensions of education effectiveness. *Studies in Educational Evaluation, 45,* 17–26.

Vermeeren, B., Kuipers, B., & Steijn, B. (2014). Does leadership style make a difference? Linking HRM, job satisfaction, and organizational performance. *Review of Public Personnel Administration, 34*(2), 174–195.

Verstegen, D. A., & King, R. A. (1998). The relationship between school spending and student achievement: A review and analysis of 35 years of production function research. *Journal of Education Finance, 24*(2), 243–262.

Vyse, G. (2019). As protests spread, lawmakers seek punishment (and protection) for teachers. *Governing: The Future of States and Localities.* www.governing.com/topics/education/gov-teacher-strike-retaliation-protection.html

Wang, H., Hall, N. C., & Rahimi, S. (2015). Self-efficacy and causal attributions in teachers: Effects on burnout, job satisfaction, illness, and quitting intentions. *Teaching and Teacher Education, 47,* 120–130.

Wang, J., Zhang, X., & Zhang, L. J. (2022). Effects of teacher engagement on students' achievement in an online English as a foreign language classroom: The mediating role of autonomous motivation and positive emotions. *Frontiers in Psychology, 13,* 950652.

Weick, K. E. (1996). Fighting fires in educational administration. *Educational Administration Quarterly, 32*(4), 565–578.

Yu, X., Wang, P., Zhai, X., Dai, H., & Yang, Q. (2015). The effect of work stress on job burnout among teachers: The mediating role of self-efficacy. *Social Indicators Research, 122,* 701–708.

CHAPTER 2

Optimizing Working Conditions for School Staff Excellence

Chapter Summary

Teacher working conditions promote school staff excellence by improving professional efficacy, satisfaction, and retention. This chapter examines the role of the principal in creating the conditions of work that build commitment to the school as a workplace and motivate teachers and other employees to be their best at work. The chapter draws on research, practice, and theory to illuminate the important role that principal leadership practices play in laying the foundation for positive working conditions. The chapter also examines the impact of working conditions during the pandemic and provides discussion questions for readers to consider.

> *Effective leaders promote the personal and professional health, well-being, and work-life balance of faculty and staff.*
>
> (PSEL Standard 6h)

> *Effective leaders tend to their own learning and effectiveness through reflection, study, and improvement, maintaining a healthy work-life balance.*
>
> (PSEL Standard 6i)

INTRODUCTION

A core premise of Talent-Centered Education Leadership (TCEL) is that not only do employees matter, but they are critical for organizational success; therefore, creating

DOI: 10.4324/9781003457060-3

working conditions that promote their well-being and engagement should be a core value for school employers. Education employers need to focus on the well-being of their workforce not only because it is the ethical thing to do but also because supportive working conditions are beneficial for organizational performance excellence, such as enhancing student outcomes (Bear et al., 2014; Kraft et al., 2016). As former North Carolina governor Michael Easley eloquently stated, "Teacher working conditions are student learning conditions" (Hirsch & Emerick, 2007).

Working conditions describe the ways in which employees experience interactions with their workplace as an organization. They shape an employee's intrinsic and extrinsic motivation and, thereby, shape their engagement and effectiveness. School working conditions are a result of many factors including administrative support and communications, shared decision-making, opportunities for professional growth and advancement, opportunities for peer collaboration and support, the structure of time, school safety and student behavior, the quality of facilities and allocation of resources, the school's culture, and the level of community support (Burkhauser, 2017). Working conditions matter greatly because they affect employee motivation, engagement, satisfaction, and retention, and these factors, in turn, influence performance outcomes such as student learning and success.

POOR WORKING CONDITIONS CONTRIBUTE TO TEACHER TURNOVER

Teacher turnover is a challenge across the teaching profession, but it is a particularly acute problem in schools with large concentrations of high-poverty, non-White, and low-achieving populations of students (Ronfeldt et al., 2013). Nationally about 16% of teachers turn over each year, with much higher rates in high-poverty compared to affluent schools (Steiner & Woo, 2021). Teachers in high-poverty schools tend to either transfer to wealthier, less diverse, and higher-achieving schools or depart the industry altogether, leaving their former less advantaged schools with a treadmill of new teachers. Because teaching is a skill that takes time to develop, these schools suffer with lower-quality beginning teachers, who often leave the school once they gain proficiency as a teacher. The repeated turnover creates a context where there is a lack of consistency and limited opportunities for the building of lasting relationships with students to support their ongoing success given the "parade of new faces" that walk through the classroom doors every year.

Indeed, repeated teacher turnover has been statistically linked to lower student achievement as a result (Ronfeldt et al., 2013). Teacher turnover affects school quality through both compositional and disruptive effects. Compositional effects describe the impact caused by more experienced, better-qualified teachers leaving to be replaced by newer, less experienced teachers. Disruptive effects describe the impact on student learning of the constant churn of teachers moving in and out of the school, which redirects school resources to hiring, impacts collaborative relationships among teachers, undermines knowledge about the curriculum, and disrupts relationships of teachers with students. The effect of turnover on learning is worse in schools with more low-income and Black students (Ronfeldt et al., 2013; Simon & Johnson, 2015).

Given the negative consequences of frequent teacher turnover, it is critical to understand its contributing factors. Recent research has shown that teacher turnover is heavily attributed to poor working conditions, and the higher turnover in high-poverty schools is further motivated by the more challenging working conditions that characterize some of these schools (Allensworth et al., 2009; Johnson et al., 2012; Simon & Johnson, 2015). The conditions that shape teacher satisfaction with their conditions of work and the choices teachers make to stay or leave the school or the profession often relate primarily to factors that the principal can influence. Specifically, the social fabric of the school – the culture, leadership, and relationships among colleagues in the school – matters most to teacher satisfaction (Johnson et al., 2012).

BOX 2.1: WHEN IT'S NOT ROSY: TEACHER WORKING CONDITIONS AND THE COVID-19 PANDEMIC

Prior to the COVID-19 pandemic, annual teacher turnover in the United States was about 16%. Teacher stress, burnout, and intent to leave increased with changes in working conditions brought on by the pandemic. Consequently, by January 2021, 23% of teachers planned to leave their jobs by the end of the year, compared to 17% of all workers. Worse yet, nearly 50% of Black teachers indicated an intention to leave their positions by the end of the year. The higher turnover intentions of Black teachers were particularly concerning because Black teachers are underrepresented in the teaching profession, and there is clear evidence to suggest that student learning and other positive outcomes are enhanced for all students, but particularly for students of color, when students have a teacher of color (Steiner & Woo, 2021).

Teaching has long been considered a high-stress profession, and volumes of research have examined the factors that cause teacher stress, burnout, and turnover. This research has shown that working conditions – including teacher salaries, school leadership, opportunities for professional collaboration, access to resources, and a positive organizational culture – are important for teacher satisfaction and retention (Kraft et al., 2021). Working conditions shape satisfaction through various means; for example, they can influence teachers' sense of efficacy. Teachers with a stronger sense of efficacy are less likely to leave their positions and classrooms (Johnson & Birkeland, 2003).

Because of the changes caused by the swift pivot to remote and hybrid learning, teachers' sense of success declined during the pandemic. However, Kraft et al. (2021) found that teachers in schools with supportive working conditions in place prior to the pandemic saw reduced declines in teacher efficacy. Preexisting positive working conditions that reduced the negative impact of the pandemic included clear communications, targeted professional development, professional collaboration, reasonable expectations, and positive feedback. These conditions provided support for navigating the challenges associated with unplanned radical change. Teachers working in schools with these supportive conditions were less likely to experience stress, depression, burnout, and the desire to quit.

Kraft et al. (2021) also found that teachers – even those in the same school – experienced their work environments differently. There was a range of opinions about the working conditions depending on which teacher was describing them. The fact that teachers within a school may perceive working conditions differently creates a management challenge for principals and re-emphasizes the avoidance of a "one-size-fits-all" approach to support. For example, beginning teachers often receive much attention through avenues such as mentorship and onboarding supports because it is understood that they are in a period that is sensitive to turnover. However, the focus on beginning teachers can result in the neglect of more experienced teachers who have different types of needs that often are unsupported (Tran & Smith, 2020). By collecting and analyzing data on employee perceptions of working conditions, the principal can identify the range of perceptions and seek clear communication with teachers across the school to ensure that working conditions within subcultures in the school are positive and supportive and are meeting teacher needs.

Discussion Questions: What steps would you take as a school leader to develop a safe and supportive work environment for your teachers? How will these conditions buffer the school from external events, especially in a turbulent and challenging education environment? How would you collect and use information to assess your teachers' sense of satisfaction and need for support? Please rationalize and justify your response based on ethical, legal, professional, and/or leadership frameworks.

THE PRINCIPAL'S ROLE IN SHAPING TEACHER WORKING CONDITIONS

Some working conditions are controlled by school districts, state or national policymakers, or community leaders. For example, low salaries, which are a product of education funding formulas and district policies, have been correlated with teacher retention and turnover (Nguyen et al., 2020; Steiner & Woo, 2021). While issues related to salaries are largely outside of the control of the school, there are many other influential conditions that can be directly influenced by school leaders.

The principal plays a central role in shaping the working conditions that matter most to teacher quality, satisfaction, and retention. In a review of research literature on teacher working conditions, Leithwood (2006) found that teacher working conditions significantly influence teachers' feelings and knowledge, and teachers' feelings and knowledge, in turn, influence teacher retention, teacher performance, and student learning. Building on this research, Leithwood and McAdie (2010) identified eight specific "internal states" of teachers that affect teacher motivation and performance. They include:

- Individual sense of professional efficacy
- Collective sense of professional efficacy
- Organizational commitment
- Job satisfaction
- Stress and burnout
- Morale
- Engagement or disengagement (from the school and/or profession)
- Pedagogical content knowledge

These states are directly affected by working conditions. Leithwood and Riehl (2003) identified three major roles that the principal plays through their leadership in a school: setting direction, developing people, and developing the organization. It is through these leadership activities that the principal creates the conditions of work that affect teacher stress, efficacy, commitment, satisfaction, morale, engagement, and teaching capacity (Leithwood & McAdie, 2010; Leithwood & Riehl, 2003). In essence, the principal's primary leadership role is to create working conditions that improve the employee experience throughout the critical moments (e.g., recruitment, orientation, development, tenure achievement) across the teacher's career cycle (Tran & Smith, 2020) and, thereby, foster teacher engagement and student success.

The argument for the pivotal role of school leaders for teacher retention is supported by research that has consistently found that teachers' perception of the administrative support they receive is the most influential factor for their retention (Boyd et al., 2011; Horng, 2009). More recent research has unpacked the various forms of administrative support and suggests that the demonstration of *respect* for teachers as professionals is critical for teacher recruitment (Tran & Smith, 2019) and retention (Tran et al., 2020), as it undergirds and serves the foundation for all other forms of support.

BOX 2.2: PRINCIPAL SELF-CARE

While we have touched on the issue of work-life balance for teachers, what gets far less attention is the work-life balance of school principals. Nationally, approximately one in every five principals leave the profession each year (Goldring & Taie, 2018), and school leadership turnover incurs significant costs not only financially (replacement cost that could have been used for teacher and student resources instead) (Jensen, 2014; Tran et al., 2018) but also in terms of lower student achievement test scores, school proficiency rates, and teacher retention (Harbatkin & Henry, 2019). With all that must be done in the school, it is easy for the work to consume the school principal's schedule, resulting in seven-day workweeks and long workdays. The risk of exhaustion is always lurking around the corner. That is why it is critical for school leaders to seek support when appropriate, build and leverage the leadership of others instead of taking on everything themselves, and maintain a manageable work-life balance. If school leaders don't want to do this for their own sake, then for the sake of their family, students, faculty, and staff. A burnt-out principal is not good for anyone.

The leadership practices that matter to promote effective working conditions do not all have to be carried out by the principal in isolation, but the principal plays a critical role in setting the tone and laying the foundation for leadership practices implemented across the school to foster and support school success. Next, we use the leadership domains defined by the Comprehensive Assessment of Leadership for Learning (CALL) to organize the school leadership practices identified by Leithwood and McAdie (2010) that shape teacher working conditions (see, e.g., Halverson & Kelley, 2017; Halverson et al., 2014; leadershipforlearning.org). The five leadership domains represent core areas of leadership practice undertaken by school leaders. While we know that important leadership practices are distributed across many actors in a school (Mayrowetz, 2008; Spillane & Diamond, 2007; Spillane et al., 2004), the principal plays an important role in providing symbolic and structural leadership to lay the foundation for the emergence of effective leadership practices and for school success. Table 2.1 summarizes the CALL domains and links leadership action in each domain to the resulting working conditions and their impact on teacher engagement, motivation, and satisfaction. The first leadership domain identified in the CALL model is establishing a clear focus on learning. The principal builds shared understanding by consistently sharing the story of the school, working to build clear consensus about the school's instructional goals, and creating and sustaining programs designed to address these goals (Halverson & Kelley, 2017).

These actions help to establish a shared history, common language, and shared understanding about the direction of the school; define the school's approach to student behavior management and instruction; and promote a sense of being part of something important that is bigger than any one individual. When done well, the result is increased professional and collective efficacy, organizational commitment, job satisfaction, and engagement.

The second CALL domain focuses on monitoring teaching and learning. Principal leadership practices in this domain include ensuring regular assessments of teaching through formal and informal walkthroughs and teacher observations. The walkthroughs do not necessarily have to be done by the principal, but the principal is responsible for ensuring that these observations occur and that teachers have opportunities to receive actionable feedback and participate in relevant professional development to support their continuous growth and improvement. Being able to build the knowledge and skills to be effective in the classroom reduces teacher stress, improves morale, and enhances pedagogical content knowledge.

The third CALL domain focuses on building opportunities for professional collaboration. Teachers are rarely trained to lead collaborative teams. Yet the ability to facilitate effective group processes is perhaps more important in teaching than in just about any other career. Teachers have limited time for team meetings, and they need to be skilled facilitators to make this collaboration time efficient and effective. Principals foster professional community by setting aside dedicated collaborative meeting time, building the capacity of teachers to lead collaborative team meetings, providing clarity about the purpose of the collaborative meeting time, modeling effective collaboration, and providing teams with feedback to improve performance. Effective collaborative teams promote a positive work culture and provide teachers with space for problem-solving with others. This leads to enhanced professional and collective efficacy, job satisfaction, and engagement in the work.

The fourth CALL domain involves leadership practices related to acquiring and allocating resources. Principals play a central role in allocating resources at the school level and in establishing opportunities for staff input on policy decisions that impact teaching and learning in the school. Key resources that need to be effectively allocated include personnel (assigning teachers to classes, setting teacher workloads), time, space, materials, and financial resources. Principals also shape district decisions by providing feedback to the district about how their decisions impact the school. An important role that the principal can play is to build relationships with district personnel and keep the lines of communication between the district and school open. As principals work to engage teachers in leadership initiatives at the school level, it is important that their efforts are not undermined by district policies. Two examples illustrate this point.

Scenario 1: The teachers at an elementary school identify writing as an important area of needed improvement. They invest time in researching writing programs and identify and purchase a writing curriculum that they feel would really help their students improve. As it turns out, the major conference that supports implementation of the writing curriculum has been scheduled on the same day as the district's annual blood pathogen training. The school asks if they can attend the writing conference and make up the blood pathogen training later, but the district denies the request because attendance at the blood pathogen training is mandatory. Implementation of the writing curriculum stops. The teachers who worked so hard to address the writing challenges of their students feel undermined and defeated.

Scenario 2: The principal at an urban high school has been working to encourage teachers to analyze school data and identify and implement solutions to student learning problems. After a review of their data, the teachers identify the challenges associated with overaged students as a problem that they think they can work on and make some successful progress. Overaged students often cause behavior and attendance problems. The teachers identify course-taking patterns that lead to course failure and ultimately overaged students. They develop interventions around these specific areas and make progress in addressing the retention problem that leads to overaged students. The district, noting their efforts, decides to adopt a districtwide program to work on the overaged student problem. However, the district's new solution, while being adopted because of the work of these teachers, is not compatible with the school's approach. Moreover, the teachers who worked so hard to identify and address the problem are asked to stop doing the work they had started and, instead, implement the district solution. The teachers decide that in the future, they will decline leadership opportunities because they feel disrespected and undermined.

Both of these scenarios are real events and provide a testament to the important role the principal should play in building a solid relationship with the district and making the case for their schools so efforts made at the school level are supported rather than undermined by district policy decisions. When principals succeed in matching teacher capacity with teaching assignments, engage teachers in decision-making, and manage up to protect the school's resources and direction, teachers will have higher job satisfaction, improved morale, and reduced stress and burnout.

The fifth CALL domain is creating a safe and effective learning environment. Leadership practices in this domain include building a shared approach to student behavior management, managing school safety, building positive relationships with family and community members, and buffering teachers from interruptions in their instructional time, such as intercom interruptions during the class period. When these behavior, safety, and support structures are in place, it can enhance professional efficacy, reduce stress and burnout, and improve teacher morale.

The leadership practices described here support the development and maintenance of positive working conditions in schools. These working conditions are important because they make the school a more attractive place to work and enable teachers to be successful at what they do. They are also correlated with reduced teacher turnover, improved teacher job satisfaction, and ultimately higher quality teaching.

Table 2.1 Leadership Practices That Shape School Working Conditions and Their Impact on Teacher Engagement, Motivation, and Satisfaction

CALL Domains of Leadership Practice	*Leadership Practices*	*Resulting Working Conditions*	*Impact on Teachers*
Focus on Learning	Build community around learning Tell and live the school's story Engage the school community in planning Build programs that promote learning and advance equity	Clear goals shared across the school Teachers find their work meaningful Well-developed and stable programs implemented Quality of communication in the school improved School improvement plans better match teacher beliefs about what they should be	Professional efficacy Collective efficacy Organizational commitment Job satisfaction Engagement
Monitoring Teaching and Learning	Conduct regular assessments of teaching and learning Provide feedback and supports to improve teaching practice	Professional development and support provided High academic expectations for students communicated Communication skills improved	Reduced stress and burnout Improved morale Pedagogical content knowledge
Building Professional Community	Build teacher capacity to lead collaborative teams Structure opportunities for professional collaboration Set clear goals for collaboration time Provide feedback about team progress Model effective collaboration	A positive and supportive school culture is promoted Teachers collaborate Participation in decision-making is shared Opportunities for collaboration and work in small teams are provided Regular feedback to teacher teams about their progress is given Friendliness is improved	Professional efficacy Collective efficacy Job satisfaction Engagement

(*Continued*)

Table 2.1 (Continued)

CALL Domains of Leadership Practice	*Leadership Practices*	*Resulting Working Conditions*	*Impact on Teachers*
Acquiring and Allocating Resources	Consider teachers, time, facilities, and finances as core resources for improvement Allocate teachers to teaching assignments according to capacity Seek funding to support school goals Provide district leaders with clear feedback regarding school needs	Teacher workload volume is manageable Adequate instructional prep time is provided A clear match between teacher capacity/training and teaching assignments is in place Principals are able to manage up	Professional efficacy Job satisfaction Reduced stress and burnout Improved morale
Establishing a Safe and Effective Learning Environment	Build clear, shared understanding of behavioral interventions and supports Carefully manage school safety Build positive relationships with parents and community Protect teacher instructional time from unnecessary interruption	Student discipline is under control Sense of safety is enhanced Parents and the wider community provide support Teaching environment is buffered from interruption	Professional efficacy Reduced stress and burnout Improved morale

Sources: Adapted from Halverson & Kelley, 2017; and Leithwood & McAdie, 2010

BOX 2.3: THE NORTH CAROLINA TEACHER WORKING CONDITIONS SURVEY

Recognizing the clear relationship between teacher working conditions and student learning outcomes, beginning in 2002, the state of North Carolina has conducted annual teacher working condition surveys and has invested in leveraging survey results for school improvement. As former Governor Michael Easley noted, "teacher working conditions are student learning conditions." The North Carolina Teacher Working Conditions survey focuses on teacher planning and collaboration time, facilities and resources (access to sufficient instructional materials, technology, professional workspace, equipment and supplies, in a safe work environment), teacher empowerment in decision-making, quality of school leadership, and access to quality professional development. Results from the surveys in North Carolina have shown that there is a clear relationship between teacher working conditions, teacher retention, and student learning. In addition, the North Carolina schools that use survey data to inform school improvement have shown a marked improvement in working conditions (Hirsch & Emerick, 2007).

Table 2.2 provides a comparison of the results of the 2018, 2020, and 2022 survey results. The table shows the percentage of teachers who agree or strongly agree with each statement.

What do these data suggest for ways that a principal could focus their leadership to improve teacher working conditions and student learning?

Source: Hirsch & Emerick, 2007; and the North Carolina Teacher Working Conditions Survey, https://nctwcs.org/

Table 2.2 North Carolina Teacher Working Conditions Survey*

	2018	*2020*	*2022*
a. Class sizes are reasonable such that (teachers) ["Teachers" means a majority of teachers in your school.] have the time available to meet the needs of all students.	59.17%	60.15%	62.20%
b. Teachers have time available to collaborate with colleagues.	74.38%	74.37%	69.36%
c. Teachers are allowed to focus on educating students with minimal interruptions.	68.29%	68.42%	67.88%
d. The non-instructional (time)[Non-instructional time includes any time during the day without the responsibility for student contact, including collaboration planning, meetings/conferences with students and families, etc.] provided for teachers in my school is sufficient.	64.05%	64.11%	57.41%

(*Continued*)

Table 1.1 (Continued)

	2018	*2020*	*2022*
e. Efforts are made to minimize the amount of routine (paperwork) [Routine paperwork means both electronic and paper forms and documents that must be completed to comply with school, district, state, and federal policies] teachers are required to do.	64.50%	63.78%	64.73%
f. Teachers have sufficient instructional time to meet the needs of all students.	70.00%	69.62%	68.69%
g. Teachers are protected from duties that interfere with their essential role of educating students.	71.52%	69.85%	66.99%

Source: https://nctwcs.org/ Reproduced with permission.

Learning Activities

Discussion Questions:

1. What are the working conditions that support teacher success? How can the principal actively work to shape these conditions?
2. Importantly, increasing attention is being paid to employee mental health. Given that "a much higher percentage of teachers reported frequent job-related stress and symptoms of depression than the general adult population" (Steiner & Woo, 2021), what support should a school or district provide to ensure that its employees are receiving the kinds of support they need to be successful? What should a principal do to ensure that their staff is managing stress successfully and has the resources needed to address challenges related to depression?
3. Work-life balance is critical to employee satisfaction. As a principal, how do you attend to your own positive work-life balance? How can you take the lessons from your own experience to better support the work-life balance of your employees?
4. Open, positive communication plays an important role in establishing a positive work environment. Leadership plays a critical role in shaping the communications in a school. What specific actions should you take as a school leader to create and sustain positive communication in the school? Specifically, how will you approach interactions with teachers? Students? Parents? District personnel? Discuss the implications for written communications, communications with individuals, and communications with groups.
5. Many of the most important working conditions in schools are shaped by the principal's leadership. However, some working conditions are the responsibility of the district or of a partnership between the district and the school. How will you work with your district to support changes in district policy and practice that impact important working conditions at the school level?

CONCLUSION

Working conditions are a critical component of Talent-Centered Education Leadership because they lay the foundations for employee satisfaction, engagement, and success. Creating a positive work environment involves establishing effective, positive, and reliable communications; identifying and addressing employee training needs; establishing opportunities for professional collaboration; promoting a positive school culture; setting challenging academic goals for students; establishing a safe environment; and providing the resources – in uninterrupted time – for instruction. Working conditions provide the conditions for employees to be successful, and successful employees have higher levels of satisfaction and lower levels of turnover.

It is important to note that employees, even in the same organization, may experience their workplace differently. Consequently, the principal should collect data about workplace conditions to better understand the differences and strive to ensure that the needs of employees across the organization are being addressed. The North Carolina example illustrates that data-informed decision-making can be used to improve working conditions, increase employee satisfaction, reduce turnover, and elevate student learning outcomes.

Increasingly, employees are striving to find meaning in their work and are motivated to stay with their employers if their employers can provide this. Most teachers enter the profession for altruistic reasons, such as helping students learn and making a positive difference in their lives. Teacher satisfaction is highest when teachers are successful at helping students learn and are provided the context and resources that cultivate this.

Summary of Key Points

- Working conditions are the result of effective school leadership practices: creating a shared focus on learning; providing feedback and support; establishing the conditions for thriving professional collaboration; allocating teacher time, facilities, and financial resources effectively; and promoting safe and effective learning environments. These leadership practices foster a clear shared sense of the importance of the work, strengthen and improve professional efficacy, support collaborative problem-solving, and ensure that teachers have the resources they need to be successful in a safe and effective learning environment.
- Effective working conditions promote professional efficacy, which increases satisfaction, reduces stress and burnout, and improves teacher retention. Teacher retention enhances teacher quality. Diverse and low-income schools often struggle with less effective working conditions; attention to improving working conditions is of particular importance in these schools.
- Positive working conditions buffer schools from organizational shocks. Teachers in schools with more positive working conditions weather the storm

caused by the introduction of a pandemic or potential policy shocks to the system. A solid foundation of effective communications, professional development, a positive organizational culture, and professional collaborative relationships, among others, provides a cushion to support sudden changes in policies that would otherwise severely negatively impact the quality of teachers' work lives.

REFERENCES

Allensworth, E., Ponisciak, S., & Mazzeo, C. (2009). *The schools teachers leave: Teacher mobility in Chicago Public Schools*. Consortium on Chicago School Research – University of Chicago.

Bear, G. G., Yang, C., Pell, M., & Gaskins, C. (2014). Validation of a brief measure of teachers' perceptions of school climate: Relations to student achievement and suspensions. *Learning Environments Research, 17*(3), 339–354. https://doi.org/10.1007/s10984-014-9162-1

Boyd, D., Grossman, P., Ing, M., Lankford, H., Loeb, S., & Wyckoff, J. (2011). The influence of school administrators on teacher retention decisions. *American Educational Research Journal, 48*(2), 303–333.

Burkhauser, S. (2017). How much do school principals matter when it comes to teacher working conditions? *Educational Evaluation and Policy Analysis, 39*(1), 126–145.

EdWeek Research, C. (2020, April 27). Survey tracker: Monitoring how K–12 educators are responding to coronavirus. *Education Week*. https://www.edweek.org/teaching-learning/survey-tracker-monitoring-how-k-12-educators-are-responding-to-coronavirus/2020/04

Goldring, R., & Taie, S. (2018). *Principal attrition and m=mobility: Results from the 2016–17 principal follow-up survey first look* (NCES 2018–066). U.S. Department of Education, National Center for Education Statistics.

Halverson, R., & Kelley, C. (2017). *Mapping leadership: The tasks that matter for improving teaching and learning in schools*. Jossey-Bass.

Halverson, R., Kelley, C., & Shaw, J. (2014). A CALL for improved school leadership. *Phi Delta Kappan, 95*(6), 57–60.

Harbatkin, E., & Henry, G. T. (2019). The cascading effects of principal turnover on students and schools. *Brookings*. www.brookings.edu/blog/brown-center-chalkboard/2019/10/21/the-cascading-effects-of-principal-turnover-on-students-and-schools/

Hirsch, E., & Emerick, S. (2007). *Teacher working conditions are student learning conditions: A report on the 2006 North Carolina Teacher Working Conditions Survey*. Center for Teaching Quality. www.teachingquality.org

Horng, E. L. (2009). Teacher tradeoffs: Disentangling teachers' preferences for working conditions and student demographics. *American Educational Research Journal, 46*(3), 690–717.

Ingersoll, R. (2003, September). *Is there really a teacher shortage?* Reprinted from a Research Report Co-sponsored by the Consortium for Policy Research in Education and the Center for the Study of Teaching and Policy. https://repository.upenn.edu/gse_pubs

Jensen, D. (2014). *Churn: The high cost of principal turnover*. School Leaders Network. https://connectleadsucceed.org

Johnson, S. M., & Birkeland, S. E. (2003). Pursuing a "sense of success": New teachers explain their career decisions. *American Educational Research Journal, 40*(3), 581–617. https://doi.org/10.3102/00028312040003581

Johnson, S. M., Kraft, M., & Papay, J. P. (2012). How context matters in high-need schools: The effects of teachers' working conditions on their professional satisfaction and their students' achievement. *Teachers College Record, 114*(10), 1–39.

Kraft, M. A., Marinell, W. H., & Shen-Wei Yee, D. (2016). School organizational contexts, teacher turnover, and student achievement: Evidence from panel data. *American Educational Research Journal, 53*(5), 1411–1449. https://doi.org/10.3102/0002831216667478

Kraft, M. A., Simon, N. S., & Lyon, M. A. (2021). Sustaining a sense of success: The protective role of teacher working conditions during the COVID-19 pandemic. *Journal of Research on Educational Effectiveness, 14*(4), 727–769. https://doi.org/10.1080/19345747.2021.1938314

Leithwood, K. (2006). *Teacher working conditions that matter: Evidence for change.* Elementary Teachers' Federation of Ontario.

Leithwood, K., & McAdie, P. (2010). Teacher working conditions that matter. *Education Canada, 47*(2). www.cea-ace.ca

Leithwood, K. A., & Riehl, C. (2003). *What we know about successful school leadership.* Laboratory for Student Success, Temple University.

Mayrowetz, D. (2008). Making sense of distributed leadership: Exploring the multiple usages of the concept in the field. *Educational Administration Quarterly, 44*(3), 424–435.

Nguyen, T. D., Pham, L. D., Crouch, M., & Springer, M. G. (2020). The correlates of teacher turnover: An updated and expanded meta-analysis of the literature. *Educational Research Review, 31*, 100355.

Ronfeldt, M., Loeb, S., & Wyckoff, J. (2013). How teacher turnover harms student achievement. *American Educational Research Journal, 50*(1), 4–36.

Simon, N. S., & Johnson, S. M. (2015). Teacher turnover in high poverty schools: What we know and can do. *Teachers College Record, 117*, 030308.

Spillane, J. P., & Diamond, J. B. (Eds.). (2007). *Distributed leadership in practice.* Teachers College, Columbia University.

Spillane, J. P., Halverson, R., & Diamond, J. B. (2004). Towards a theory of leadership practice: A distributed perspective. *Journal of Curriculum Studies, 36*(1), 3–34.

Steiner, E. D., & Woo, A. (2021). *Job-related stress threatens the teacher supply: Key findings from the 2021 state of the U.S. teacher survey.* RAND Corporation. www.rand.org/pubs/research_reports/RRA1108-1.html

Tran, H. (2021). *Retaining teachers with talent centered education leadership* (SC-Teacher Report). https://sc-teacher.org/retaining-teachers-through-talent-centered-education-leadership/

Tran, H., Hardie, S., & Cunningham, K. M. (2020). Leading with empathy and humanity: Why talent-centred education leadership is especially critical amidst the pandemic crisis. *International Studies in Educational Administration (Commonwealth Council for Educational Administration & Management (CCEAM)), 48*(1), 39–45.

Tran, H., McCormick, J., & Nguyen, T. T. (2018). The cost of replacing South Carolina high school principals. *Management in Education, 32*(3), 109–118.

Tran, H., & Smith, D. (2019). Insufficient money and inadequate respect: What obstructs the recruitment of college students to teach in hard-to-staff schools. *Journal of Educational Administration, 57*(2), 152–166.

Tran, H., & Smith, D. A. (2020). Designing an employee experience approach to teacher retention in hard-to-staff schools. *NASSP Bulletin, 104*(2), 85–109.

CHAPTER 3

Talent Motivation

Chapter Summary

The potential success of teachers is influenced by many factors, not the least of which is their motivation. To engage and sustain this motivation, employers work with employees to co-construct the intentional design of the employee experience so employees *want* to, rather than *need* to, come to work. Doing so will unlock the discretionary efforts of employees and fully engage them to be catalysts for organizational excellence. This chapter helps leaders set the stage for a great workplace by addressing these issues.

Effective leaders empower and motivate teachers and staff to the highest levels of professional practice and to continuous learning and improvement.

(PSEL Standard 6f)

INTRODUCTION

Research has consistently found that teachers are the most important school input for student outcomes (Bowen & Mills, 2017; Blazar & Kraft, 2017). Students of teachers with high value-added student test scores, for example, have been found more likely to attend college, enroll in more selective institutions, and earn higher salaries (Chetty et al., 2014). Yet the success of teachers is influenced by many factors, not the least of which is their motivation.

DOI: 10.4324/9781003457060-4

The expectancy theory of motivation argues that an individual's performance is not only contingent on their motivation, engagement, and involvement but is further predicated on their knowledge, skills, and abilities (Guest, 1997). The latter requires a work environment that promotes the recruitment, selection, and development of educational talent. Cultivating and maintaining such a humanistic environment is a critical role for talent-centered school administrators (Tran, 2022). This does not mean that school employers should purely cater to employees' every whim. In fact, employees do not expect privileges to be handed to them without stipulations, rather they appreciate when performance accountability and standards are upheld. An employee who constantly avoids disciplinary action despite violating the behavioral code of conduct (e.g., unexcused excessive absences) sends the message to their fellow employees that the standards are, at best, hollow and meaningless or, even worse, discriminatory. Just like with students, a culture of high but clear expectations for employees increases the potential for positive results.

Consequently, a high-performance working system can establish the nourishing context that links employee motivation to performance. High-performance work systems tightly coordinate mutually supportive HR activities in the service of improving performance. These activities include, but are not limited to, rearranging work schedule and job redesign, enhancing workforce contributions, setting workplace practices for employee empowerment, proactively recruiting and selecting high-performing talent, implementing HR development programs, conducting performance monitoring, sustaining a culture of continuous improvement, and designing rewards and compensation for improving motivation for performance (Armstrong & Taylor, 2020). Given its importance, the next section will elaborate on the topic of motivation in more detail.

MOTIVATION

In order to truly leverage Talent-Centered Education Leadership (Tran, 2022) it is necessary to understand employee motivation. Unfortunately, education policy and reform initiatives are often undergirded by an outdated philosophy of motivation from the early 20th century, known in the scholarship as instrumentality theory. Instrumentality theory has its foundation in scientific management and Taylorism, based primarily on the idea that employee performance can be motivated solely by management control via rewards and punishment (Armstrong & Taylor, 2020). This is often the theory undergirding many performance/merit pay initiatives that have been in vogue again in recent years, yet they often ignore the most important aspects of the workplace, namely the human elements such as intrinsic motivation and the power of social relationships. Focusing on the topic of merit and performance pay as an example, the next section will review their respective literatures to better understand the opportunities and limitations associated with such efforts.

Merit Pay and Performance Pay

In the 20th century, human resources management policies in schools were largely disconnected from the educational goals of schools. Rather than reinforcing educational goals, teacher compensation systems evolved to address inequities in prior compensation systems which typically paid men more than women, White teachers more than teachers of color, and secondary school teachers more than elementary teachers. First introduced in 1921, the single salary schedule eliminated much of the subjectivity of prior systems, favored equality, and rewarded additional education and years of experience rather than teacher performance. The single salary schedule addressed many problems inherent in the prior systems, but it did little to incentivize teacher performance (Kelley, 1997; Odden & Kelley, 1997, 2002).

Critics of the single salary schedule questioned whether different pay incentives would attract more effective individuals who would otherwise choose a profession that rewarded strong performance, effort, and skills. Performance pay was touted as a mechanism to improve student achievement and as a redress for teacher supply problems (Shifrer et al., 2017; Glazerman et al., 2011). Specifically, performance pay programs were purported to be able to attract high-potential professionals who would otherwise resist entry into the teaching profession that lacks salary differentiation between high and low performers (Bowen & Mills, 2017). This sorting effect is said to occur because high-performing individuals are attracted to jobs that pay for performance and resist working at institutions that pay employees without performance-based differentiation (Erikkson et al., 2009). At least, aligning incentives in the compensation system with school or district educational goals seemed like a good idea (Kelley, 1996; Odden & Kelley, 1997).

Recent decades have brought much enthusiasm for promoting the use of teacher pay to incentivize improvements in student outcomes, with performance pay initiatives being the most popular (U.S. Department of Education, 2009; Podgursky & Springer, 2007). Although some positive findings have been identified in the literature (Chiang et al., 2015; Balch & Springer, 2015; Sojourner et al., 2014), results from the bulk of experimental and nonexperimental evaluations have largely not been found to be promising either for student outcomes (Imberman & Lovenheim, 2015; Marsh et al., 2011; Springer et al., 2012a) or increasing the supply of quality teachers through a compositional effect (Goodman & Turner, 2013; Bowen & Mills, 2017). Shifrer et al. (2017), for example, examined the effects of an urban school districts' teacher performance pay program on student achievement and teacher retention and even accounted for award amount. Based on results from a regression discontinuity analysis, they found that financial awards were not consistently related to either outcome. On the student performance side, numerous studies, including those designed as multiyear randomized control trials, have not supported a link between incentive pay and student outcomes (Springer et al., 2012a, 2012b; Marsh et al., 2011). Similarly, results from Goodman and Turner's (2013) experimental research design found no changes in teacher supply as a result of schools being eligible for group-based teacher incentive programs, which coincides with the evidence that suggests performance pay does not alter the teacher workforce composition (Bowen & Mills, 2017; Goodman & Turner, 2013). In fact, Bowen and Mills (2017) found that explicit extrinsic rewards for factors such as performance "may not increase retention and possibly even dissuade current or potential, high-quality educators from the profession because they find intrinsic motivation crowding-out effects to outweigh the financial gain" (p. 25).

Why should we expect that performance pay might not increase teacher quality or improve student learning outcomes? First, incentive systems are very challenging to design, as they can easily produce both intended and unintended consequences (Odden & Kelley, 2002). Ideally, a performance pay system would be designed to complement the full range of strategic human resource policies and be aligned with the educational goals of the district. This is known as *strategic human resources management* (Heneman & Milanowski, 2004; Tran, 2015). Thus, teacher professional development opportunities would enhance knowledge and skills; evaluation systems would provide meaningful feedback and support for performance improvement; and organizational mission, goals, professional development, and improvement efforts would all point towards the same performance indicators and strategies for improvement. The failure of researchers to identify a solid and consistent relationship between pay-for-performance systems and teacher quality or performance improvement highlights the significant challenge in designing performance pay systems that produce the intended effects (Bowen & Mills, 2017; Goodman & Turner, 2013).

When designed poorly, performance pay systems may deter intrinsically motivated people from applying to or staying with the organization because they undermine the altruistic desires among teachers to make meaningful impacts on the lives of the youth due to their deep commitment to the students. It is commonly noted that teachers' bonds with students are often the most rewarding parts of their job (Kelchtermans, 2017).

Herzberg et al. (1959) improved our understanding of intrinsic versus extrinsic motivation in their seminal presentation of the motivation-hygiene theory. The theory suggests workplace factors that result in job satisfaction (known as motivators) are distinct from those that result in job dissatisfaction (known as hygienes). For example, while low pay may deter or drive individuals away from the teaching profession, higher pay, especially in isolation, does not necessarily attract and retain teachers.

Recent research has supported the argument that the limitations in providing financial rewards in the public sector make the theory particularly relevant to public sector employees, by distinctly linking motivators (as opposed to hygienes) with job satisfaction (Hur, 2018). Even among public workers, it is arguable that the theory is especially relevant for teachers. There is a saying that people do not enter the teaching profession for money. Many educators who have persevered through the years and thrived in the profession originally came into teaching because of a "calling" (Yinon & Orland-Barak, 2017) or a "sense of mission" (Freedman & Appleman, 2009). Relatedly, findings from past studies have supported the argument that individuals often enter the teaching profession because of intrinsically motivated altruistic reasons. These reasons include enthusiasm for teaching youth (Curtis, 2012), helping children (Struyven et al., 2013), making a positive difference in society (Brunetti, 2001; Curtis, 2012; Tran et al., 2015), and improving social equity (Fokkens-Bruinsma & Canrinus, 2012). In Mintrop's (2018) in-depth study of how teachers in three schools (that volunteered for managerial performance management) balanced neo-managerial versus professional concerns, he found that many teachers rebuffed the incentive system that emphasized hygiene factors in favor of teachers' commitment to student justice and service. In fact, he explained that "[w]hile bonus money did play a reinforcing role, the distinguishing criterion between those who rebuffed the system and those who embraced it was the meaningfulness of system elements for one's own performance expectations and desires to learn" (p. 200).

Enduring satisfaction, engagement, and the consequent employment sustainability necessitate talent management policies that prioritize mitigating detrimental effects of hygiene factors, including policies that address low salaries and challenging environmental work context. Yet intrinsic motivating factors, such as providing administrative support so that the employee's work is manageable and meaningful, must also be attended to. This suggests that while hygiene needs (e.g., the ability to earn a living, pay bills, and care for one's family) need to be addressed, addressing only hygiene needs will not mitigate teacher motivational problems. Instead, sustainable and effective talent motivational strategies must first comprehensively address teachers' hygiene needs to minimize negative extrinsic factors, then address motivator needs to captivate their intrinsic desire/interest.

Returning to the topic of performance pay, some educators may view such programs as overly restrictive, prescriptive, and controlling. It is also often perceived as a threat to collaboration with other teachers and teachers' professional autonomy from administrators or the government. For example, organizational identification of the top-performing teacher for a financial bonus may create an incentive for that teacher not to share their resources and skills with their colleagues. Moreover, poor implementation due to factors such as perception that the administrators lack the ability to distinguish between employee performances, favoritism in identification of high performers, and employees' poor understanding of the program details and eligibility for receipt of incentives, results in a lack of trust in the entire program. For these reasons, reforming teacher pay via a performance pay framework is often resisted by many educators (Springer et al., 2012a). This, coupled with the fact that there is relatively slim evidence that supports the effectiveness of performance pay at fulfilling its dual objectives of motivating teachers to improve their performance (Chiang et al., 2015; Balch & Springer, 2015; Sojourner et al., 2014) or attracting/retaining higher-quality individuals into teaching (Fulbeck, 2014; Springer et al., 2014) when compared to studies with no effect or null findings (Bowen & Mills, 2017; Goodman & Turner, 2013; Shifrer et al., 2017), suggests that performance pay is not the "magic bullet" for employee motivation that many promote it to be.

Those who are familiar with the evolution of HRM philosophies and practices should not be too surprised at the lack of success of performance pay programs in education. As mentioned earlier, the stick (i.e., the noncompliance punishment) and carrot (i.e., the compliance reward) philosophy undergirding many of the recent manifestations of performance pay initiatives have outdated origins (Lai, 2017). In the 1960s and 1970s, more evolved theories of motivation were introduced that focused on cognitive processes that are concerned with how people interpret their work environment. For example, Vroom (1964) proposed the valency-instrumentality-expectancy (VIE) theory that suggested employees will be motivated if they value the outcome (valency), believe that what they will do is instrumental to leading to the outcome (instrumentality), and trust in the likelihood of receiving the outcome should they expend the necessary effort (expectancy). This theory captures additional nuances to employee motivation than prior theories did. For example, continuing with the performance pay scenario, a school district may communicate that rewards will be allocated to the highest-performing teachers. However, based on past experiences, teachers may believe that the rewards will be too small to influence behavioral changes (low valency), doled out on a political basis (low instrumentality), or that the district will not have the funds to pay out the rewards since a high number of teachers met the criteria (low expectancy). In this situation, we would not expect the performance pay program to be highly motivating (see, e.g., Kelley, 1998).

With regard to valency, modern talent management practices suggest that it is important to intentionally consider people over processes in employer's recognition efforts (Morgan, 2017). For example, while it may be nice to recognize all workers who have been with the school for ten years by rewarding each of them with a gift card, this approach is not very personal. Personalizing the recognition activities to the talent would be more in line with Talent-Centered Education Leadership (Tran, 2022). The individual approach to talent management is essential in facilitating inclusivity in an increasingly diverse work environment.

BOX 3.1: MANAGING FOR STYLISTIC DIFFERENCES IN A DIVERSE WORKPLACE

A one-size-fits-all approach to employee management seldom works for everyone. It is often the case that the status quo, which has traditionally benefited the majority, has marginalized the minority. For example, a school leader may host meetings (whether in-person or virtually) to discuss problems and seek input from the workforce on how to resolve them. However, research has suggested that across professions and industries, men often dominate the speaking time in such meetings (Karpowitz et al., 2012; Nittrouer et al., 2018) and are more likely to interrupt women who are speaking (Hancock & Rubin,

2015; McKinsey & Company & Leanin.org, 2019). Reasons why women speak less can be numerous including the fear of being perceived as overly aggressive, emotional, and less competent at work (Brescoll, 2011; McKinsey & Company & Leanin.org, 2019). Women may also be more rapport-oriented than men (Tannen, 1995), which can result in their voices and ideas being overshadowed by men, who may seek to gain dominance and authority when they speak. This can create a chilling effect on the marginalized and not allow for full participation by all participants when dialogue is being sought for important work-related topics and decision-making, resulting in the disengagement of those who are neglected. Moreover, there is often a perception that those who speak have more ideas (receiving credit for those ideas, even if the interrupting speaker merely elaborated on the idea proposed by someone else), confidence, competence, and leadership potential. This further exacerbates the inequity and perpetuates further implicit bias in decision-making.

While the terms *diversity* and *inclusion* are often used in tandem, they are not interchangeable. Diversity speaks to representation (e.g., bringing them in), whereas inclusion speaks to the sense of belonging of those that are represented (e.g., welcoming them so they feel included). An inclusive environment meets people where they are as opposed to strictly assimilating them into the dominant norms that may have sustained inequity by continuously disadvantaging certain groups of people (e.g., the feedback of custodians and food services professionals may not have received much value by employers in the past) (Tran & Jenkins, 2022).

School leaders can create more inclusive environments by allowing equitable proportion of speaking "airtime" (and the receipt of appropriate credit for ideas) by different meeting members (Tannen, 1995) and by understanding that people have different ways of expressing their communications (e.g., differences in pause length, succinctness in communication). Leaders can intentionally seek out opposing views to stated or presented perspectives to have more robust discussions on the topic and facilitate a sense of belonging. They should create a safe space so that everyone feels confident in voicing their opinion and experiences, which allows the organization to gain a diversity of perspectives to connect with their stakeholders.

It is worth noting that when those who have been typically silenced are allowed to speak (especially on topics such as negative experiences related to their demographic identity traits such as gender and race), this may result in uncomfortable "difficult to have" conversations that may feel easier to avoid than to confront. However, talent-centered education leaders must be courageous enough to have honest dialogues about heavy topics to truly progress the workspace and seek commonality where differences may exist.

For school leaders, now more than ever before, it is critical to understand how to motivate each member of the school. Instead of the carrot-and-stick approach, Lai (2017) suggests that

> motivation is less about *employees doing great work* and more about employees *feeling great about their work*. The better employees feel about their work, the more motivated they remain over time. When we step away from the traditional carrot or stick to motivate employees, we can engage in a new and meaningful dialogue about the work instead.
>
> (para 3, emphasis in original)

Lai goes on to explain that this type of motivation starts with communicating the relevance of the employee's work contribution towards the organization's goals of improving student outcomes. Leaders should be proactive in identifying and removing barriers and challenges so that workers can focus on their work without interruptions or distractions. Finally, the contribution of employees should be recognized and appreciated in meaningful ways. When employees are properly motivated, they become engaged with the organization, setting the context for their mutually reinforcing boundless potential to flourish.

EMPLOYEE ENGAGEMENT

While employees typically begin their employment engaged, they tend to disengage across time (Morgan, 2017). Engagement demonstrates an individual's commitment to the organization. It represents the positive feelings and dedication an employee has for their job (Truss et al., 2006). A highly engaged employee displays additional discretionary effort for their job beyond what is entailed in their contract. For example, an engaged teacher may take the extra time and effort to display positive organizational citizenship behavior, such as mentoring struggling new teachers without being explicitly asked to do so. This type of discretionary behavior has been found to differ by 48% in high-complex jobs between "superior" versus "standard" performers (Hunter et al., 1990).

Engaged employees are enthusiastic about their work and accomplishing the organization's objectives and mission. There is often criticism within education concerning the "reform of the month" phenomenon, where teachers may be drained and disengaged by the constant reform churn. Consequently, engagement is critical to ensure appropriate implementation of policies and programs to reap their full potential.

The three ways in which employee engagement is experienced include trait engagement (i.e., employees hold positive views of their work), state engagement (i.e., the degree of engagement employees feel daily), and behavioral engagement (i.e., employees going "above and beyond" typical performance such as taking personal initiative to address organizational matters) (Rooy & Oehler, 2013).

Many of the traits associated with good school leadership have been found to be related to employee engagement, including clarifying expectations, purpose, and procedures; recognizing and appreciating individual employee strengths and efforts; allowing for employee's influence in decision-making; providing adequate support (advising and resources) and development; providing autonomy; supporting work accountability; and treating employees equitably and fairly (Lewis et al., 2014; MacLeod & Clarke, 2009; Macey & Schneider, 2008). Engaged employees have been found to perform better and are less likely to be absent and turn over (Stairs & Galpin, 2010; Messersmith et al., 2011) than their disengaged counterparts.

The relationship between employee engagement (and its associated components of employee motivation, organizational citizenship behavior, and job satisfaction) and organizational performance is complex, yet many education reform advocates often push to skip the complexity to promote "incentive" policies designed to stimulate employee actions for performance improvement directly through monetary rewards or punishment (Tran & Smith, 2020). These policies and practices have largely been found to be ineffective in education and the business world. The result of a lack of employee engagement is burnout and turnover.

On the other hand, while we know that relationships matter, they can be a double-edged sword. For instance, although teachers' relationship with their students, colleagues, and administrators can be their strongest source of support, it can also be the most destructive working factor in their professional lives (Kelchtermans, 2017) and, therefore, must be intentionally attended to. Jenkins and Delbridge (2013) found leaders who attended to those relationships and working climate gained higher levels of engagement among their employees than leaders who attempted to directly influence performance behavior through extrinsic motivators and skipping these intangibles. Because teachers are generally intrinsically motivated to teach and often choose a career in teaching because of a "calling" for meaningful work, the structure and the design of the work itself, including substantive performance feedback and classroom autonomy, can be sources of employee engagement (Macey & Schneider, 2008).

TALENT-CENTERED EDUCATION LEADERSHIP

While the issues of motivation, support, and recognition can be each handled individually, modern cutting-edge human resources management (HRM) suggests that the intentional cultivation and design of a supportive employee experience (EEX) through a Talent-Centered Education Leadership approach yields much promise. Talent-Centered Education Leadership (TCEL) is, as the name implies, a human-centered talent management process where employers work with employees to co-construct and customize each worker's EEX in response to their individual needs, thereby personalizing each EEX for the talent (Tran, 2022; Tran & Smith, 2020). Instead of forcing people to fit into narrow predefined work positions, talent-centered leaders design and co-create the work around the talent, with the recognition that while positions are replaceable, people are not. For example, if Susan leaves her position as the school-site secretary with our organization, the employer can fill the position with someone else, but Susan (with all her unique talents, personality, and interests) can never be replaced.

With TCEL's EEX approach, it is important for employers to get to know their talent as people and learn what work the employees enjoy doing. They should engage in dialogue with each employee about their needs, favorite projects, greatest work moments, aspirations, motivations, and professional goals (Goler et al., 2018; Morgan, 2017). This can happen with employees starting with their first week on the job so that the role can be individually designed in a motivating and meaningful way. Akin to differentiated instruction for students in the classroom, this differentiated management of each employee requires that leaders truly listen to their employee's personal work narratives and communicate with (i.e., not just "talk at") them. This attention should improve the quality of work-life for those in the school as well as create a more inclusive and engaging work environment as specific instances of potential marginalization, discrimination, and negative experiences are recognized and resolved. Talent-centered leaders care about their employees, their success, and their lives (Goler et al., 2018). In sum, school leaders come to know their employee as a "whole" person. Consequently, they work with their employees to co-design jobs that are so talent-centered that the members of the workforce would not want to leave because of the deep support they receive and the pride they have for their employer.

BOX 3.2: DISTRIBUTE LEADERSHIP TASKS TO MAKE THE WORK SUSTAINABLE

School leaders should not only be attentive to the well-being of their employees but also be mindful of their own welfare. Lai (2017) reminds us that the motivation of the workforce is often connected to the motivation of the leaders themselves. It does not benefit anyone to have an overworked and stressed-out principal. These factors can lead to principal disengagement and eventually turnover. Therefore, as a school leader, it is important to be honest about how engaged and motivated you are for the work you do and your employer. Reflect on your current level of motivation and what might be done to increase your own enthusiasm for the work that you do. Your motivation has the potential to be contagious for those who work with/for you. Schools with high principal turnover often have high teacher turnover, and the trickle-down result is lower student performance (Bartanen et al., 2019). Distributing leadership responsibilities can help to alleviate some of that work burden from the school administrator and give teachers and other employees an opportunity to have more influence and gain new work experiences. Job rotations and enrichment described in Table 3.1 are powerful practices that can be used towards this endeavor and have the potential benefit of strengthening the engagement of employees who go through the experience.

THE EMPLOYEE EXPERIENCE APPROACH

Within the employee experience (EEX) framework, addressing material hygiene factors alone can serve as a short-term "quick-fix to organizational engagement issues," but real, sustainable "[e]ngagement in work in the experience economy stems from meaning and purpose" (Plaskoff, 2017, p. 141). When personal directed goals of workers are complemented by motivating factors in the workplace that further emphasize the meaningfulness of their work, achievement of positive work outcomes results (Barrick et al., 2013). Extrinsic hygiene factors (e.g., challenging public relations, depressed salaries and benefits, unsafe school environment) and intrinsic motivators (e.g., sense of reward from work, intellectual stimulation) often work simultaneously influencing teachers' perceptions of their employment in both positive and negative ways.

Yet throughout an employee's career with a given employer, their personality traits, goals, and motivating and requisite support needs will undoubtedly change. Consistent with the broader body of research, Rinke's (2011) longitudinal examination of the career perspectives of urban teachers found that they look for ongoing opportunities for developmental support and professional growth to build their careers but that the type of opportunities sought after differs by the teacher. Specifically, they found that beginning teachers seek to work in contexts where they can feel a sense of self-efficacy from their classroom success. More experienced teachers often yearn for more autonomy, discretion over pedagogy, and broader work opportunities (Tran & Smith, 2020). Even at the entry point, some teachers enter the profession with the intent to stay in the position for the duration of their working career, while others aspire for leadership positions and still others plan to come in to make an impact and then leave within several years. Understanding the career motivations of teachers across their tenure can help school leaders better plan their EEX and the needs of their staff.

The EEX approach to talent management entails an organizational shift from a process focus to an experience focus. It considers all the "moments that matter" to employees across the spectrum of employee-employer interactions and uses that to design the ideal workforce experience (Mazor, 2018). It has been increasingly adopted by organizations in their talent management efforts. For example, many employers, such as Samsung, Amazon, Cisco, Whirlpool, Deloitte, Microsoft, LinkedIn, Schneider Electric, General Electric, and Riot Games have been intentionally working on designing the EEX. Still other companies, like AirBnB and Adobe, specifically allocate a position in their organization for head of EEX.

The EEX is a never-ending series of back-and-forth interactions between the employer and the employee (Morgan, 2017; Tran & Smith, 2020). The intentional design of the EEX for the organization's talent is a human-centric endeavor. Its approach is different than earlier forms of talent management approaches because it

> treats work not as mere employment, but as a life journey, with the employee as the hero. The employee journey has many milestones and interactions

> (or touchpoints), and the quality of employee experiences has a direct influence on employee satisfaction, engagement, commitment, and in the end performance. . . . Rather than the traditional "transactional" [HR] strategy, the organization must more deeply understand, the needs, wants, fears and emotions of each employee"
>
> (Plaskoff, 2017, p. 137)

An EEX approach to talent management requires that employers consider employees' holistic journeys and generate innovative ideas to address persistent issues (not settling for the first idea that arises) to intentionally design a supportive EEX. The goal is for employers to create a work environment where employees *want* to rather than *need* to come to work (Morgan, 2017). Administrators play a critical role in developing, shaping, and co-constructing the EEX with their faculty and staff, and have the opportunity to help the academic workforce become more successful than they already are. The consideration of the total EEX from entry to exit is part of a Talent-Centered Education Leadership approach (Tran & Smith, 2020) that prioritizes empathy with employees as humans in response to their needs (both extrinsic and intrinsic) as opposed to a strict focus on how to use humans as resources to meet organizational needs.

Professional growth opportunities and the empowerment of learning conditions should be present throughout teachers' entire careers to create a work environment that mitigates demotivation and teacher attrition for the "wrong reasons" (e.g., inadequate development and support) (Kelchtermans, 2017). In their meta-analytic review of the motivators of teacher attrition, Borman and Dowling (2008) concluded that "teacher attrition rates and the reasons for attrition vary across the lifespan and career path and points to the need for longitudinal analyses that are sensitive to differences emerging over time in teachers' career choices" (p. 400).

Huberman (1989), leveraging a stage theory of development, was among the first to detail the teacher career cycle comprehensively, separating it into distinct phases: the beginning, mid-career, and late-career. While presented linearly, Huberman argues that the model may progress nonlinearly, especially after the stabilization phase, and teachers may skip or transition back and forth between phases. Likewise, Ballantine and Hammack (2014) suggest three major stages of the teacher career cycle, which differentially impact their commitment: the early survival years, the stable middle years, and the disengaged final years. As teachers progress through the phases, they can either engage in critical reflection and growth or disengage and eventually withdraw from the profession. Tran and Smith (2020) drew from stage cycle theory to provide differentiated support through an EEX framework.

Of course, teacher motivations and career plans may change. Their sense of stable professional identity, efficacy, job satisfaction, work engagement, commitment, and resilience are critical for teacher engagement and retention (Day & Hong, 2016). Furthermore, employers should differentiate among career phases and academic contexts (e.g., elementary versus secondary, English-language learners versus special education) when confronting teacher turnover, given the varying needs of teachers of differing experience levels and locations.

For example, in Rosenholtz and Simpson's (1990) study of elementary school teachers, the commitment of beginning teachers was more influenced by the addressing of boundary issues external to the core of teaching (e.g., constant

Table 3.1 Huberman's (1989) and Hammack's (2015) Stage Cycle Theory With Tran and Smith's (2020) Differentiated Supports Across the Employee Experience

Career Stage	*Description and Risks*	*What can be done*
Early-Career Teachers (1–3 years of experience)	Career Entry and Survival Years **Description:** This is when teachers begin to learn how to teach and acclimate to their school environment and work with their colleagues, students, and broader community. Some are doing career exploration to determine whether this job will be a good fit for them. **Risks:** Teachers can become overwhelmed by the job, responsibilities, and pressures associated with the position and lose their sense of self-efficacy for the role. This increases the likelihood of their departure from the school or the profession altogether. In fact, the largest concentration of teacher attrition occurs during this time (Gray & Taie, 2015).	School leaders should set realistic expectations and clear guidance for new teachers, providing them with actionable feedback for improvement. Administrative support is crucial. Induction support for first-year teachers has been found to be promising for teacher retention (Ronfeldt & McQueen, 2017). See Chapter 6 for more details.
Mid-Career Teachers (4–6 years of experience)	Stabilization Years **Descriptions:** These teachers are more confident than beginning teachers, as they begin to feel comfortable with their pedagogical abilities. **Risks:** These teachers may yearn for novel work experiences and actively seek new challenges. Furthermore, they may be more sensitive to reduction of classroom autonomy and discretion, which they view not only as disrespectful but also as hampering their ability to provide the best instruction for their students. If these issues are not addressed in their current position, the teachers may look elsewhere (e.g., outside the school or even occupation).	These more seasoned teachers can be provided opportunities to be mentors so that they can gain more career fulfillment, all the while helping new teachers and reducing the administrative burden of school administration. If the teachers are expected to remain teaching while serving in this additional role, their teaching load should be reduced to accommodate the additional work.

(*Continued*)

Table 3.1 (Continued)

Career Stage	*Description and Risks*	*What can be done*
Late-Career Teachers (7–18 years of experience)	Experimental or Activism Years **Descriptions:** These later-career teachers yearn for even more challenges, such as implementing new instructional pedagogy and content or even taking on leadership roles. **Risks:** The skills of these teachers can stagnate without new opportunities and experiences.	Late-career teachers may benefit from job rotation (allowing the teacher to experience working in different positions with different assigned job responsibilities to broaden their experience) and enrichment (adding additional responsibilities typically reserved for higher-ranking positions) to deepen and add variety to their experience, as well as provide more opportunities to exercise their creativity. Expanding teachers' professional opportunities in positions such as instructional coaches and facilitators could re-engage teachers. As before, if the teachers are expected to remain teaching while serving in these additional roles, their teaching load should be reduced to accommodate the additional work.

classroom interruptions and buying needed class materials with personal funds) that represent hygiene factors and affect teachers' survival needs. Meanwhile, mid-career and veteran teachers were more strongly influenced by factors affecting the core of instruction (e.g., provision of more autonomy and discretion for the direct provision of instruction for student learning), as they typically have figured out how to manage the boundary issues. These results suggest that in order for school leaders to create the conditions for learning to occur, they should emphasize addressing boundary issues for new teachers and enhancing the core task of instruction for more senior teachers (Tran & Smith, 2020).

Barnatt et al. (2017) longitudinally examined how the career trajectories for beginning teachers with similar backgrounds resulted in different outcomes. Results from their qualitative analysis suggest that no single factor or policy thoroughly explains the variation in teaching career outcomes for their sample, but, rather, teachers' careers are affected by teachers' sensemaking of how they fit into the teaching world and the interaction between that world and themselves. Relatedly, based on a nationally representative school and staffing survey data set, You and Conley (2015) examined factors that predicted secondary (middle and high school) teachers' intention to turn over across different career stages (i.e., beginners, mid-careers, and veterans). They found a direct relationship between administrative support and mid-career teachers' intention to turnover (a result of teacher disengagement), and an indirect relationship between the two through job satisfaction, work, and career commitment for beginning and veteran teachers. Teacher empowerment factors such as classroom autonomy and discretion affected career commitment for mid-career and veteran teachers. Studies like these consistently demonstrate the importance of school leaders' influence on teachers' workplace sentiments.

BOX 3.3: WHEN IT'S NOT ROSY: EEX SCAFFOLDING FRAMEWORK EXERCISE

Tran and Smith (2021) identified design thinking as a potential approach to address the persistent "wicked problem" of teacher disengagement and turnover. Within this context, design thinking represents a set of principles and way of thinking that guides the intentional design of solutions for this problem that can be addressed in a multitude of ways. Aligning design thinking with EEX, school leaders and their design teams (e.g., administrators, district, and school staff/faculty) collaborate to address the question: How can schools intentionally design teachers' work experience to improve teacher engagement and, subsequently, retention?

Unlike the traditional centralized approach, where problem identification and solution proposals occur at the top (e.g., with the HR department), with a design thinking EEX talent management approach, administration collaborates with the talent closest to the issue to co-design the EEX together. And while systematic structures are often perceived as restricting the broad innovative potential of design thinking, Glen et al. (2015) presented a six-phase scaffolding framework activity to help learners understand design thinking. These phases include 1) problem finding, 2) observation, 3) visualization and sense-making, 4) ideation, 5) prototyping and testing, and 6) viability testing. See Table 3.2 for more information about each phase and a learning exercise for readers (or users of the approach) to further illustrate the framework.

By providing growth opportunities for teachers, principals can help them develop their sense of self-efficacy, which mediates the relationship between workplace characteristics and teachers' engagement and retention (Rosenholtz & Simpson, 1990). This type of support is particularly important in high-poverty rural and urban settings because a) they are more likely to have more boundary issues external to the classroom that can disrupt classroom teaching and b) there

Table 3.2 Glen et al. (2015)'s Scaffolding Framework

Design Thinking Phases	*Users Objective*	*Purpose*
1. Problem Finding	Develop the initial problem statement. For this activity, begin with the following: The teacher work experience should be intentionally designed to improve teacher engagement and retention.	Helps inform question development and observational protocol for data collection.
2. Observation	Observe and interview potential users for this activity: teachers. The problem identified from the prior phase will serve as the guide for the data collection and sensemaking. Collect and analyze relevant documents (e.g., teacher welfare policies, photographs of work environment).	"At the heart of design thinking is forming empathy for the end user. The most powerful means for students to develop empathy is through direct, in person, observation and interviews of the target population in the context of their lives or work" (p. 186). Careful observation can help refine problem definition.
3. Visualization and Sensemaking	There are many ways users can visualize and make sense of themes and patterns. One approach involves writing down all the relevant information gathered from data collection (e.g., observations, document retrievals) on a whiteboard and grouping the information based on themes for further examination. This phase helps with refining the problem statement to identify the "job to be done" based on insights derived from examination and analysis of the data. Example approach: Create an Empathy Map. This can be done by drawing four quadrants on the wall and grouping items from your observations and interviews around things the subject said, did, thought, and felt. From the map, generate ideas regarding the needs of the subjects and insights about the map. (Bootcamp Bootleg, 2010)	Identifies themes and patterns to help make sense and interpret the data.

Design Thinking Phases	*Users Objective*	*Purpose*
4. Ideation	Brainstorm as many ideas, interpretations, and solutions as possible to address the problem of focus. These ideas should be written down. They can be motivated by responding to the "job to be done . . ." statement. One way to begin generating ideas is to start with the phrase "how might we . . ." and let the group finish the sentence. For example, "How might we . . . make it so that the faculty and staff want to come to work every day?" or "How might we . . . create a work environment where the workforce feels supported and engaged at the school?"	Brainstorm a list of ideas.
5. Prototyping and Testing	The first rough draft of the determined idea can be briefly (approximately 90 seconds) presented to the potential clientele (e.g., the school employer) to gather feedback (e.g., cost relative to benefits of the plan). The idea here is not to confirm a finalized idea but rather to use the idea as a foundation for conversation and dialogue for further refinement. These conversations can shed light on why certain ideas may not be practical, viable, or even desirable to the constituents.	Generate many iterative and quick prototypes for frequent testing and for purposes of engaging in deep dialogue with the clientele. Satisfactory completion of the ideation phase includes the generation of a wide range of solutions and selection of the most promising among them. The ideas with the most consensus among the team should be selected for trial. However, it is important to not stop once a good idea is reached, as the generation of a broad array of ideas is critical to the process. In fact, it is understood that many of the ideas that will be generated will not be used or require substantive refinement.
6. Viability Testing	Once the final revisions have been made to the idea, experimentation and feedback should be used to test assumptions concerning its practicality. It is in this phase that a compelling case should be developed for the idea in order to gain resource support to enact the plans of action	Feasibility and viability of the ideas are tested in the context of use and feedback is obtained.

are more structural and environmental barriers to students' academic success in those contexts. However, this requires that principals buffer external influences so that teachers can focus on teaching. A buffer allows teachers to more quickly develop their mastery of teaching and ability to adapt and contextualize what they teach to their students to maximize their pedagogical impact. Meeting these needs will develop teachers' self-efficacy, which will allow teachers in those environments to feel confident that they can make a meaningful impact in the lives of students.

Given that isolation often results in professional burnout that leads to turnover, administrators should take advantage of promoting teacher learning and job satisfaction by encouraging collaborative learning environments (Margolis, 2008). The presence of supportive professional learning communities has been linked to teacher retention (Brown & Wynn, 2009; Watkins, 2005) and student achievement (Vescio et al., 2008). Furthermore, administrative support, including mentorship and professional development, should be intentionally differentiated based on each teacher's specific needs that are foundational for the growth of their professional identities as opposed to one-size-fits-all micromanagement approaches and policies that ignore the complexities of the dynamic interaction that occurs between individual teachers and the educational context in which they work (Barnatt et al., 2017). Administrative support has been consistently found to be one of the most important factors for teacher retention, with teachers who have more negative perceptions of their administrators being more likely to transfer/leave (Boyd et al., 2011; Ladd, 2011; Kraft et al., 2016). Therefore, school leaders should learn how to provide differentiated levels of support and development based on individual teacher needs. A wide breadth of scholarship has suggested that school leaders are more likely to design a more positive EEX for their workers when they maintain: supportive school cultures that motivate and recognize teachers; are present, development-oriented, strong instructional leaders; engender trust; and do not display overly controlling micromanagement tendencies. This has been evidenced by their teachers' stronger teacher retention as well as perceptions of their leadership being more effective (Horng, 2009; Simon & Johnson, 2015; Kraft et al., 2016; Tran & Bon, 2015).

EMPATHIZE WITH TEACHERS TO DETERMINE THEIR NEEDS

The heart of design-thinking activity and the first step towards building the teacher employee journey map with the EEX approach is to *empathize* with teachers (Mazor, 2018; Plaskoff, 2017). For example, in high school teacher Sydney Jensen's (2019) TedTalk presentation, she questioned who will support teachers as they experience "secondary trauma" or "compassion fatigue" through their provision of daily emotional support for their students who navigate diverse and difficult circumstances. She stressed the importance of providing mental health and wellness support not only to students but also to teachers, who absorb students' trauma. With a Talent-Centered Education Leadership approach (Tran, 2022), school leaders should hold a key role in facilitating that support, which can range from providing the time and space for support group–style meetups with other teachers to unload some of the emotional weight, to professional mental health assistance provided by trained counselors to help teachers navigate feelings of powerlessness and self-blame in response to student hardships.

Relatedly, developing teachers' emotional resiliency is paramount. Day and Hong (2016) explain that emotional resiliency is the balance of commitment and agency that goes beyond coping (survival) to include the management of the everyday challenges (e.g., student learning and behavioral issues, lack of parental involvement, heavy workload, accountability pressure, and additional government attention and scrutiny) in a way that success is achieved. According to their work, emotional resilience is particularly critical for teachers working in economically disadvantaged schools, where the environment may be more emotionally intense given the heavier dependence of students on teachers' attention and the provision of stability and safety that the school may offer. However, their capacity for emotional resilience will be heavily influenced by the type of support they receive.

At the end of the day, teaching is emotional work, especially in disadvantaged and high-need communities. To connect with their students, teachers often empathize with them, worry about them, and, in the process, gain secondary trauma by sharing the mental load with them. Emotional strain can develop from the caring relationship, as teachers adapt to their stressors and risks. Therefore, supporting teachers' capacities for emotional resilience is a key part of the school leader's role and part of that support includes enhancing the faculty's "collective efficacy and shared beliefs of professional control, influence and responsibility" (Day & Gu, 2014, p. 11). Teachers' commitment as an altruistic motivation for teaching in high-need communities can only be sustained if school leaders ensure that the working conditions nurture their emotional resilience and allow them to have the capacity to make a meaningful impact; otherwise, the school is doomed to experience a revolving door of inexperienced teachers, as staff either leave in search for schools that offer such support or exit the profession altogether (Day & Hong, 2016).

Simply telling teachers to take better self-care without substantively changing the working conditions and accumulating workload is, at best, useless and, at worse, insulting. Instead, school leaders can build strong relationships with their faculty by demonstrating empathy for their teachers' needs and cultivating an atmosphere of trust. They can facilitate a culture of belonging and care for teachers by maintaining a clear coherent and consistent vision, distributing decision-making authority as appropriate (Day & Hong, 2016), and addressing the multitude of factors that influence teachers' work sentiments. In doing so, school employers should consider the personal, individual, and environmental factors that influence teacher engagement across their career experience and generate multiple potential strategies to address the problem (Farley-Ripple et al., 2012; Tran & Smith, 2020). The next section will address each of these factors in more detail.

PERSONAL FACTORS

Personal factors encompass demographics, values, morals, emotions, knowledge, skills, and self-efficacy. Policy interventions aimed at improving teacher recruitment and retention have largely neglected personal characteristics. Take, for example, the issue of stress. Stress has been linked with illness, disease, and increased physician visits (Nerurkar et al., 2013). Meanwhile, teaching is widely recognized as one of the most stressful professions in the US due, in large part, to intense scrutiny and work demands, rates of job disengagement/dissatisfaction, burnout, absenteeism, depression, cynicism, and rising turnover in the last few decades (Emerson et al., 2017; Robertson-Kraft & Zhang, 2018; Schelvis et al., 2014). Despite this, policies specifically directed at the reduction of teacher stress are scarce. Recent scholarship suggests mindfulness-based interventions as a potentially fruitful initiative for stress reduction (Bamber & Schneider, 2016). This intervention emphasizes focusing on the present through practices such as meditation and diet improvement but is neither commonplace in schools nor often a topic of policy discussion.

Work-related stress is merely a symptom, however, and addressing it still leaves the root cause of the stress unconfronted. To reduce that stress and support teacher needs, principals must create the conditions that allow for learning to occur. That involves buffering factors external to direct classroom instruction that may impede teaching (e.g., student behavioral issues, lack of resources and material, excessive paperwork), especially for new teachers, so that they can concentrate on teaching and allowing more experienced teachers elevated levels of instructional autonomy in their teaching (Rosenholtz & Simpson, 1990). Accomplishing the former will negate teachers from dealing with boundary tasks such as constant classroom interruptions and buying needed class materials from their own personal funds, both of which represent hygiene factors that could make teaching at the school less attractive. However, addressing them does not necessarily make their job more attractive (i.e., they are not motivators). Therefore, it is important to address the motivator factors that directly relate to the core of teaching. Doing so will result in more teacher buy-in for the school's work and simultaneously demonstrate respect for their professional expertise. Both the motivating and hygiene factors jointly influence teacher engagement (and ultimately retention) and require the school leader's attention. Interpreted within Herzberg's theoretical motivation-hygiene theory, failing to buffer boundary issues allows the flourishing of hygiene factors that could potentially negatively affect personal factors that promote not only the disengagement and turnover but also the attrition of new teachers.

Another example of an influential but related personal factor for teacher retention is self-efficacy. Ultimately, teacher satisfaction is derived from the sense of self-efficacy (i.e., their ability to achieve success with meeting the learning needs of their students) that is associated with the provision of direct effective classroom instruction that truly makes a difference for student learning

(Johnson & Birkeland, 2003; Rosenholtz & Simpson, 1990). Teachers who feel more self-efficacy about their teaching ability will be less stressed. Consequently, they are attracted to staying in schools that enable them to develop that sense of self-efficacy that is critical for job satisfaction and teacher retention (Ortan et al., 2021). This requires a supportive environment that is attuned to teacher needs and is evidenced from the performance feedback principals provide to teachers and actionable recommendations for improvement. When teachers feel that the work they do matters (i.e., performance efficacy) and is fulfilling, they are incentivized to come back to work the next day. However, before enhancing the core tasks of instruction, the boundary issues must be addressed.

Self-efficacy influences entry and retention into teaching, particularly at "hard-to-staff" schools. Tran et al. (2015) surveyed 64 early childhood education preservice teachers, finding positive associations between not only the students' self-efficacy and their openness to teaching in rural districts with teacher shortages but also the students' sense of public service and their openness to teaching in hard-to-staff rural districts. These findings suggest two areas potentially impactful to recruiting and retaining teachers – promoting and encouraging a sense of belonging and fostering preservice teachers' confidence to teach in hard-to-staff districts.

INDIVIDUAL BEHAVIOR

Individual behavior includes teachers' work content, roles and responsibilities, education, and training. Results from Marston's (2010) mixed-methods study of California elementary, high school, and college teachers from 1997 to 2005 demonstrated that the most important motivators for teacher retention across all school levels were intrinsic work-related professional factors like working with students, seeing them learn, and enjoying course materials. Teachers across all levels rated extrinsic practical factors (e.g., job security, salary/benefits) as the least important motivator to continuing in the classroom. Curtis (2012) surveyed/interviewed 1,571 middle and high school math teachers across the US, similarly finding that many began teaching to fulfill intrinsic personal desires to work with youth, make a difference in the lives of others, and work with a beloved subject matter.

Accordingly, when examining teacher retention and turnover, some scholars have focused on the intrinsic motivators of individual teachers, such as their sense of self-efficacy and desire for recognition (Fuller et al., 1982; Rosenholtz, 1989). Brunetti (2001) surveyed high school teachers from a California district, interviewing teachers about job satisfaction. Despite unattractive work conditions, teachers communicated high levels of satisfaction and cited working with students as the most important motivator, followed by a passion for the subject, classroom excitement, autonomy, and collegiality. These responses insinuate that personal and individual factors contribute to value-added influence on the teaching experience, despite the work environment. This, of course, does not mean that environmental conditions do not matter.

ENVIRONMENTAL CONDITIONS

Environmental factors include working conditions, physical workspaces, salary, administrative support, student demographics, and school performance. Many of these factors require maintenance (hygiene issues) in that employers must address them to prevent job dissatisfaction. It is important to note that diminished dissatisfaction does not necessitate increased satisfaction (Herzberg et al., 1959), an observation evident in the empirical literature. Such is the case with salary. In sum, employers must be attentive to the holistic needs of their employees in their intentional design of the optimal supportive employee experience.

BOX 3.4: CREATE OPPORTUNITIES FOR WORK-RELATED PERKS

Many school employers have limited resources to provide many, if any, work-related perks to their employees. However, there is a difference between making the perks available and funding for their provision. There are many free opportunities for school leaders to enhance the access to perks such as negotiating with vendors to make different types of food available for the school population during lunch hours. One high school principal we know was able to obtain donated workout equipment and refurbish an unused room in the school to create a workout space for staff to recognize their contributions and promote employee self-care.

Learning Activities

Discussion Questions:

1. One way to understand how the school can become a more desirable place to work is to truly take the time to understand its employees. How might you go about doing this?
2. How can the school show that it is authentically working towards better understanding of and caring for employees as opposed to merely telling them that they do so (i.e., providing "lip service" by repeatedly talking about how the school cares without substance to back up the statements)?
3. How will the school demonstrate its commitment to empowering faculty and staff, giving them a voice, providing opportunities for professional growth, and caring for the people in the school?

4. Given the importance of the process for the EEX approach, how might school leaders ensure that attention to EEX is not treated in a transactional and compliance-driven way (e.g., a necessary evil that needs to be done to fast-track implementation towards a "solution to the problem") but, rather, provide employees with a thoughtful, meaningful, and positive experience?
5. How might the EEX approach be used to improve the work-life for the non-teaching staff of the school (e.g., custodians, maintenance workers, nutrition specialists)?

MANAGING UP

It has been said that "[t]here is no great strategy, only great execution" (Gratton, 2000). And it is the line manager, such as the school principal, who is responsible for strategy implementation and delivery as they are the ones who "bring policies to life" (Purcell, 2003) by putting them into practice. Principals play a critical role in the potential effectiveness of HR policies because they have the power to be indifferent, uninvolved, or downright resistant to the policies. This can translate into the same sentiments from the school faculty, if they sense a lack of enthusiasm or care from their school leader, which will result in less than desirable performance outcomes (most frequently, no change in status quo). This type of disconnect often exists when the culture of the organization is comprised of factions of them (upper management) versus us (school employees).

School leaders play a mediating role between district HR and school employees. They are well-positioned to clarify the intent of HR policies and practices to allay suspicions about the motives of district HR. Unfortunately, in some districts, school leaders occupy an adversarial role with HR. Instead of seeing HR as a watchdog or compliance officer, school leaders should develop an education partnership with the HR department. Within this context, HR and school administrators collaborate on the planning and implementation of HR practices. Two-way communication between the parties allows for less miscommunication and improves mutual understanding of the strengths, weaknesses, opportunities, and threats that are facing the organization, as well as their associated HR implications. The HR department can be a valuable resource for school leaders, providing them with support, advice, data, resources, and training to implement HR decisions and policies in schools.

ETHICS

While strategic talent management often emphasizes the improvement of organizational effectiveness through its employees, it is also about the ethics of how people are treated and, more specifically, how HR policies and practices can enhance employee well-being (Armstrong & Taylor, 2020). In fact, these two points are not contradictory. Franklin D. Roosevelt once said, "If you treat people right, they will treat you right . . . ninety percent of the time" (as cited in Tanner, 2021). That's a pretty good investment and, of course, applies directly to the employer-employee relationship.

Because HRM involves addressing human concerns, the issue of ethical treatment of employees as it relates to employment decision-making processes is particularly relevant. In an environment of accountability where administrators are heavily scrutinized for student performance and have limited time to respond to a multitude of competing demands, it can be easy to neglect issues related to the school workforce in favor of directing attention to student matters. In this context, employee issues like ethics and fairness are often overlooked for "bottom-line" school results. Kelchtermans (2017) argues that the school plays a key role in preventing teacher disengagement and turnover through its influences on buffering external policy influences that hurt teacher morale and bolstering internal working conditions that support professional learning and growth that improve teacher job satisfaction. Through this support, school leaders enable teachers to exercise their professional agency through collaboration and collegiality against the tide of mounting accountability pressure that promotes individualism (e.g., individual accountability) and the narrowing of teacher professionalism.

While performance accountability is often touted as a vehicle to cultivate a culture of excellence, often neglected is another integral component to sustain such cultivation: the fair treatment of employees. Rawls (1973) proposed several definitions of justice that promote fairness, among them, procedural and distributive justice. Procedural justice deals with fairness within employment processes, which should be applied consistently and equitably. Examples of this include grievance or promotional procedures that arrive at decisions logically as opposed to personal bias or preferences in decision-making. Distributive justice deals with fairness in the allocation of resources. For example, pay incentives are allocated fairly based on an accurate assessment of performance or some other objective criteria.

In Strike and Solitis' (2015) discussion of the ethical issues faced by educators, two ethical principles that have relevance for education HRM were presented: 1) the principle of benefit maximization and 2) the principle of equal respect for persons. The former relates to making decisions that will result in benefits for the most amount of people. The latter relates to treating people as intrinsically worthwhile and with equal value as moral agents. More specifically, employees should not be treated as a means to an end but rather as ends themselves (i.e., they are not merely instruments to help the employer achieve its goals, but rather their needs matter as well). Their time and feedback should be respected in a meaningful way. For example, holding a pointless meeting to gather faux "consensus" from the faculty when the decision has already been made is disrespectful to both the faculty's time and feedback.

Ethical treatment should underlie the foundation of HRM, especially as it relates to how people are treated. How employees are treated not only affects their feelings but their behaviors and performance as well. In education, there is a nobility and missionary-like purpose associated with responding to the needs of students that make it easy for employers to do so at the expense of addressing the needs of teachers and other school workers. This should be avoided in order to deter the dehumanization of the workplace.

The school leader can play a pivotal role in shaping the culture and climate of the school. The culture represents the norms and unwritten rules that are adhered to by the school community, whereas the climate refers to "how people perceive (see and feel about) the culture existing in their organization" (Armstrong & Taylor, 2020, p. 124). Both can have a significant influence on student performance (Destler, 2016; Leithwood & Sun, 2018; Smith & Shouppe, 2018). As it relates to ethics, school leaders can cultivate a negative culture where unethical behavior is promoted, a wall of silence exists in the presence of harassment, and retaliation is condoned, or they can cultivate a positive culture where employees are respected, engaged, motivated, supported, and thriving. School leaders are role models, and there will typically be a higher expectation for standard of conduct for them relative to their employees. How they act can have a powerful influence on what their workers view as "acceptable" at the school, so one great way to promote an ethical work environment is to lead by example and operate as an ethical professional.

CONCLUSION

The traditional stick-and-carrot method of workforce motivation has failed to yield promising results. Talent-Centered Education Leadership can potentially improve workplace engagement and motivation when employees are provided opportunities to do what they love at work, feel their jobs become more enjoyable, are able to utilize their strengths, and gain meaningful development and learning opportunities from their employer to meet their own priorities. By working with the talent to co-design each employee experience, the talent has a voice in identifying and developing solutions for workplace problems.

Summary of Key Points

- Successful linkage between employee and organizational success is heavily dependent on the employee's motivation.
- Education policy and reform initiatives are often undergirded by an outdated philosophy based primarily on the idea that employee performance can be motivated solely by management control via rewards and punishment. These methods, as demonstrated in performance and merit pay initiatives, have not yielded much research support.
- Herzberg, Mauser, and Snyderman's motivation-hygiene theory suggests workplace factors that result in job satisfaction (known as motivators) are distinct from those that result in job dissatisfaction (known as hygienes).

- Vroom proposed the valency-instrumentality-expectancy theory that suggested employees will be motivated if they value the outcome (valency), believe that what they will do is instrumental to leading to the outcome (instrumentality), and trust in the likelihood of receiving the outcome should they expend the necessary effort (expectancy).
- While hygiene needs (e.g., the ability to earn a living, pay bills, and care for one's family) need to be addressed, addressing only hygiene needs will not mitigate teacher motivational problems. Instead, sustainable and effective talent motivation strategies must first comprehensively address teachers' hygiene needs to minimize negative extrinsic factors, then address motivator needs to captivate their intrinsic desire/interest.
- Consistent with Talent-Centered Education Leadership, employers should intentionally design the employee experience of their organization so that employees *want* to, rather than *need* to, come to work. Doing so will unlock the discretionary efforts of employees that will serve as the catalyst for organizational excellence.
- Tran and Smith (2020) drew on Huberman's (1989) stage cycle theory to provide differentiated support through an EEX framework. School employers should consider the personal, individual, and environmental factors that influence teacher engagement across their career experiences and generate multiple potential strategies to address the problem.
- Because HRM involves addressing human concerns, the issue of ethical treatment of employees as it relates to the employment decision-making process is particularly relevant.

REFERENCES

Armstrong, M., & Taylor, S. (2020). *Armstrong's handbook of human resource management practice.* Kogan Page Publishers.

Balch, R., & Springer, M. G. (2015). Performance pay, test scores, and student learning objectives. *Economics of Education Review, 44,* 114–125.

Ballantine, J. H., & Hammack, F. M. (2014). A unique perspective for understanding schools. In *Schools and society: A sociological approach to education* (pp. 13–17).

Bamber, M. D., & Schneider, J. K. (2016). Mindfulness-based meditation to decrease stress and anxiety in college students: A narrative synthesis of the research. *Educational Research Review, 18,* 1–32.

Barnatt, J., Gahlsdorf Terrell, D., D'Souza, L. A., Jong, C., Cochran-Smith, M., Viesca, K. M., Gleeson, A. M., McQuillan, P., & Shakman, K. (2017). Interpreting early career trajectories. *Educational Policy, 31*(7), 992–1032.

Barrick, M. R., Mount, M. K., & Li, N. (2013). The theory of purposeful work behavior: The role of personality, higher-order goals, and job characteristics. *Academy of Management Review, 38*(1), 132–153.

Bartanen, B., Grissom, J. A., & Rogers, L. K. (2019). The impacts of principal turnover. *Educational Evaluation and Policy Analysis, 41*(3), 350–374.

Blazar, D., & Kraft, M. A. (2017). Teacher and teaching effects on students' attitudes and behaviors. *Educational Evaluation and Policy Analysis, 39*(1), 146–170.

Bootcamp Bootleg. (2010). *Hasso Plattner Institute of Design at Stanford University.* http://dschool.stanford.edu/wp-content/uploads/2011/03/BootcampBootleg2010v2SLIM.pdf

Borman, G. D., & Dowling, N. M. (2008). Teacher attrition and retention: A meta-analytic and narrative review of the research. *Review of Educational Research, 78*, 367–409.

Bowen, D., & Mills, J. N. (2017). Changing the education workforce? The relationships between teacher quality, motivation, and performance pay. *Teachers College Record, 119*(4), 1–32.

Boyd, D., Grossman, P., Ing, M., Lankford, H., Loeb, S., & Wyckoff, J. (2011). The influence of school administrators on teacher retention decisions. *American Educational Research Journal, 48*(2), 303–333.

Brescoll, V. L. (2011). Who takes the floor and why: Gender, power, and volubility in organizations. *Administrative Science Quarterly, 56*(4), 622–641.

Brown, K., & Wynn, S. R. (2009). Finding, supporting, and keeping: The role of the principal in teacher retention issues. *Leadership and Policy in Schools, 8*(1), 37–63.

Brunetti, G. J. (2001). Why do they teach? A study of job satisfaction among long-term high school teachers. *Teacher Education Quarterly, 28*(3), 49–74.

Chetty, R., Friedman, J. N., & Rockoff, J. E. (2014). Measuring the impacts of teachers II: Teacher value-added and student outcomes in adulthood. *American Economic Review, 104*(9), 2633–2679.

Chiang, H., Wellington, A., Hallgren, K., Speroni, C., Herrmann, M., Glazerman, S., & Constantine, J. (2015). *Evaluation of the teacher incentive fund: Implementation of pay for performance after two years.* Mathematica Policy Research. www.mathematica-mpr.com//our-publications-and-findings/publications/evaluation-of-the-teacher-incentive-fund-implementation-and-impacts-of-payforperformance-after-two

Curtis, C. (2012). Why do they choose to teach--and why do they leave? A study of middle school and high school mathematics teachers. *Education, 132*(4), 779–789.

Day, C., & Gu, Q. (2014). Response to Margolis, Hodge and Alexandrou: Misrepresentations of teacher resilience and hope. *Journal of Education for Teaching, 40*(4), 409–412.

Day, C., & Hong, J. (2016). Influences on the capacities for emotional resilience of teachers in schools serving disadvantaged urban communities: Challenges of living on the edge. *Teaching and Teacher Education, 59*, 115–125.

Destler, K. N. (2016). Creating a performance culture: Incentives, climate, and organizational change. *The American Review of Public Administration, 46*(2), 201–225.

Emerson, L. M., Leyland, A., Hudson, K., Rowse, G., Hanley, P., & Hugh-Jones, S. (2017). Teaching mindfulness to teachers: A systematic review and narrative synthesis. *Mindfulness, 8*(5), 1136–1149.

Erikkson, T., Teyssier, S., & Villeval, M. (2009). Self-selection and the efficiency of tournaments. *Economic Inquiry, 47*(3), 530–548.

Farley-Ripple, E. N., Raffel, J. A., & Christine Welch, J. (2012). Administrator career paths and decision processes. *Journal of Educational Administration, 50*(6), 788–816.

Fokkens-Bruinsma, M., & Canrinus, E. T. (2012). Adaptive and maladaptive motives for becoming a teacher. *Journal of Education for Teaching, 38*(1), 3–19.

Freedman, S. W., & Appleman, D. (2009). "In It for the Long Haul" – How teacher education can contribute to teacher retention in high-poverty, urban schools. *Journal of Teacher Education, 60*(3), 323–337.

Fulbeck, E. S. (2014). Teacher mobility and financial incentive. A descriptive analysis of Denver's procomp. *Educational Evaluation and Policy Analysis, 36*(1), 67–82.

Fuller, B., Wood, K., Rapoport, T., & Dornbusch, S. M. (1982). The organizational context of individual efficacy. *Review of Educational Research, 52*(1), 7–30.

Glazerman, S., Chiang, H., Wellington, A., Constantine, J., & Player, D. (2011). *Impacts of Performance pay under the teacher incentive fund: Study design report.* Mathematica Policy Research, Inc.

Glen, R., Suciu, C., Baughn, C. C., & Anson, R. (2015). Teaching design thinking in business schools. *The International Journal of Management Education, 13*(2), 182–192.

Goler, L., Gale, J., Harrington, B., & Grant, A. (January 11, 2018). Why people really quit their jobs. *Harvard Business Review.* https://hbr.org/2018/01/why-people-really-quit-their-jobs\

Goodman, S. F., & Turner, L. J. (2013). The design of teacher incentive pay and educational outcomes: Evidence from the New York City bonus program. *Journal of Labor Economics, 31*(2), 409–420.

Gratton, L. (2000). *Living strategy: Putting people at the heart of corporate purpose.* FT Press.

Gray, L., & Taie, S. (2015). *Public school teacher attrition and mobility in the first five years: Results from the first through fifth waves of the 2007–08 beginning teacher longitudinal study.* First Look. NCES 2015-337. National Center for Education Statistics.

Guest, D. E. (1997). Human resource management and performance; A review of the research agenda. *The International Journal of Human Resource Management, 8*(3), 263–276.

Hammack, P. L. (2015). Theoretical foundations of identity. In K. C. McLean & M. Syed (Eds.), *The Oxford handbook of identity development* (pp. 11–30). Oxford University Press.

Hancock, A. B., & Rubin, B. A. (2015). Influence of communication partner's gender on language. *Journal of Language and Social Psychology, 34*(1), 46–64.

Heneman, H. G., III, & Milanowski, A. T. (2004). Alignment of human resource practices and teacher performance competency. *Peabody Journal of Education, 79*(4), 108–125.

Herzberg, F., Mausner, B., & Snyderman, B. (1959). *The motivation to work* (2nd ed.). John Wiley & Sons, Inc.

Horng, E. L. (2009). Teacher tradeoffs: Disentangling teachers' preferences for working conditions and student demographics. *American Educational Research Journal, 46*(3), 690–717.

Huberman, M. (1989). The professional life cycle of teachers. *Teachers College Record, 91*(1), 31–57.

Hunter, J. E., Schmidt, F. L., & Judiesch, M. K. (1990). Individual differences in output variability as a function of job complexity. *Journal of Applied Psychology, 75*(1), 28.

Hur, Y. (2018). Testing Herzberg's two-factor theory of motivation in the public sector: Is it applicable to public managers? *Public Organization Review, 18,* 329–343.

Imberman, S. A., & Lovenheim, M. F. (2015). Incentive strength and teacher productivity: Evidence from a group-based teacher incentive pay system. *Review of Economics and Statistics, 97*(2), 364–386.

Jenkins, S., & Delbridge, R. (2013). Context matters: Examining 'soft' and 'hard' approaches to employee engagement in two workplaces. *The International Journal of Human Resource Management, 24*(14), 2670–2691.

Jensen, S. (2019). How can we support the emotional well-being of teachers? *Tedtalk.* https://www.ted.com/talks/sydney_jensen_how_can_we_support_the_emotional_well_being_of_teachers

Johnson, S. M., & Birkeland, S. E. (2003). Pursuing a "sense of success": New teachers explain their career decisions. *American Educational Research Journal, 40*(3), 581–617. https://doi.org/10.3102/00028312040003581

Karpowitz, C. F., Mendelberg, T., & Shaker, L. (2012). Gender inequality in deliberative participation. *American Political Science Review*, 533–547.

Kelchtermans, G. (2017). 'Should I stay or should I go?': Unpacking teacher attrition/retention as an educational issue. *Teachers and Teaching, 23*(8), 961–977.

Kelley, C. (1996, February 28). A new teacher-pay system could better support reform. *Education Week*, pp. 35, 38.

Kelley, C. (1997). Teacher compensation and organization. *Educational Evaluation and Policy Analysis, 19*(1), 15–28.

Kelley, C. (1998). The Kentucky school-based performance award program: School-level effects. *Educational Policy, 12*(3), 305–324.

Kraft, M. A., Marinell, W. H., & Shen-Wei Yee, D. (2016). School organizational contexts, teacher turnover, and student achievement: Evidence from panel data. *American Educational Research Journal, 53*(5), 1411–1449.

Ladd, H. F. (2011). Teachers' perceptions of their working conditions: How predictive of planned and actual teacher movement? *Educational Evaluation and Policy Analysis, 33*(2), 235–261.

Lai, L. (2017, July 27). Motivating employees is not about carrots or sticks. *Harvard Business Review*. https://hbr.org/2017/06/motivating-employees-is-not-about-carrots-or-sticks

Leithwood, K., & Sun, J. (2018). Academic culture: A promising mediator of school leaders' influence on student learning. *Journal of Educational Administration, 56*(3), 350–363.

Lewis, R., Donaldson-Feilder, E., & Tharani, T. (2014). *Managing for sustainable employee engagement*. CIPD.

Macey, W. H., & Schneider, B. (2008). The meaning of employee engagement. *Industrial and Organizational Psychology, 1*(1), 3–30.

MacLeod, D., & Clarke, N. (2009). *Engaging for success: Enhancing performance through employee engagement*. Office of Public Sector Information.

Margolis, J. (2008). What will keep today's teachers teaching? Looking for a hook as a new career cycle emerges. *Teachers College Record, 110*(1), 160–194.

Marsh, J., Springer, M. G., McCaffrey, D. F., Yuan, K., Epstein, S., Koppich, J., Kalra, N., DiMartino, C., & Peng, A. (2011). *A big apple for educators: New York City's experiment with schoolwide performance bonuses: Final evaluation report*. RAND Corporation. www.rand.org/pubs/monographs/MG1114.html

Marston, S. H. (2010). Why do they teach? A comparison of elementary, high school, and college teachers. *Education, 131*(2), 437–454. https://eric.ed.gov/?id=EJ930614

Mazor, A. H. (2018). *Reimagine and craft the employee experience: Design thinking in action*. https://www2.deloitte.com/content/dam/Deloitte/global/Documents/HumanCapital/gx-cons-reimagine-and-craft-the-employee-experience.pdf

McKinsey & Company & Leanin.org. (2019). *Women in the workplace*. https://wiw-report.s3.amazonaws.com/Women_in_the_Workplace_2019.pdf

Messersmith, J. G., Patel, P. C., Lepak, D. P., & Gould-Williams, J. S. (2011). Unlocking the black box: Exploring the link between high-performance work systems and performance. *Journal of Applied Psychology, 96*(6), 1105.

Mintrop, R. (2018). Neo-liberal managerialism and professionalization in US schools. In *Education policies and the restructuring of the educational profession* (pp. 189–204). Springer.

Morgan, J. (2017). *The employee experience advantage: How to win the war for talent by giving employees the workspaces they want, the tools they need, and a culture they can celebrate.* John Wiley & Sons.

Nerurkar, A., Bitton, A., Davis, R. B., Phillips, R. S., & Yeh, G. (2013). When physicians counsel about stress: Results of a national study. *JAMA Internal Medicine, 173*(1), 76–77.

Nittrouer, C. L., Hebl, M. R., Ashburn-Nardo, L., Trump-Steele, R. C., Lane, D. M., & Valian, V. (2018). Gender disparities in colloquium speakers at top universities. *Proceedings of the National Academy of Sciences, 115*(1), 104–108.

Odden, A., & Kelley, C. (1997). *Paying teachers for what they know and do: New and smarter compensation strategies to improve schools.* Corwin Press.

Odden, A., & Kelley, C. (2002). *Paying teachers for what they know and do: New and smarter compensation strategies to improve schools* (2nd ed.). Corwin Press.

Ortan, F., Simut, C., & Simut, R. (2021). Self-efficacy, job satisfaction and teacher well-being in the K–12 educational system. *International Journal of Environmental Research and Public Health, 18*(23), 12763.

Plaskoff, J. (2017). Employee experience: The new human resource management approach. *Strategic HR Review, 16*(3), 136–141.

Podgursky, M. J., & Springer, M. G. (2007). Teacher performance pay: A review. *Journal of Policy Analysis and Management, 26*(4), 909–949.

Purcell, J. (2003). *Understanding the people and performance link: Unlocking the black box.* CIPD Publishing.

Rawls, J. (1973). Theory of justice: Reply to Lyons and Teitelman. *The Journal of Philosophy, 69*(18), 556–557.

Rinke, C. R. (2011). Career trajectories of urban teachers: A continuum of perspectives, participation, and plans shaping retention in the educational system. *Urban Education, 46*(4), 639–662.

Robertson-Kraft, C., & Zhang, R. S. (2018). Keeping great teachers: A case study on the impact and implementation of a pilot teacher evaluation system. *Educational Policy, 32*(3), 363–394.

Rooy, D. V., & Oehler, K. (2013). *The evolution of employee opinion surveys – the voice of employee as a strategic business management tool.* Society for Industrial and Organizational Psychology White Paper Series. Society of Human Resource Management. www.shrm.org/ResourcesAndTools/hr-topics/employee-relations/Documents/SIOP%20-%20Employee%20Engagement,%20final.pdf

Rosenholtz, S. J. (1989). Workplace conditions that affect teacher quality and commitment: Implications for teacher induction programs. *The Elementary School Journal, 89*(4), 421–439.

Rosenholtz, S. J., & Simpson, C. (1990). Workplace conditions and the rise and fall of teachers' commitment. *Sociology of Education*, 241–257.

Schelvis, R. M., Zwetsloot, G. I., Bos, E. H., & Wiezer, N. M. (2014). Exploring teacher and school resilience as a new perspective to solve persistent problems in the educational sector. *Teachers and Teaching, 20*(5), 622–637.

Shifrer, D., Turley, R. L., & Heard, H. (2017). Do teacher financial awards improve teacher retention and student achievement in an urban disadvantaged school district? *American Educational Research Journal, 54*(6), 1117–1153.

Simon, N., & Johnson, S. M. (2015). Teacher turnover in high-poverty schools: What we know and can do. *Teachers College Record, 117*(3), 1–36.

Smith, T., & Shouppe, G. (2018). Is there a relationship between schools' climate ratings and student performance data? *National Teacher Education Journal, 11*(1).

Sojourner, A. J., Mykerezi, E., & West, K. L. (2014). Teacher pay reform and productivity. Panel data evidence from adoptions of Q-comp in Minnesota. *The Journal of Human Resources, 49*(4), 945–981.

Springer, M. G., Pane, J. F., Le, V., McCaffrey, D. F., Burns, S. F., Hamilton, L. S., & Stetcher, B. M. (2012a). *No evidence that incentive pay for teacher teams improve student outcomes. Results from a randomized trial.* Rand Corporation. www.rand.org/pubs/research_briefs/RB9649.html

Springer, M. G., Pane, J. F., Le, V., McCaffrey, D. F., Burns, S. F., Hamilton, L. S., & Stetcher, B. M. (2012b). Team pay for performance. Experimental evidence from the Round Rock pilot project on team incentives. *Educational Evaluation and Policy Analysis, 34*(4), 367–390.

Springer, M. S., Rodriguez, L. A., & Swain, W. A. (2014). *Effective teacher retention bonuses: Evidence from Tennessee* (Working paper). Tennessee Consortium on Research, Evaluation & Development.

Stairs, M., & Galpin, M. (2010). Positive engagement: From employee engagement to workplace happiness. In P. A. Linley, S. Harrington, & N. Garcea (Eds.), *Oxford handbook of positive psychology and work* (pp. 155–172). Oxford University Press.

Strike, K. A. (1988). The ethics of teaching. *The Phi Delta Kappan, 70*(2), 156–158.

Strike, K. A., & Soltis, J. F. (2015). *The ethics of teaching.* Teachers College Press.

Struyven, K., Jacobs, K., & Dochy, F. (2013). Why do they want to teach? The multiple reasons of different groups of students for undertaking teacher education. *European Journal of Psychology of Education, 28*, 1007–1022.

Tannen, D. (1995). *The power of talk: Who gets heard and why.* Harvard Business Review. https://hbr.org/1995/09/the-power-of-talk-who-gets-heard-and-why

Tanner, R. (2021, September 3). *Three critical leadership lessons from the Roosevelts. Management is a journey.* https://managementisajourney.com/three-critical-leadership-lessons-from-the-roosevelts/

Tran, H. (2015). Personnel vs. strategic human resource management in public education. *Management in Education, 29*(3), 112–118.

Tran, H. (2022). Revolutionizing school HR strategies and practices to reflect talent centered education leadership. *Leadership and Policy in Schools, 21*(2), 238–252.

Tran, H., & Bon, S. C. (2015). Assessing multiple stakeholders' perceptions of an effective principal evaluation system. *Education Leadership Review, 16*(2), 1–18.

Tran, H., Hogue, A. M., & Moon, A. M. (2015). Attracting early childhood teachers to South Carolina's high needs rural districts: Loan repayment vs. tuition subsidy. *Teacher Education Journal of South Carolina, 8*, 98–107.

Tran, H., & Jenkins, Z. (2022). Embracing the future of education work with talent centered education leadership. *Journal of Education Human Resources, 40*(2), 266–276.

Tran, H., & Smith, D. A. (2020). Designing an employee experience approach to teacher retention in hard-to-staff schools. *NASSP Bulletin, 104*(2), 85–109.

Tran, H., & Smith, D. A. (2021). Talent-centered education leadership: Using the employee experience to improve teacher-school relations. *Journal of Cases in Educational Leadership, 24*(1), 42–54.

Truss, C., Soane, E., Edwards, C., Wisdom, K., Croll, A., & Burnett, J. (2006). *Working life: Employee attitudes and engagement*. CIPD.

U.S. Department of Education. (2009). *Race to the top executive summary*. http://www2.ed.gov/programs/racetothetop/executive-summary.pdf

Vescio, V., Ross, D., & Adams, A. (2008). A review of research on the impact of professional learning communities on teaching practice and student learning. *Teaching and Teacher Education, 24*(1), 80–91.

Vroom, V. H. (1964). *Work and motivation*. Wiley.

Watkins, P. (2005). The principal's role in attracting, retaining, and developing new teachers: Three strategies for collaboration and support. *The Clearing House: A Journal of Educational Strategies, Issues and Ideas, 79*(2), 83–87.

Yinon, H., & Orland-Barak, L. (2017). Career stories of Israeli teachers who left teaching: A salutogenic view of teacher attrition. *Teachers and Teaching, 23*(8), 914–927.

You, S., & Conley, S. (2015). Workplace predictors of secondary school teachers' intention to leave: An exploration of career stages. *Educational Management Administration & Leadership, 43*(4), 561–581.

PART 2

Getting the Right People

CHAPTER 4

Planning for Talent Needs

Recruitment and Retention

Chapter Summary

While there is a lack of consensus concerning the presence of a national K–12 teacher shortage, much less controversial is the fact that teacher staffing challenges remain persistent for certain subject areas (e.g., math, science, and special education) and school types (e.g., urban, rural, high-poverty, majority non-White, and low-achieving schools). The problems have been exacerbated by a trend of declining enrollment in teacher preparation programs as well as the COVID pandemic and its associated "Great Resignation," which has spurred increased teacher turnover since the onset of the pandemic. Furthermore, hiring diverse candidates to match the ever-growing diversity of students has been a perennial challenge. With escalating teacher turnover and declining interest in the teaching profession, this chapter addresses the question: How can school leaders create attractive workplace conditions to better recruit and retain teachers? The chapter also addresses differentiated geographic challenges, workplace inclusion, and strategic talent management.

Effective leaders recruit, hire, support, develop, and retain effective and caring teachers and other professional staff and form them into an educationally effective faculty.
(PSEL Standard 6a)

DOI: 10.4324/9781003457060-6

INTRODUCTION

In recent years, a wave of teacher strikes has rippled across the nation. While the reasons for the strikes varied (e.g., inadequate funding, low teacher pay), a pervasive pattern of unfavorable teacher working conditions undergirds the movement. These conditions have contributed to what some are calling a "national teacher shortage," with recent estimates suggesting the nation is short approximately 112,000 teachers in response to labor demand. This is exacerbated by an additional 109,000 employed individuals who are uncertified for their positions (Sutcher et al., 2019), leaving scores of students in oversized classrooms with unqualified teachers. The "teacher shortage" constitutes a serious talent management problem that is often narrowly addressed by just focusing on hiring more teachers without regard to the problem of their frequent turnover. Darling-Hammond (2010) notes that "the quality of school leaders is critical to recruiting and retaining teachers, as the principal's ability to organize a productive environment, access resources, buffer the school from outside distractions, motivate adults, and support their learning is critical to teachers' satisfaction and efficacy" (p. 10). And while there is empirical research that suggests administrative support by school principals is perceived by both current and prospective teachers to be the most influential factor affecting how they feel about their workplace (Horng, 2009; Ingersoll, 2001; Ladd, 2011; Tran & Smith, 2020b), school leaders have shared that they often do not know how to provide that support and need HR (e.g., employee development) support themselves (Barber et al., 2010). Due to declining interest in the teaching profession and turnover in the classroom, this chapter continues to elaborate on the discussion started in Chapter 2 concerning: How can school leaders create attractive workplace conditions that foster teacher recruitment and retention?

FACTORS THAT INFLUENCE RECRUITMENT AND RETENTION

It is important for school employers to ensure they have the talent they need by proactively addressing people-sourcing issues such as recruitment, absenteeism, and turnover. Many states have responded to teacher shortage issues by easing career entry requirements (Murnane & Steele, 2007; Stotsky, 2015), yet alternatively certified teachers have been found to be more likely to leave the profession than their traditional counterparts (Redding & Smith, 2016). While nontraditional routes into the teaching profession, such as Teach for America, have been suggested as a potential remedy for the teacher supply shortages, teachers from these types of programs are recruited in much smaller numbers and have lower retention rates than teachers from traditional pathways (Boyd et al., 2006, 2012). Despite these nontraditional options stepping in to fill voids in some communities, the teacher supply problem continues to persistently plague many "hard-to-staff" schools, partly because the underlying causes of the teacher shortages are often not addressed (Boyd et al., 2011; Ladd, 2011; Tran & Smith, 2020b).

TEACHER RECRUITMENT

While there is a lack of consensus concerning the presence of a national teacher shortage (Huffman, 2015; Taie & Goldring, 2017), much less controversial is the fact that teacher staffing challenges remain persistent for certain subject areas (e.g., math, science, and special education) and school types (e.g., urban, rural, high-poverty, majority non-White, and low-achieving schools) (Aragon, 2016). The problems have been exacerbated by a trend of declining enrollment in teacher preparation programs (signaling less interest in the teaching profession) (Partelow, 2019) as well as the COVID pandemic and its associated "Great Resignation," which has spurred increased teacher turnover since the onset of the pandemic (García & Weiss, 2022; Goldhaber & Theobald, 2022; Steiner & Woo, 2021). Furthermore, hiring diverse candidates to match the ever-growing diversity of students remains a challenge nationwide (D'amico et al., 2017). School employers that are active and strategic with their recruitment intentionally work to expand their recruitment pools, while those that remain passive and reactionary to applicants do not proactively recruit and, therefore, can only hire those who happen to apply (DeArmond et al., 2010; Tran, 2015). The latter strategy may work for schools that maintain a sufficient pool due to their inherent attractiveness (e.g., favorable location or reputation), but the approach will have limited value for hard-to-staff schools that may be perceived as unattractive to begin with. For organizations that aim to actively recruit potential employees, there are several popular sources and strategies that they can apply.

Online Recruiting

The use of online recruiting is becoming increasingly common given its potential to reach a wider audience, its relatively inexpensive operational costs post setup, and the internet's near ubiquity in modern society. While some districts merely post job advertisements on their official websites, other organizations use more progressive strategies that recruit via online databases (e.g., databank of vacancies or potential applicant pool) and maintain active recruitment via social media (e.g., Meta, LinkedIn, X) in their staffing efforts. When it comes to the former, it is important for webpages with recruitment content to be up-to-date and have a specific contact number (e.g., a number to a specific HR representative as opposed to a number for the whole school district generally) for candidates who have additional comments or who require technical assistance (Young, 2008). When it comes to the latter, social media is a relatively new terrain for employers and comes with its share of opportunities and risks. While the use of social media allows employers to reach wide audiences at a potentially low cost, both current and former employees can also comment on these platforms, using them as forums to air grievances and speak negatively about the employer. The former can help recruit potential applicants; the latter can deter them. Consequently, Watkins (2021) suggests that social media should be intentionally managed with clear protocols and policies established to help mitigate potential public relations and legal risks.

External Partnerships

Another valuable source of potential educators is partnerships with institutions of higher education (Harrison & Tran, 2020). These alliances have the potential to improve staffing opportunities for schools in hard-to-staff regions (Tran et al., 2018) and recruit diverse candidates (Dobbin & Kalev, 2018) if they are used with intention. However, collaboration among schools, communities, and higher education cannot occur protractedly; instead, there needs to be ample opportunities for K–12 and postsecondary educators to work together in ways that are mutually beneficial for school districts and the communities within which they are situated. For example, universities can work with school districts and communities to facilitate recruitment fairs for hard-to-staff rural communities. This partnership is mutually beneficial since it provides employment for the university's students, who then become educators for these communities and schools. Similarly, school employers with underrepresentation of Black educators can collaborate with historically Black colleges and universities (HBCUs) for targeted recruitment efforts to increase employment interest from potential Black candidates. The key is intentionality and the leveraging of proactive, as opposed to reactive, recruitment.

Hiring Incentives

School employers have used a variety of hiring incentives such as signing bonuses, strategic compensation (e.g., "frontloading" the salary schedule so that a larger percentage of raises occur for less experienced newer teachers), and provision of workday flexibility (e.g., working a four-day workweek) to recruit high-quality candidates for employment purposes. While each individual recruitment practice may have its own utility, the use of more recruitment practices in tandem often results in the hiring of more qualified teachers (Balter & Duncombe, 2008). Unfortunately, many employers are not in a position to offer financial incentives. To the extent that they cannot, they should be markedly more creative with providing potential applicants with a clear and convincing argument as to why it would be advantageous to apply for their job vacancies.

Employers should remember that during the recruitment process, both sides are courting and selecting each other. A common mistake made by many employers is that they forget they are also attracting candidates and not just testing them to determine if they want to hire the individual. When addressing employee recruitment and retention, employers should consider their employee value proposition, which communicates what is offered to prospective or existing employees to demonstrate their value for working and remaining in the school and why their organization should be the "employer of choice." Values can range from factors such as attractive location, positive work environment, employer's reputation, and career and learning opportunities. Just as it is important to understand why the candidate represents a great fit for the organization, the opposite is also true: Candidates need to be convinced why the organization would be a great employer for them. Employer branding is one way to communicate this information.

Employer Branding

Employer branding is important in tight labor markets, such as the one for teachers in high-poverty urban and rural schools. Employer branding may serve as a potential mechanism to address the teacher shortages commonly faced by many hard-to-staff schools. Unfortunately, current theory and practice have yet to connect school employer branding to educator talent management, which is at the heart of the strategic agenda for school improvement.

There are many ways that school employers can rely on employer branding in the hiring process. One way is for schools to have informational meetings (DeArmond et al., 2010) to showcase their culture and programs to provide a more realistic job preview for prospective candidates (Tran et al., 2020b).

Successful "employers of choice" are able to address employees' needs associated with being employed in a great place (Purcell et al., 2003) and a good job (e.g., one that values their input, provides them proper training, conducts fair and constructive evaluations, and offers supportive coaching and feedback). High-poverty, hard-to-staff schools have experienced some success with appealing to candidates' public service interests and relying on mission-based student-centered recruitment messages (Shuls & Maranto, 2014).

BOX 4.1: RECRUITMENT SUGGESTIONS

School leaders and employers should:

- Avoid overstating job requirements. While it may seem clever to "shoot for the moon," unreasonably high and unrealistic job requirements limit the candidate pool. This limitation is further exacerbated when compensation is not proportionate to workplace expectations and employees' talents are not relied upon to the degree communicated in the job advertisement. All of this jointly results in employees feeling undervalued.
- Be careful of implicit bias which can result in unintentional discrimination against those in protected class categories such as age, race, disability, and sex in job advertisements. For example, specifically stating that the organization is looking for "young and energetic new teachers" may be construed as discriminatory against the protected class category of age.
- Ensure that job advertisements clarify the knowledge, skills, and abilities (KSAs) associated with the role; the job duties associated with the position;

and the qualifications, training, and experience required of the jobholder. Ensure that the stated requirements are necessary for the job and that they do not unintentionally result in discriminatory hiring outcomes for people in protected class categories.

For example, requiring excessive job experience before consideration of hire may seem valid on its face, but if this requirement is truly unnecessary for the job's execution and results in disproportionate amounts of protected class people (e.g., women) being deemed ineligible for the position, then the use of this kind of job criteria may be deemed illegal (see Chapter 5 for more details).

- Pay attention to the source of where candidates are being drawn from: such as local and nationally renowned universities, locally developed workforce or "grow your own" initiatives, job fairs, former employees and job candidates, or referrals from current employees.

  Then, examine the success rates of the sources. For example, where have the organization's best employees come from? Are the sources producing a diverse array of candidates? Remember, diversity and quality are not mutually exclusive. If a source has a pattern of producing a diverse pool of quality candidates, employers should be sure to emphasize actively recruiting from this source.
- Conduct analysis of factors of the organization that are likely to attract or deter candidates. Strengths and weaknesses of the employer can be solicited through employee feedback (e.g., surveys, focus groups, exit interviews). For example, if employees are leaving the organization, why are they doing so? Who is leaving and when? The strengths can be advertised, while the weaknesses can be improved upon.
- Recruit early or year-round to maximize the chances of attracting the best candidates before they are hired elsewhere. The timing of the search is paramount; late recruitment leads to late hires, most of whom will typically be less qualified candidates (Liu & Johnson, 2006).
- Have resource plans that include identifying capable paraeducators and training them to become teachers.
- Avoid posting for subjective personal qualities in job advertisements such as "motivated" and "determined," because these statements are difficult to validate and often ignored by the candidates. Most candidates will state that they possess such traits if asked, which suggests that stating them will not hold much practical value for recruitment purposes.
- Assess the cost-effectiveness of advertisements by determining the applicant yield obtained from each source relative to the cost of the source (i.e., cost per reply).

- Conduct a thorough background check of candidates including checking the validity/obtainment of requisite credentials and degrees, talking with their past employers, etc. There have been some high-profile cases that exposed the fact that employees and even high-ranking education leaders were able to hold their positions based on inaccurate information communicated on their résumés and applications.
- Remember that the hiring process is two-way and the beginning of the employee experience (see Chapter 3) for the hired employee. The employer should treat prospective employees with courtesy and respect throughout the entire process. For example, this means employers should provide candidates with timely feedback on their application status, even if they are not hired. Candidates who are treated poorly during the job search process by an employer will likely tell others about their experience, thereby jeopardizing the reputation of the employer.
- Send job candidates details about the workplace to save time at the interview stage so that they can ask more targeted questions that require personal elaboration.

Prioritizing People

Tran and Smith (2020a) identified the relative preferences of college students when considering possible teaching positions in a rural, hard-to-staff school district. Their study sought to determine which factors were perceived to be the most important by respondents for the purposes of their recruitment as teachers in a rural district with severe teacher turnover. Through their quantitative and qualitative analyses, they found administrative support, as well as teachers' strong connection with students and self-confidence, to be the most important factors for college students' consideration for teaching at a rural, high-turnover school district.

With Talent-Centered Education Leadership (Tran, 2022), talent is prioritized above processes. Prioritizing the people is particularly helpful during the hiring phase as this prioritization helps set a good tone for the employee experience (see Chapter 3 for more information) and builds a positive reputation that will further attract more employees. For example, when organizational protocols and policies result in candidates waiting an inordinate amount of time before they are hired (weeks, or even months), potential good hires are lost to other more responsive employers, which causes hiring to become late (sometimes after the school year has started) and based on limited information (Liu & Johnson, 2006; Tran & Smith, 2020b). When employers keep their talent at the center of their decision-making, the talent is expected to respond positively. More intentionality in the recruitment process helps increase the likelihood of a better fit between the employer and the employee, which can help mitigate future turnover.

TEACHER RETENTION

While both teacher recruitment and retention challenge teacher supply, Ingersoll (2001) famously noted that teacher shortages often result from the latter, with the revolving door of turnover influenced heavily by organizational factors such as weak administrative support, lack of input on decision-making, and student disciplinary problems. Educator stability is necessary to develop consistency in high-performing school cultures (Balu et al., 2009). Constant educator turnover is associated with numerous negative outcomes such as higher replacement costs, diminishing trust, and lower student achievement, which become more pronounced in economically disadvantaged schools (Ronfeldt et al., 2013; Watlington et al., 2010). Kelchtermans (2017) argues that teacher attrition is a "prime issue" where multiple factors such as professional/career development, workplace motivation, life choices, working conditions, and the social status of the teaching profession converge. Unfortunately, strategies aimed at mitigating teacher shortages "have focused primarily on recruiting promising teachers into high-poverty schools, often with little attention to systematically supporting and retaining them once they are there" (Simon & Johnson, 2015, p. 2).

Teachers voluntarily leave their positions through attrition (leave the teaching profession), migration (leave to teach at another school) (Ingersoll, 2003), or shifting to other positions (e.g., administration) (Olsen & Anderson, 2007). Guarino et al. (2006) conducted an extensive review of the literature that examined 1) the characteristics of those in the teaching profession, 2) school and district characteristics associated with successful teacher recruitment and retention, and 3) the most promising staffing strategies. First, they found that White women made up the majority of teachers. There were also tentative findings that suggest that individuals with higher academic ability were less likely to teach. This finding may be biased towards elementary school teachers, who make up the majority of teachers. The results also suggest that altruism is the primary motivator for those who enter into teaching. Teachers who are more likely to leave the profession include those who are at the beginning or end of their career, who teach science and math, who are White, and who have higher academic ability. Schools and districts with high percentages of non-White, high-poverty, and low-performing students tend to see higher turnover. When it comes to successful staffing strategies, Guarino et al.'s (2006) review of the research found much support for the importance of mentoring and induction programs (especially collegial support), teacher autonomy, and administrative support for teacher retention. Teachers generally left their positions for jobs that offered more intrinsic rewards, higher pay, and better working conditions. Many of these findings were supported by earlier research and continue to be supported in recent scholarship.

Borman and Dowling (2008) conducted a comprehensive meta-analysis on the influences of voluntary teacher attrition (not resulting from retirement or transfer) and found evidence for the importance of various factors across teachers' careers. These factors include the characteristics and identity of the teacher (e.g., gender, experience, qualifications, certification status, familial status, subject-matter training in math and science) and their workplace (e.g., work-related resources, salary offerings, geographic locale, poverty status, district spending, school size). They also found that working conditions such as the degree of teacher networking, administrative support, and collaboration significantly moderate the relationship between the aforementioned factors and teacher attrition. School leaders often have tremendous influence on working conditions and occupy a critical role in influencing teacher retention. In fact, it is commonly said that employees join organizations but leave their managers (Armstrong & Taylor, 2014).

Retention Incentives

Some school employers use extrinsic financial incentives in their efforts to retain teachers. For example, employees may receive an annual monetary retention bonus for each year they stay. Scholarly literature suggests that retention bonuses can have a positive effect on teacher retention (Springer et al., 2016). However, as discussed in Chapter 3, specifics of the program design and implementation impact program effectiveness (Clotfelter et al., 2008). Further, Ondrich et al. (2008) demonstrate that urban teachers are less likely to leave districts that pay higher salaries than local nonteaching entities. This difference reinforces the idea that local labor markets are influenced by teaching salaries. Unfortunately, decision-makers narrow their focus too often on inadequate financial incentives (e.g., barely perceivable salary increases) that are insufficient to address morale issues in isolation, even if the amounts were substantive to begin with (which in many cases they are not). Even worse is the damage of trust that occurs when financial incentives are promised but not delivered (e.g., employee meeting performance target for a bonus but not receiving the bonus due to lack of funding).

BOX 4.2: RETENTION TIPS

School leaders and employers should:

- Calculate employee turnover and retention. Armstrong and Taylor (2014) suggest several HR analytical methods to do so. One way to calculate turnover is to use the following **turnover rate formula**:

  number of leavers in a year/average number of employees during the same period (x100)

- Lower scores suggest less turnover. This method is popular due to its simplicity. A method of retention calculation is **the stability index**, which is calculated with the following formula:

  number with one year's service or more/number employed a year ago (x100)

- Higher scores suggest less turnover here. One suggested target stability for organizations is between 75–85%. Of course, you can designate a different time frame than one year. Turnover is not necessarily the opposite of retention; organizations can have multiple turnovers for the same position in one year, which would increase the turnover rate but not necessarily the retention rate.
- Realize that while it is often not calculated by employers, employee replacement can be costly (Tran et al., 2018; Watlington et al., 2010). These costs range from expenses related to recruitment; separation of the departing employee; and orientation/onboarding/training to the time invested by HR, district, and school personnel involved in the replacement process. Understanding the cost of turnover can better inform the cost-effectiveness of retention efforts. For example, while providing developmental opportunities to improve teacher morale may be costly, it may cost less than current annual turnover expenses. As a result, even from a purely financial perspective, investment into retention efforts may be a better use of funds than constant employee replacement.

  Follow up and check with new employees on how well they are doing post-hire and ensure that they have settled into the workplace properly. It is better to identify problems early. Induction and early onboarding mentorship can help reduce turnover.

Prioritizing People

Teaching activities such as home grading, lesson planning, and investing in classroom resources with funds out of their own paycheck result in heavy commitment in time, finances, and emotions from teachers. This, coupled with the ever-growing increase in paperwork, monitoring and data analysis related to test-based accountability, and professional expectations of the role of education in society, has made teacher work-life balance particularly challenging. For example, Harrison et al. (2015) found that beyond dealing with their own health problems, work-life balance issues, such as caring for aging parents and young children, primarily motivated the work absences in their sample of over 600 Texas teachers. Teachers also noted that workplace-related stress resulting from increasing workload demands (without the provision of corresponding support and sufficient planning time) also stimulated what they referred to as "mental health day" absences. Excessive absences often connote and reflect employee dissatisfaction and disengagement.

If school leaders better understand the underlying reasons for excessive absences, then they will be better able to address the absenteeism effectively. This investigation can occur in several ways. For example, school leaders can examine and analyze absence data to identify patterns of absences. Questions that can be addressed in this phase include: When are absences more likely? Who is most likely to be absent? What is the cost of absences? Beyond cost, what else is affected by absences? It may be particularly important to authentically engage and discuss with employees not only the reasons for absences but also how might the absences be mitigated. Furthermore, attention should be paid to discerning different types of absences and how they are treated and viewed within the work culture. For example, is there a stigma against teachers who take their earned personal days off? Is that perceived as demonstrating a lack of commitment to their students, even if they are taking it for the purposes of addressing their own health or family obligations? School leaders should facilitate a work environment that mitigates and addresses stress while countering the neglect of family and personal lives because of workplace management. Excessive absences can be a precursor for turnover.

Relatedly, while using the restroom is a basic human necessity, in many schools, teachers are not practically able to do so for the entirety of the school day because they have an obligation as an adult to supervise the students. Many school leaders take this situation for granted as an unchangeable reality. But is it really? Is there absolutely no way to accommodate teachers' restroom use during the school day? If a school leader desires, how could they make it work? School leaders who exemplify Talent-Centered Education Leadership (Tran, 2022) understand that its foundation is based on humanizing the workplace.

INCLUSION

At its core, TCEL encourages employers to create inclusive work environments that value their employees and respond to the needs of the workforce, regardless of their demographic status or identities. TCEL allows for the cultivation of an atmosphere of belonging for individuals across the spectrum of disability, veteran status, race, age, gender, and other social groups, to go beyond representation to successfully integrate them into the organization. This should not be approached to purely satisfy legal compliance regulations but rather through an authentic engagement with the people at work from a diversity-conscious approach, based on transparency and respect for the workforce.

It is easy to see why organizations often focus on compliance, given that illegal discrimination based on a lack of attention to diversity issues has cost many employers millions of dollars in lawsuits. In response, many organizations have invested in diversity programs to improve their workplace climate, yet linkage between the programs to climate improvement is important if the efforts are meant to be meaningful. Much of what we know about the efficacy of diversity programs on improving the diversity of the workforce comes from research in private businesses and the public sector more broadly. For instance, despite their popularity, most anti-bias diversity training programs, in isolation, do not appear to increase diversity as they are often too surface-level to substantively change the tacit assumptions and behaviors undergirding employment practices

(Dobbin & Kalev, 2013). Additionally, such programs are often too episodic in duration to cultivate enduring change and focus too much on controlling employees through negative messaging, force, threats, and punishments to mitigate their bias (Dobbin & Kalev, 2013, 2018; Rynes & Rosen, 1995). Moreover, while participants may learn how to answer questions associated with diversity training exams correctly, their behavior often does not change in accordance.

Rather than serving as a conduit for positive change, the lack of success of anti-bias diversity training programs suggests that employers often treat them as a public relations tool, a compliance checkbox that is offered because it is symbolically or legally beneficial to do so. Coupled with platitudes regarding its value, diversity training represents an opportunity for virtue-signaling optics to publicly demonstrate that the employer is responsive to outside pressure without necessarily being culturally responsive internally. In having such a program, employers can look like they address their biases, and their employees can feel better about their decisions since they "went through the training," regardless of its impact on behavior and decision-making.

Hundreds of studies spanning a century have found that anti-bias training is not only ineffective and often quite costly to implement (Dobbin & Kalev, 2018; Paluck & Green, 2009), but it also can be counterproductive. Specifically, the training may trigger and embolden the very biases it is designed to quell if recipients feel excluded and attacked in the training because of their own demographic traits (e.g., being White or a straight male) (Kulik et al., 2007; Rynes & Rosen, 1995) or because they are forced to receive training that they view as limiting their autonomy and freedom of thought (Homan et al., 2015).

A more effective approach to motivate change is to engage employees by involving them in creating solutions to address diversity problems, increasing the likelihood that they will become willing and voluntary champions of diversity. For example, the use of a diversity task force comprised of a diverse body of constituents, including members of underrepresented groups, provides an opportunity for members to increase their contact with different types of people. In service of setting diversity goals, evaluating progress towards goal achievement, and overseeing diversity processes and programs, diversity task forces increase cross-cultural interactions and allow for more understanding and empathy between individuals from different backgrounds, thus promoting cultural awareness. Furthermore, a task force can activate another powerful influencer towards diversity improvement: transparency. Specifically, diverse task forces create transparency because members have to explain their decisions in front of their peers. Social accountability increases the chances that decisions are made based on quality, if for no other reasons than the fact that most will want to at least appear fair (if they are not acting with conviction towards fairness) in front of others, in order to maintain social desirability (Castilla, 2015).

Another way to increase transparency to improve diversity is to showcase diversity metrics (in areas such as hiring and performance pay) disaggregated by protected class categories such as race, sex, and disability status. This provides a spotlight on potential discrimination that might exist within different departments and in the organization as a whole. Such illumination gives the employer an opportunity to be proactive as opposed to reactive in responding to a court ruling. A review of turnover trends might suggest a pattern of concentrated turnover for underrepresented employees, potentially suggesting a work atmosphere that promotes systemic exclusion. Surveys of the workforce might provide an additional pulse check of the organization's current inclusion climate. Exit surveys and interviews with departing employees can help employers better understand areas that warrant workplace improvement. An inclusive work environment can be enhanced by considering multiple forms of data and evidence of performance.

As the data are collected, employers should listen and attempt to understand the feedback as opposed to taking a defensive stance to justify present actions without consideration of how those actions might be transformed. Issues like sexual harassment and abuse flourish in workplaces where victims are not listened to or where complaints are trivialized. For example, when someone reports that a certain administrator has been harassing them and the response they receive is, "I have known that administrator for years, and he would never do that" and no further substantive investigation or action is taken, victims will be less likely to speak up in the future. A failure of follow-through is a major reason why much abuse and discrimination fails to be reported. Leaders have an obligation to maintain a workplace free of harassment and bullying.

Beyond engagement and transparency, organizations can improve their diversity efforts if they do not treat them in isolation as a specialty initiative but rather as an embedded and integrated set of standards within the organization's operations. School administrators, like other operational managers, often are concerned with the main organizational output of the institution – one of which for schools is student learning.

Diversity and HR work, in general, are often treated as something that just needs to be done, a box that has to be checked to get it out of the way (i.e., diversity is not the focus), and even worse, they are often perceived as a waste of time. Integrating diversity efforts into the routinized operations increases the likelihood that employees will be internally motivated to commit to change (Dobbin & Kalev, 2018).

Mentorship programs that allow more seasoned employees to show their less experienced colleagues the "ropes" and share tacit knowledge have the potential to make the workforce more diverse. Because most of the informal mentorship opportunities occur between people who are similar, organizations can assign mentorship in formal programs that allow for more interactions and engagement between people from different demographic backgrounds. Similarly, the use of cross-training and self-managed teams can also increase contact between individuals from different backgrounds to reduce bias and dismantle stereotypes. These types of programs may garner more support and engagement than mandatory training because they are not framed as "diversity efforts" (and therefore less polarizing as some see "diversity" as code for anti-White) despite having the potential to improve the organization's diversity endeavors (Dobbin & Kalev, 2016; Kulik et al., 2007).

While the establishment of organizational policies can be powerful and clarity-inducing, they are not discrimination-proof. Quick fixes rarely fix anything at all, as employees often learn to work around the system. For example, in situations where there is minimal variation in performance ratings, administrators have more discretion to operate in a less-than-transparent manner by promoting employees based on hidden or tacit criteria. Similarly, employer policy mandating the posting of job vacancies for open application does not inhibit the hiring agents from "stacking the deck" in favor of the individual they have predetermined as the hiring target (e.g., the "inside" person), thereby treating the entire hiring process as a symbolic sham that wastes the time of everyone involved.

Structural responsibility for diversity and inclusion (D&I) can also be beneficial. Because school administrators often have numerous responsibilities and duties they must attend to, they may not be able to devote the type of focus to D&I that it warrants, increasing the risk that these important issues are treated superficially or not at all.

Consequently, assigning the responsibility to oversee D&I efforts to a specific individual/unit (e.g., assistant principal of diversity or the diversity manager) can be invaluable, although the individual should not be the only person responsible for diversity. The individual should report directly to top management so that they have the authority to be taken seriously in a context with competing demands. Furthermore, this can promote social accountability from other employees to reduce bias in decision-making in pursuit of setting and achieving D&I goals.

Many employers mistakenly believe that if they hire a diverse candidate or two, their diversity issues will go away. Unfortunately, this perspective is short-sighted, as workplace equity can only be achieved through sustaining a culturally responsive and inclusive work environment (Tran et al., 2020a). Otherwise, the perpetuation of bias remains unresolved. For instance, in a culturally unresponsive context, diverse hires may be seen as "diversity hires," perceived to have been selected for employment, not because of their qualities or performance but rather their non-job–related demographic traits (e.g., race). Employees here fail to recognize that performance, quality, and diversity are not mutually exclusive. Broadening the diversity of the workforce does not mean the organization should reduce its standards or candidates' qualifications for hire. In fact, having more diversity has been associated with improved organizational performance, for both profit in the private business sector (Hunt et al., 2018) and student learning outcomes in education (DuBois & Schanzenbach, 2017; Gershenson et al., 2018).

While intentional illegal discrimination can be the underlying motivation for bias-perpetuating decision-making and behavior, it can occur even from those who espouse pro-equity views as a result of implicit bias that sustains the homosocial reproduction of the workforce (Holgersson, 2013; Tallberg, 2009). Biases are transmitted to us in our everyday lives, ingrained through socialization by our upbringing, the media, and broader society at large (Dobbin & Kalev, 2018). Biases can be perpetuated in the workplace when administrators and hiring personnel are more likely to favor and trust individuals who are more similar to them (e.g., in-group preferences such as men preferring men) than not, resulting in discriminatory employment practices. The result is inequitable opportunities for those who differ from decision-makers and upper management and are out of network with them because of those dissimilarities.

According to Dobbin and Kalev (2018), while the positive effects of diversity training, in isolation, may be questionable for improving representation for underrepresented workers of color, its potential is improved when used as part of a larger comprehensive diversity effort that targets change to discriminatory structural and organizational practices and behavior, such as addressing discriminatory hiring and promotional criteria, not just individual biases. For example, training and mentoring programs are more effective when coupled with responsibility structures like diversity managers.

The bulk of traditional diversity efforts were designed to acclimate workers to the preexisting structures and cultures of the workplace, without the workplace acclimating to the employees. Yet, times are changing, and as Hecht (2020) notes, "[t]oday's racial equity and inclusion efforts must flip that premise on its head. Instead of trying to change some people to fit the organization, we must focus on transforming our organizations to fit all people" (para 5). This viewpoint reflects a TCEL (Tran, 2022) philosophy that prioritizes acknowledging and valuing each individual worker, responding to the needs of the workforce, and humanizing the workplace.

Employers have long treated employees as human *resources*, as both expendable and replaceable. It has been such an internalized perspective that even employees think of themselves that way, subordinating themselves to the needs and goals of the organization. In education, the risk is particularly high given that the goals of the organization are often to improve student learning outcomes and the altruistic motivation of teachers who join the profession to make a positive impact on students' lives. Therefore, dehumanizing educators in service of students is often viewed as not only justifiable but noble. Yet the status quo has neither served educators nor students well and often perpetuates institutional exclusion and marginalization for both.

While the issues and factors mentioned previously impact schools of all types, different types of schools have varying needs. When it comes to staffing concerns, one particularly salient point of difference between schools is geographic. Because high-poverty urban and rural schools face the fiercest staffing challenges, the next two sections highlight unique aspects of their respective locales.

Urban Schools

There are many contextual factors associated with urban schools that can serve as barriers to employee recruitment and retention. For instance, urban communities are often plagued with issues of poverty including unemployment, homelessness, and low household incomes. As a result, schools in urban communities often operate with fewer resources and educate many more students from economically disadvantaged households than their nonurban counterparts, both of which provide unique challenges for urban teaching. Beyond insufficient classroom materials, parents from urban communities may have less capacity to be involved and financially contribute to their schools. Furthermore, urban schools are often much larger than their counterparts, and as a result, they operate within more complex bureaucracies and face fiercer enrollment competition from neighboring schools (Tran & Smith, 2020c). Many high-poverty urban schools struggle with large class sizes, lack of parental involvement, low academic performance, and insufficient resources for their underserved (often non-White) students (Farinde et al., 2016). These schools are also often located in areas with high crime rates. Metal detectors, zero-tolerance misconduct policies, security guards, and disciplinary personnel are commonplace in high-poverty urban schools.

Moreover, urban schools are constantly under the microscope of government attention and focus. For example, they are spaces where the lion's share of educational reform churn occurs, with policymakers and other powerbrokers attempting to control, further bureaucratize, and shape urban education, all the while restricting teacher autonomy and agency in the process (Carlson, 2017; Mirra & Morrell, 2011). With heavy accountability pressures and large concentrations of students who are underperforming relative to the state performance metrics, there may be temptation for the school to promote a tacit expectation of socially promoting students to the next grade level despite their failure to achieve the prerequisite skill mastery. However, these promotions will result in more difficult working conditions for teachers in higher level grades as they struggle to work with the incoming academically unprepared students.

While urban communities often have a diverse body of students, it is common for the school's teaching staff to not reflect that diversity. In such situations, teachers often lack experiences with students from cultures different from their own and may harbor negative attitudes and low expectations for students based on misconceptions associated with race and class differences (Cochran-Smith & Zeichner, 2009). Relatedly, student disciplinary issues may also be more pervasive in high-poverty urban schools, with infractions ranging from intentional interruptions to physical violence (Smith & Smith, 2006). While some argue that at least a portion of these disciplinary infractions may result from bias (Blake et al., 2011; Staats, 2016), the perception of the students' behavioral problems and lack of enforcement of disciplinary protocols, nonetheless, contribute to teacher turnover (Allensworth et al., 2009). Multicultural leadership is necessary in such a context to improve the cultural responsiveness of school personnel, policies, and practices (Ahram et al., 2011).

High-poverty schools typically have high teacher demand, but low teacher supply (Rinke, 2011). To exacerbate the issue, teachers in those schools are more likely to have lower qualifications (across most common metrics of quality) (Goldhaber et al., 2015), have less experience, and leave their schools for those with wealthier students after they have gained some experience (Miller, 2012). Consequently, teacher shortages represent an issue of equity (Tran & Smith, 2020a).

Inclusion in Urban Schools

Inclusion is particularly important in urban schools given the equity and diversity concerns there. Inclusive and talent-centered leaders recognize that there is a difference between equity and equality, where equality relates to sameness (e.g., everyone gets the same support) and equity relates to fairness (e.g., those who need differential support get differential support) (Tran, 2018). For example, there are many teachers who seek to teach in high-poverty urban schools who come at teaching from a social justice advocacy approach, with an intentional desire to enhance educational equity. These teachers may feel isolated in schools that adopt a "color-blind" approach that insists on equal treatment of all, despite the different backgrounds and communities of the students. The adults in these schools may also refrain from acknowledging cultural differences, and the discussion of such topics may be silenced because of discomfort with acknowledging its effect. This type of perspective can lead to an exclusive work environment. In such a school, an elementary school teacher who speaks Spanish to her Spanish-speaking students as a form of cultural connection may be chastised by her colleagues or supervisor, as her skill set may not be appreciated as a legitimate asset in a school where "everyone should be speaking English" (Kohli, 2008). This narrow definition of professionalism could affect not only her perception of self-efficacy as a teacher but retention as well.

Because of the underrepresentation of teachers of color in the industry, many urban schools do not have teachers who reflect their community of students of color. This lack of congruence between students and teachers may contribute to issues of cultural mismatch or misunderstanding (Weisman & Hansen, 2008). For example, it may be harder for a teacher to understand and relate to the circumstances of a student when they do not share a similar background. This lack of familiarity from the teachers can result in assumptions that lead to lower expectations of those students.

On the other hand, when race is acknowledged within a school, care must be taken to ensure it is not relied upon in ways that reproduce inequities. For example, in high-poverty urban environments, Black teachers have expressed experiencing increasing expectations to serve as experts in stereotypical racialized roles (Mabokela & Madsen, 2007) and as representative of their race or the diversity representative. They are often the person many students of color come to for additional extracurricular support, and are perceived as angry if they disagree with their colleagues, having an authoritarian persona, and receiving a disproportionate assignment of disciplinary responsibilities for the Black youth in their schools. These tokenized occurrences are problematic on many fronts. For example, some of these Black teachers have been critical of the view that they should serve as disciplinary agents for their urban schools and, as a result, reinforce systemic inequity when they believe that students of color are being inequitably disciplined (Brockenbrough, 2015). These experiences are exacerbated when they translate to a narrowing of the contributions of teachers of color, resulting in neglect of their strengths in other areas of teaching and leadership (Kohli, 2018). The result is an increase in work responsibilities that can lead to burnout.

In contrast, talent-centered leaders can intentionally cultivate a culture of inclusion. An inclusive work culture is one that looks beyond legal compliance of diversity of representation (e.g., having a diverse work context) to create a work environment where diverse employees are welcomed, celebrated, and appreciated. Such a context should be free of microaggressions that work to jeopardize the inclusionary atmosphere, microaggression being the subtle verbal and nonverbal everyday insults or denigration related to the victim's social group status such as race or gender (Krull & Robicheau, 2020). These can range from intentionally and repeatedly mispronouncing someone's name or pronoun (e.g., using the pronoun *he* to refer to someone who identifies as a *she*) to outright explicit attacks (e.g., using the word *gay* in a pejorative manner when describing behavior) on the person with the intention to hurt them based on their group affiliation.

Kohli (2018) argues that the ethos of schooling must shift from a pure performance perspective to one that is attuned to humanizing schools as spaces that acknowledge the differences in histories, strengths, and struggles of its diverse body of teachers and students to promote their success. The complex bureaucracies associated with many large urban school districts create power structures that may stifle the power and agency of individuals. Supportive leadership is needed for teachers to counterbalance the structural neglect they experience in K–12 schools.

Administrative support, teacher coaching, constructive teacher evaluation, and teacher education programs have been linked to student success in the urban context (Grissom et al., 2013). Moreover, organizational management skills (e.g., managing the "school business" including budgeting, maintenance, hiring, safety, professional development) have been found to be predictive of multiple school outcomes including student achievement gains, teacher and parent assessment of school climate, and teacher retention (Grissom & Loeb, 2011; Horng et al., 2010). Still, the needs of urban institutions may differ from those of rural ones. In the next section, special attention will be directed to schools in the rural context.

Rural Schools

While high-poverty rural school employers share many of the challenges of high-poverty urban schools (e.g., limited resources, students who struggle academically) that contribute to difficulties with teacher recruitment and retention, there are also important differences. One major distinction is the fact that rural districts often operate with smaller organizational systems, which means rural administrators often wear "many hats," sometimes occupying the role of both a principal and superintendent (Canales et al., 2010) or taking on additional responsibilities in their position (Stewart & Matthews, 2015), such as teaching or driving the school bus.

According to Townsell (2007), rural principals often become involved in all aspects of school decision-making in a manner that differs from nonrural principals, given the lack of administrative support they receive, and they need to have an acute awareness of the culture of the community. Rural principals play an important role in helping acclimate new teachers to the community environment. By doing so, they can help mitigate teachers' feelings of social, cultural, and professional isolation, promoted by the geographic isolation common to many rural locales (Townsell, 2007). In rural environments, there is often a social expectation that rural principals are not just school leaders but community leaders as well (Pendola & Fuller, 2018). Rural principals can leverage these community connections to help integrate teachers with the community. Because rural educators often have less access to professional networks, their needs for support often differ from their nonrural counterparts.

Masumoto and Brown-Welty (2009) conducted a case study analysis of three high-poverty, underresourced, yet high-performing, rural schools and found the schools compensated for the lack of resources by partnering extensively with external partners such as parents, business professionals, professional organizations, and universities in formal and informal capacities. Two-way communication between the entities allowed parties to be responsive to each other's needs, increasing the active engagement of parents and communities with the school. This relationship suggests the importance of partnership skills for rural principals as rural leaders. Bauch (2001) identifies six rural-specific community attributes that school leaders can depend on for support. They include social capital, sense of place, parent involvement, strong church ties, school-community-business partnership, and community as curriculum.

Like with poor urban schools, poor rural schools often become a "training ground" for new employees, where they only work in such schools to gain enough experience to move to schools that are perceived to be less challenging (Tran et al., 2020b). Yet rurality is not a monolith. While rural schools that are closer in proximity to their urban counterparts face stiffer competition to retain teachers, remote rural schools often experience difficulty attracting them there in the first place (Miller, 2012). Rural superintendents have identified their communities' geographic and social isolation as significant barriers to attracting qualified candidates (Hammer et al., 2005). The region's lack of adequate housing, poor access to medical care, close-knit guard against "outsiders" of the community, and lack of amenities (e.g., beaches, shopping malls, grocery outlets, museums, zoos, universities), especially relative to their wealthier metropolitan counterparts, all further contribute to its lack of appeal (Miller, 2012; Harrison & Tran, 2020).

Global trends in rural teacher recruitment barriers identified in the early 1970s in Eastern Europe and the United States mostly remain today. These barriers include large student-teacher ratios, rural-to-urban population migration, lack of prestige associated with the teaching profession, lower relative salaries, and unavailability of housing in rural communities (Laderriere, 1971). Teachers' first employment usually occurs in districts that are close in physical and cultural proximity to where they went to college (Fowles et al., 2014), but because of the lack of universities located in rural regions, there is a smaller supply of rural teacher candidates relative to teachers in other regions.

Tran et al.'s (2020b) review of the rural teacher staffing literature expanded on many of the aforementioned rural staffing challenges, such as large concentrations of rural teachers teaching out of their subject of expertise, having to teach multiple subjects/grade levels, being highly visible (and therefore more open to criticism) in the community, among others. (see Figure 4.1 for a full list of challenges from the literature). Their work also highlighted several advantages of rural staffing such as small class sizes; stronger engagement with the local community; stronger school-wide camaraderie between leaders, teachers, and students; and more teacher autonomy in rural schools (see Figure 4.2 for a full list of advantages from the literature). They further supplemented these lists based on their own original research with rural educators to expand on the challenges to include factors such as small-town politics, lack of industry, cultural isolation, and barriers for those not familiar with rural life, as well as advantages such as tighter networks, family-oriented culture, and school camaraderie. While the challenges are often acknowledged as deterrents and barriers to rural teacher recruitment, the advantages and opportunities are rarely leveraged and advertised by rural employers to attract potential employees for recruitment purposes, representing a potential missed opportunity.

Figure 4.1 Challenges of Teaching in Rural Areas

Source: Reproduced with permission from Tran et al., 2020b/The Rural Educator

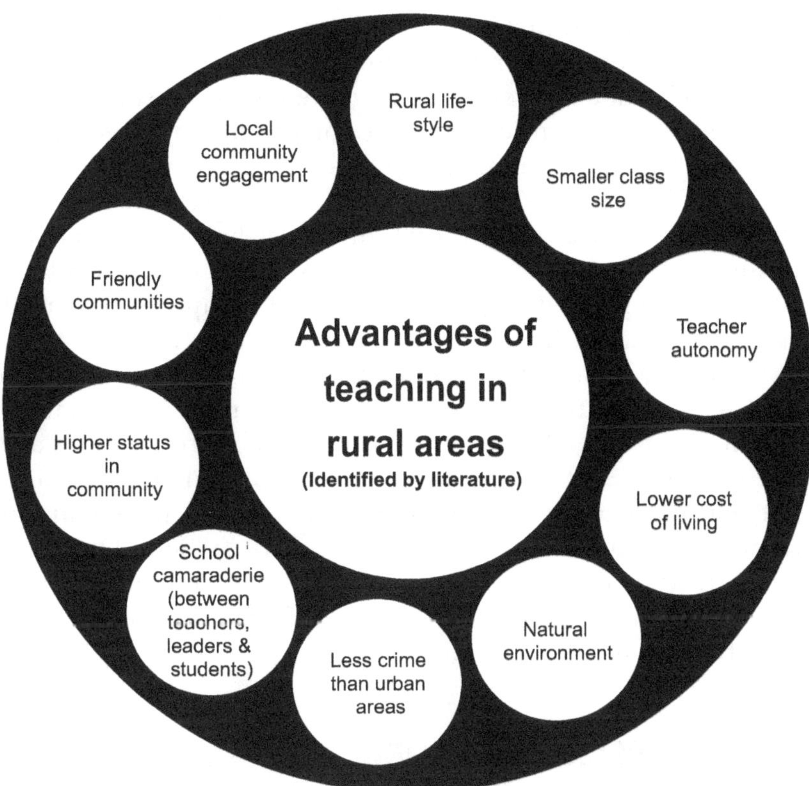

Figure 4.2 Advantages of Teaching in Rural Areas

Source: Reproduced with permission from Tran et al., 2020b/The Rural Educator

Employer Branding in Rural Schools

Rural schools (especially those that are high-poverty and remote) are often considered unattractive places to work and, as a result, are usually described and viewed through a deficit lens that emphasizes the negative aspects of the work environment. One potential marketing strategy that rural school employers could leverage to help improve the attractiveness is an asset-oriented view of employer branding, specifically through place marketing. Eshuis et al. (2013) explain that place marketing has been used to increase the competitive attractiveness of locales by branding the location with a positive image. Within the rural teacher recruitment context, the marketing aspect treats prospective rural teachers as customers and targets the messages to meet their needs. Place marketing applies a marketing framework to advertise attractive aspects of geographic locales. Within the context of rural teacher staffing, place marketing allows for place-conscious recruiting.

Interpreted from Herzberg et al.'s (1959) motivator-hygiene perspective, place marketing has potential as a recruitment branding strategy because it draws directly on the motivating factor of the work itself in the rural context, such as stronger connection to students and small class sizes that allow for more individualized teaching attention for students. Recommendations often focused solely on addressing the hygiene factors of salaries (i.e., offering higher "combat" wages to compensate for the harder-to-staff rural contexts) to mitigate the disadvantages by reducing potential job dissatisfaction while neglecting the need to attune to increasing potential job satisfaction. Moreover, from a practical perspective, impoverished rural school districts often have low property value to draw revenue from, which results in lower teacher salaries to begin with (Tran, 2018). That, coupled with rural superintendents' admission of the difficulty of sustaining financial recruitment incentives (Hammer et al., 2005) and the ability of wealthier districts to offer more financially attractive incentives than their rural counterparts, makes focusing on rural advantages a potentially more relevant and viable recruitment strategy. Still, the benefits of focusing on rural advantages do not suggest that financial incentives should be avoided if they are available but that relying on financial incentives alone is insufficient. Data concerning the potential effectiveness of the various recruitment and retention strategies should be collected and analyzed so that the information can be used to further improve future employment endeavors.

DATA-INFORMED DECISION-MAKING

As mentioned earlier, data and metrics can be useful tools to help leaders better understand their school's work environment. Human capital represents the knowledge, skills, and abilities that are critical for organizational performance. Human capital management (HCM) relies on metrics and data to inform HR decision-making, assessing the impact of HR practices on educational outcomes (Armstrong & Taylor, 2014). Critical questions to address in HCM include (but are not limited to) how to continuously measure meaningful data to understand the linkages between human capital and the education strategy, how to refine and develop the data as appropriate, how not to succumb to analysis paralysis, and how to collect the data in a cost-efficient manner that does not unduly occupy the time of school personnel.

Human capital data can help school leaders identify potential problems (such as development and/or staffing diversity needs) early to address them proactively. Furthermore, it is not critical to possess advanced statistical expertise to record and report basic HR data (Armstrong & Taylor, 2014). However, data should not be collected just for the sake of collection. Nor should all decisions be made solely based on the data, as other factors (e.g., feasibility of implementation, likelihood of political resistance) should also be considered. Rather, data should be used to help *inform* rather than dictate decision-making. Armstrong & Taylor (2014) described four major types of HCM measurements. They include workforce data (e.g., turnover rate, absence rate, demographics); people developmental data (e.g., skill gaps, qualifications); perceptual data (e.g., satisfaction, exit interviews); and performance data (e.g., teacher-value added). Care should be taken to ensure data accuracy as well as utility for decision-makers. It doesn't make sense to collect data nobody understands how to use.

Strategic Talent Management

There has been increasing recognition that school leaders often employ strategic talent management practices in their efforts to improve student achievement. These practices range from intentional hiring to workforce development and dismissals of ineffective personnel (Grissom & Bartanen, 2019). The extent to which these represent effective practice depends on how they are implemented. For example, Grissom et al. (2015a) remind us that although many talent management practices (e.g., hiring and retaining) are harder for school administrators to control, that is not the case with teacher-student assignments, where they largely have more influence to strategically assign teachers for improvement of school performance and equity outcomes. These researchers (2017) also found evidence to suggest that school principals, especially in lower-performing schools with more accountability pressure, often assigned their higher-performing teachers to tested grades. In elementary schools, this behavior can be problematic given that they also found evidence to suggest this results in the reassignment of less effective teachers to students in earlier grades (K–2). This assignment pattern depresses the students' math and reading potential, which also hurts their achievement in later grades. School leaders should take into consideration the potential long-term impacts of their talent management decisions and distinguish between gaming the system to appear to improve student learning outcomes and creating an environment that results in substantive meaningful improvement in student learning outcomes (Grissom et al., 2017).

Relatedly, it has been tradition in many schools to give beginning teachers the most challenging assignments relative to their veteran peers, and they often experience collegial isolation with little administrative support (Borman & Dowling, 2008; Gordon & Maxey, 2000). In a national study, Donaldson and Johnson (2010) found that principals in low-income schools tended to assign new teachers to more difficult assignments (e.g., multiple secondary subjects), which resulted in higher teacher turnover. Inequities can be compounded because while new teachers are typically less effective than their more seasoned counterparts (Ladd & Sorensen, 2017; Rockoff, 2004), they are often assigned to the lower-performing and most disadvantaged students in the school. The issue here stems from a culture that privileges seniority to the potential detriment of new teacher retention. Part of the reason this inequity in staffing endures, despite its potential harm to students, is the inequity in teacher-student assignments that results from what Grissom et al. (2015b) refer to as the "micropolitics of educational inequality" in schools. This refers to the political power that more experienced teachers have in influencing student assignments. In fact, they found evidence to support the existence of this political imbalance in their research, as experienced teachers were more involved in influencing teacher-student assignments and were assigned fewer low-performing, Black, and economically disadvantaged students. These patterns present an interesting question:

Discussion Questions: Should the most effective teachers be assigned to the academically neediest students?

Discussion Questions: What about gifted and talented students? Should they be assigned less effective teachers than academically disadvantaged students? Why or why not?

Based on multiple measures of teacher and principal performance in a multi-year longitudinal data analysis, Grissom and Bartanen (2019) found that higher-performing principals were more often associated with strategic retention – i.e., lower teacher turnover (on average, especially with high performers) and higher teacher turnover among low performers although this pattern is more evident in advantaged schools with less school leadership turnover. School leaders have numerous channels to strategically retain their faculty. For example, they may facilitate higher turnover for low-performing teachers through mechanisms such as failing to renew their contract, "counseling" them out by providing them candid feedback about their underperformance relative to the school's performance expectations, suggesting that they may be a better "fit" with another school (Drake et al., 2016), or pursuing administrative means for involuntary termination should struggling teachers not improve in response to their formal performance intervention plans. Teachers identified as low performers often leave on their own accord.

On the other hand, school leaders may provide higher-performing teachers with better working conditions and more mentor and teacher leadership roles (Jacob et al., 2012). A work environment with high-performance expectations can both encourage high performers to stay and encourage low performers to leave. There is some evidence to suggest that the strategic retention of more effective teachers, coupled with the increased turnover of less effective teachers, is associated with higher academic growth in schools (Loeb et al., 2012). It is important to note that geographic context affects the utility of strategic retention efforts. For example, Grissom and Bartanen (2019) found that suburban schools have more capacity than their rural and urban counterparts to leverage strategic retention. In the case of rural schools that have few teacher applicants to begin with, inducing turnover comes at the risk of having fewer teachers for their students.

BOX 4.3: A WARNING ABOUT MANAGING FOR PERFORMANCE

School leaders must be careful when strategically managing based on performance. How performance is measured is critical. Performance assessments should be valid, meaningful, fair, and ideally based on multiple measures. This means an adequate performance evaluation system is a necessary precondition for implementing strategic retention (see Chapter 5). Leaders should further ensure employees have reasonable control over their measured performance outcome and that decisions based on this performance are not shaped by biases that result in discriminatory decision-making. For example, it would be inequitable and illegal if people of certain protected class groups (e.g., race, age) were categorically considered to be less effective and provided less favorable working conditions as a result. Furthermore, many education organizations operate with a culture of "sameness," and these stakeholders' cultures are more likely to resist strategic human resources management (HRM) efforts, as they view equality to mean equity. These cultural issues must be intentionally tended (e.g., through dialogue and consensus-building) prior to instituting performance-based management.

To maximize the benefits associated with strategic talent management, employee motivation and behavior need to be understood. School leaders depend on their influence on employee behavior to accomplish organizational goals and objectives. While this influence has traditionally been exercised through control, increasingly scholars and practitioners have been advocating for the adoption of an engagement strategy (Truss et al., 2006). This perspective mirrors thinking in the broader HR management field, which has long evolved away from an employee control philosophy towards one of engendering employee commitment and, more recently, engagement (Armstrong & Taylor, 2014). Walton (1985) argues that workers respond best when given broader responsibilities, discretion, and input as opposed to being tightly controlled. Therefore, it is unsurprising that support mechanisms that have been found to be related to teacher retention include increases in autonomy, distributed decision-making, and teacher professional development (Urick, 2016).

BOX 4.4 WHEN IT'S NOT ROSY: WHEN RELATIONSHIPS TURN SOUR

Relationships are critical, especially in education. Developing a culture where employees maintain strong social bonds with one another may increase employee engagement and mitigate turnover (Cappelli, 2000). While it is ideal that employees work with their employers, that positive relationship may not always be there. Let's say, for example, that you are leading a school and are working hard to create a positive work experience for your employees. However, there is a particular disengaged employee who is not only unappreciative of your efforts but seems to also actively undermine everything that you do. He not only frequently complains about your suggestions but has verbally noted on several occasions that current leadership in the school is lacking and he wishes the old school principal (your predecessor) were still around. He makes you feel uncomfortable when he is in the same room as you because the conversations between the two of you often turn "ugly" and end in an argument. That said, the employee has not violated any organizational policies that warrant discipline and performs his job adequately.

Discussion Questions: How might you deal with this situation? Does it even warrant your attention, or should you just ignore it and operate as usual? Why or why not? Please rationalize and justify your responses based on ethical, legal, professional, and/or leadership frameworks.

Learning Activities

Discussion Questions:

1. Review your employer's most recent job descriptions for a specific job position (e.g., assistant principal or elementary school teacher). Is there potentially discriminatory and outdated language in them? What is it? How might the job description be rewritten to avoid biases and improve its validity?
2. How does your work environment allow for a space for open dialogue for sensitive issues such as discussions about race, gender, and sexual orientation? If it does not, how might it? Does the school provide an opportunity for such vulnerable dialogue or are such discussions considered "divisive?" Please explain your answer.
3. How does your employer acknowledge and recognize that differences between workers (e.g., teachers) may translate into differential types of needs? If it does not, how might it?
4. How often does your school leadership engage in dialogue about organizational equity?
5. How can leaders create an environment where employees feel comfortable bringing their full selves to work?
6. If you had to make a choice between the two, would you prefer an exceptional teacher who only teaches for a few years and leaves or an average career length teacher? Why?
7. How would you brand a school (pick one that you are familiar with) for the purposes of marketing for new employees? How would you brand the

community? Consider how these statements could be used in recruiting new teachers to the school/community.

CONCLUSION

School leaders occupy a critical role in the recruitment and retention of teachers. Effective school leaders can develop and maintain an attractive work environment that is grounded in equity, high expectations, professionalism, support, and respect. An unsupportive administration can exacerbate the challenges of a high-poverty and high-needs school by micromanaging, intimidating, and generally leading with an oppressive culture of fear and threats that contributes to turnover (Farinde et al., 2016).

The social dimensions of school are critical working conditions (Simon & Johnson, 2015). School-based communities, even informal ones, are important for teacher retention. In this chapter, beyond discussing factors that influence teacher recruitment and retention, we also discussed differentiated geographic challenges, workplace inclusion, and strategic talent management. In sum, school leaders should be intentional and responsive with their Talent-Centered Education Leadership (Tran, 2022).

Summary of Key Points

- There are many factors that influence teacher recruitment and retention, and these factors can vary significantly by the school's geographic location.
- Schools that have more inclusive decision-making, providing teachers with more administrative support, respect, and acknowledgment as professionals experience greater teacher retention (Borman & Dowling, 2008; Ingersoll, 2001)
- Talent-Centered Education Leaders maintain an inclusive work environment. This type of environment goes beyond diversity of representation to cultivate an environment of belonging for the workforce.
- School leaders can strategically retain high performers while inducing turnover of low performers through various formal and informal means, but they must be cautious that these actions are fair and nondiscriminatory and be mindful of cultural issues that may first need to be addressed to cultivate the conditions appropriate for strategic HRM.

REFERENCES

Ahram, R., Stembridge, A., Fergus, E., & Noguera, P. (2011). *Framing urban school challenges: The problems to examine when implementing response to intervention*. www.RTInetwork.org/learn/diversity/urban-school-challenges

Allensworth, E., Ponisciak, S., & Mazzeo, C. (2009). *The schools teachers leave: Teacher mobility in Chicago public schools*. Consortium on Chicago School Research.

Aragon, S. (2016). *Teacher shortages: What we know*. Education Commission of the States. www.ecs.org/ec-content/uploads/Teacher-Shortages-WhatWeKnow.pdf

Armstrong, M., & Taylor, S. (2014). *Armstrong's handbook of human resource management practice* (13th ed.). Kogan Page Publishers.

Balu, R., Béteille, T., & Loeb, S. (2009). Examining teacher turnover: The role of school leadership. *Politique Américaine*, (3), 55–79.

Balter, D., & Duncombe, W. D. (2008). Recruiting highly qualified teachers: Do district recruitment practices matter? *Public Finance Review*, *36*(1), 33–62.

Bauch, P. A. (2001). School-community partnerships in rural schools: Leadership, renewal, and a sense of place. *Peabody Journal of Education*, *76*(2), 204–221.

Barber, M., Whelan, F., & Clark, M. (2010). *Capturing the leadership premium. How the world's top school systems are building leadership capacity for the future*. McKinsey and Company. http://mckinseyonsociety.com/Education_Roundtable.pdf

Blake, J. J., Butler, B. R., Lewis, C. W., & Darensbourg, A. (2011). Unmasking the inequitable discipline experiences of urban Black girls: Implications for urban educational stakeholders. *The Urban Review*, *43*(1), 90–106.

Borman, G. D., & Dowling, N. M. (2008). Teacher attrition and retention: A meta-analytic and narrative review of the research. *Review of Educational Research*, *78*(3), 367–409.

Boyd, D., Grossman, P., Hammerness, K., Lankford, H., Loeb, S., Ronfeldt, M., & Wyckoff, J. (2012). Recruiting effective math teachers: Evidence from New York City. *American Educational Research Journal*, *49*(6), 1008–1047.

Boyd, D., Grossman, P., Ing, M., Lankford, H., Loeb, S., & Wyckoff, J. (2011). The influence of school administrators on teacher retention decisions. *American Educational Research Journal*, *48*(2), 303–333.

Boyd, D., Grossman, P., Lankford, H., Loeb, S., & Wyckoff, J. (2006). How changes in entry requirements alter the teacher workforce and affect student achievement. *Education Finance and Policy*, *1*, 176–216.

Brockenbrough, E. (2015). "The discipline stop" Black male teachers and the politics of urban school discipline. *Education and Urban Society*, *47*(5), 499–522.

Canales, M., Tejeda-Delgado, C., & Slate, J. R. (2010). Superintendents/principals in small rural school districts: A qualitative study of dual roles. *International Journal of Educational Leadership Preparation*, *5*(1), 1–10.

Cappelli, P. (2000). A market-driven approach to retaining talent. *Harvard Business Review*, *78*(1), 103–111.

Carlson, D. (2017). *Teachers and crisis: Urban school reform and teachers' work culture* (Vol. 1). Routledge.

Castilla, E. J. (2015). Accounting for the gap: A firm study manipulating organizational accountability and transparency in pay decisions. *Organization Science*, *26*(2), 311–333.

Clotfelter, C., Glennie, E., Ladd, H., & Vigdor, J. (2008). Would higher salaries keep teachers in high-poverty schools? Evidence from a policy intervention in North Carolina. *Journal of Public Economics*, *92*(5–6), 1352–1370.

Cochran-Smith, M., & Zeichner, K. M. (Eds.). (2009). *Studying teacher education: The report of the AERA panel on research and teacher education*. Routledge.

D'amico, D., Pawlewicz, R. J., Earley, P. M., & McGeehan, A. P. (2017). Where are all the Black teachers? Discrimination in the teacher labor market. *Harvard Educational Review*, *87*(1), 26–49.

Darling-Hammond, L. (2010). *The flat world and education: How America's commitment to equity will determine our future*. Teachers College, Columbia University.

DeArmond, M., Gross, B., & Goldhaber, D. (2010). Is it better to be good or lucky? Decentralized teacher selection in 10 elementary schools. *Educational Administration Quarterly, 46*(3), 322–362.

Dobbin, F., & Kalev, A. (2013). The origins and effects of corporate diversity programs. In *The Oxford handbook of diversity and work* (pp. 253–281). Oxford University Press.

Dobbin, F., & Kalev, A. (2016). Why diversity programs fail. *Harvard Business Review*. https://hbr.org/2016/07/why-diversity-programs-fail

Dobbin, F., & Kalev, A. (2018). Why doesn't diversity training work? The challenge for industry and academia. *Anthropology Now, 10*(2), 48–55.

Donaldson, M. L., & Johnson, S. M. (2010). The price of misassignment: The role of teaching assignments in teach for America teachers' exit from low-income schools and the teaching profession. *Educational Evaluation and Policy Analysis, 32*(2), 299–323.

Drake, T. A., Goldring, E., Grissom, J. A., Cannata, M. A., Neumerski, C., Rubin, M., & Schuermann, P. (2016). Development or dismissal? Exploring principals' use of teacher effectiveness data. In J. A. Grissom & P. Youngs (Eds.), *Improving teacher evaluation systems: Making the most of multiple measures* (pp. 169–183). Teachers College Press.

DuBois, C. C., & Schanzenbach, D. W. (2017). *The effect of court-ordered hiring guidelines on teacher composition and student achievement* (No. w24111). www.nber.org/papers/w24111

Eshuis, J., Braun, E., & Klijn, E. H. (2013). Place marketing as governance strategy: An assessment of obstacles in place marketing and their effects on attracting target groups. *Public Administration Review, 73*(3), 507–516.

Farinde, A. A., Allen, A., & Lewis, C. W. (2016). Retaining Black teachers: An examination of Black female teachers' intentions to remain in K–12 classrooms. *Equity & Excellence in Education, 49*(1), 115–127.

Fowles, J., Butler, J. S., Cowen, J. M., Streams, M. E., & Toma, E. F. (2014). Public employee quality in a geographic context: A study of rural teachers. *The American Review of Public Administration, 44*(5), 503–521.

García, E., & Weiss, E. (2022). *Policy solutions to deal with the nation's teacher shortage—a crisis made worse by COVID-19*. Economic Policy Institute. https://policycommons.net/artifacts/1407481/policy-solutions-to-deal-with-the-nations-teacher-shortage-a-crisis-made-worse-by-covid-19/2021743/ on 22 Apr 2022. CID: 20.500.12592/80xmzc

Gershenson, S., Hart, C., Hyman, J., Lindsay, C., & Papageorge, N. W. (2018). *The long-run impacts of same-race teachers* (No. w25254). http://ftp.iza.org/dp10630.pdf

Goldhaber, D., Lavery, L., & Theobald, R. (2015). Uneven playing field? Assessing the teacher quality gap between advantaged and disadvantaged students. *Educational Researcher, 44*(5), 293–307.

Goldhaber, D., & Theobald, R. (2022). *Teacher attrition and mobility in the pandemic* (CALDER Policy Brief No. 30–0322). National Center for Analysis of Longitudinal Data in Education Research.

Gordon, S. P., & Maxey, S. (2000). *How to help beginning teachers succeed* (2nd ed.). Association.

Grissom, J. A., & Bartanen, B. (2019). Strategic retention: Principal effectiveness and teacher turnover in multiple-measure teacher evaluation systems. *American Educational Research Journal, 56*(2), 514–555.

Grissom, J. A., Kalogrides, D., & Loeb, S. (2015a). Using student test scores to measure principal performance. *Educational Evaluation and Policy Analysis, 37*(1), 3–28.

Grissom, J. A., Kalogrides, D., & Loeb, S. (2015b). The micropolitics of educational inequality: The case of teacher–student assignments. *Peabody Journal of Education, 90*(5), 601–614.

Grissom, J. A., Kalogrides, D., & Loeb, S. (2017). Strategic staffing? How performance pressures affect the distribution of teachers within schools and resulting student achievement. *American Educational Research Journal, 54*(6), 1079–1116.

Grissom, J. A., & Loeb, S. (2011). Triangulating principal effectiveness: How perspectives of parents, teachers, and assistant principals identify the central importance of managerial skills. *American Educational Research Journal, 48*(5), 1091–1123.

Grissom, J. A., Loeb, S., & Master, B. (2013). Effective instructional time use for school leaders: Longitudinal evidence from observations of principals. *Educational Researcher, 42*(8), 433–444.

Guarino, C. M., Santibanez, L., & Daley, G. A. (2006). Teacher recruitment and retention: A review of the recent empirical literature. *Review of Educational Research, 76*(2), 173–208.

Hammer, P. C., Hughes, G., McClure, C., Reeves, C., & Salgado, D. (2005). *Rural teacher recruitment and retention practices: A review of the research literature, national survey of rural superintendents, and case studies of programs in Virginia*. Appalachia Educational Laboratory at Edvantia (NJ1).

Harrison, D., Labby, S., & Sullivan, S. (2015). Absent Texas teachers: Reasons and revelations. In *The Texas forum of teacher education* (Vol. 5, pp. 18–32). Texas Association of Teacher Educators. https://www.academia.edu/21515342/THE_TEXAS_FORUM_OF_TEACHER_EDUCATION_ABSENT_TEXAS_TEACHERS_REASONS_AND_REVELATIONS

Harrison, T., & Tran, H. (2020). How can higher education engage with rural communities to address their teacher shortages. In Henry Tran, Douglas A. Smith, David G. Buckman (Eds.) *Stakeholder engagement improving education through multi-level community relations* (pp. 105–120). Rowman & Littlefield.

Hecht, B. (2020, June 16). Moving beyond diversity toward racial equity. *Harvard Business Review*. https://hbr.org/2020/06/moving-beyond-diversity-toward-racial-equity

Herzberg, F., Mausner, B., & Snyderman, B. (1959). *The motivation to work* (2nd ed.). John Wiley & Sons, Inc.

Holgersson, C. (2013). Recruiting managing directors: Doing homosociality. *Gender, Work & Organization, 20*(4), 454–466.

Homan, A. C., Buengeler, C., Eckhoff, R. A., van Ginkel, W. P., & Voelpel, S. C. (2015). The interplay of diversity training and diversity beliefs on team creativity in nationality diverse teams. *Journal of Applied Psychology, 100*(5), 1456.

Horng, E. L. (2009). Teacher tradeoffs: Disentangling teachers' preferences for working conditions and student demographics. *American Educational Research Journal, 46*(3), 690–717.

Horng, E. L., Klasik, D., & Loeb, S. (2010). Principal's time use and school effectiveness. *American Journal of Education, 116*(4), 491–523.

Huffman, K. (2015, August 9). Opinion: Teacher shortage cry misses real crisis in teaching supply. *The 74 million*. www.the74million.org/article/opinion-the-teacher-shortage-cry-misses-the-real-crisis-in-the-teaching-supply/

Hunt, V., Prince, S., Dixon-Fyle, S., & Yee, L. (2018). Delivering through diversity. *McKinesey & Company*. www.mckinsey.com/~/media/mckinsey/business%20functions/organization/our%20insights/delivering%20through%20diversity/delivering-through-diversity_full-report.ashx

Ingersoll, R. M. (2001). Teacher turnover and teacher shortages: An organizational analysis. *American Educational Research Journal, 38*(3), 499–534.

Ingersoll, R. M. (2003). The teacher shortage: Myth or reality? *Educational Horizons, 81*(3), 146–152.

Jacob, A., Vidyarthi, E., & Carroll, K. (2012). *The irreplaceables: Understanding the real retention crisis in America's urban schools*. TNTP.

Kelchtermans, G. (2017). 'Should I stay or should I go?': Unpacking teacher attrition/retention as an educational issue. *Teachers and Teaching, 23*(8), 961–977.

Kohli, R. (2018). Behind school doors: The impact of hostile racial climates on urban teachers of color. *Urban Education, 53*(3), 307–333.

Krull, M., & Robicheau, J. (2020). Racial microaggressions and racial battle fatigue: Work life experiences of Black school principals. *Journal of Education Human Resources, 38*(2), 301–328.

Kulik, C. T., Pepper, M. B., Roberson, L., & Parker, S. K. (2007). The rich get richer: Predicting participation in voluntary diversity training. *Journal of Organizational Behavior: The International Journal of Industrial, Occupational and Organizational Psychology and Behavior, 28*(6), 753–769.

Ladd, H. F. (2011). Teachers' perceptions of their working conditions: How predictive of planned and actual teacher movement? *Educational Evaluation and Policy Analysis, 33*(2), 235–261.

Ladd, H. F., & Sorensen, L. C. (2017). Returns to teacher experience: Student achievement and motivation in middle school. *Education Finance and Policy, 12*(2), 241–279.

Laderriere, P. (1971). *Training, recruitment, and utilization of teachers in primary and secondary education*. Organization for Economic Cooperation and Development.

Liu, E., & Johnson, S. M. (2006). New teachers' experiences of hiring: Late, rushed, and information-poor. *Educational Administration Quarterly, 42*(3), 324–360.

Loeb, S., Kalogrides, D., & Béteille, T. (2012). Effective schools: Teacher hiring, assignment, development, and retention. *Education Finance and Policy, 7*(3), 269–304.

Mabokela, R. O., & Madsen, J. A. (2007). African American teachers in suburban desegregated schools: Intergroup differences and the impact of performance pressures. *Teachers College Record, 109*(5), 1171–1206.

Masumoto, M., & Brown-Welty, S. (2009). Case study of leadership practices and school-community interrelationships in high-performing, high-poverty, rural California high schools. *Journal of Research in Rural Education, 24*(1), 1–18.

Miller, L. C. (2012). Situating the rural teacher labor market in the broader context: A descriptive analysis of the market dynamics in New York State. *Journal of Research in Rural Education, 27*(13), 1–31. http://jrre.psu.edu/articles/27-13.pdf

Mirra, N., & Morrell, E. (2011). Teachers as civic agents: Toward a critical democratic theory of urban teacher development. *Journal of Teacher Education, 62*(4), 408–420.

Murnane, R. J., & Steele, J. L. (2007). What is the problem? The challenge of providing effective teachers for all children. *The Future of Children, 17*(1), 15–43.

Olsen, B., & Anderson, L. (2007). Courses of action: A qualitative investigation into urban teacher retention and career development. *Urban Education, 42*(1), 5–29.

Ondrich, J., Pas, E., & Yinger, J. (2008). The determinants of teacher attrition in upstate New York. *Public Finance Review, 36*(1), 112–144.

Paluck, E. L., & Green, D. P. (2009). Prejudice reduction: What works? A critical look at evidence from the field and the laboratory. *Annual Review of Psychology, 60,* 339–367.

Partelow, L. (2019). *What to make of declining enrollment in teacher preparation programs.* Center for American Progress. www.americanprogress.org/issues/education-k-12/reports/2019/12/03/477311/make-declining-enrollment-teacher-preparation-programs

Pendola, A., & Fuller, E. J. (2018). Principal stability and the rural divide. *Journal of Research in Rural Education, 34*(1).

Purcell, J., Kinnie, K., Hutchinson, R., Rayton, B., & Swart, J. (2003). *People and performance: How people management impacts on organizational performance.* CIPD.

Redding, C., & Smith, T. M. (2016). Easy in, easy out: Are alternatively certified teachers turning over at increased rates? *American Educational Research Journal, 53*(4), 1086–1125.

Rinke, C. R. (2011). Career trajectories of urban teachers: A continuum of perspectives, participation, and plans shaping retention in the educational system. *Urban Education, 46*(4), 639–662.

Rockoff, J. E. (2004). The impact of individual teachers on student achievement: Evidence from panel data. *American Economic Review, 94*(2), 247–252.

Ronfeldt, M., Loeb, S., & Wyckoff, J. (2013). How teacher turnover harms student achievement. *American Educational Research Journal, 50*(1), 4–36.

Rynes, S., & Rosen, B. (1995). A field survey of factors affecting the adoption and perceived success of diversity training. *Personnel Psychology, 48*(2), 247–270.

Shuls, J., & Maranto, R. (2014). Show them the mission: A comparison of teacher recruitment incentives in high need communities. *Social Science Quarterly, 95*(1), 239–252.

Simon, N. S., & Johnson, S. M. (2015). Teacher turnover in high-poverty schools: What we know and can do. *Teachers College Record, 117*(3), 1–36.

Smith, D. L., & Smith, B. J. (2006). Perceptions of violence: The views of teachers who left urban schools. *The High School Journal, 89*(3), 34–42.

Springer, M. G., Swain, W. A., & Rodriguez, L. A. (2016). Effective teacher retention bonuses: Evidence from Tennessee. *Educational Evaluation and Policy Analysis, 38*(2), 199–221.

Staats, C. (2016). Understanding implicit bias: What educators should know. *American Educator, 39*(4), 29.

Steiner, E. D., & Woo, A. (2021). *Job-related stress threatens the teacher supply: Key finding from the 2021 state of the US teacher survey* (Technical appendixes, Research Report, RR-A1108-1). RAND Corporation.

Stewart, C., & Matthews, J. (2015). The lone ranger in rural education: The small rural school principal and professional development. *The Rural Educator, 36*(3).

Stotsky, S. (2015). *An empty curriculum: The need to reform teacher licensing regulations and tests.* Rowman & Littlefield.

Sutcher, L., Darling-Hammond, L., & Carver-Thomas, D. (2019). Understanding teacher shortages: An analysis of teacher supply and demand in the United States. *Education Policy Analysis Archives, 27,* 35–35.

Taie, S., & Goldring, R. (2017). *Characteristics of public elementary and secondary school teachers in the United States: Results from the 2015–16 national teacher and principal survey first look (NCES 2017-072).* National Center for Education Statistics, U.S. Department of Education. https://nces.ed.gov/pubs2017/2017072.pdf

Tallberg, T. (2009). *The gendered social organisation of defence: Two ethnographic case studies in the Finnish defence forces.* Svenska handelshögskolan.

Townsell, R. (2007). Human resource management in small rural districts: The administrator's role in recruitment, hiring and staff development. *Online Submission, 20*(3).

Tran, H. (2015). Personnel vs. strategic human resource management in public education. *Management in Education, 29*(3), 112–118.

Tran, H. (2018). *Taking the mystery out of South Carolina school finance* (2nd ed.). ICPEL Publications.

Tran, H. (2022). Revolutionizing school HR strategies and practices to reflect talent-centered education leadership. *Leadership and Policy in Schools, 21*(2), 238–252.

Tran, H., Buckman, D. G., & Johnson, A. (2020a). Using the hiring process to improve the cultural responsiveness of schools. *Journal of Cases in Educational Leadership, 23*(2), 70–84.

Tran, H., Hardie, S., Gause, S., Moyi, P., & Ylimaki, R. (2020b). Leveraging the perspectives of rural educators to develop realistic job previews for rural teacher recruitment and retention. *Rural Educator, 41*(2), 31–46.

Tran, H., McCormick, J., & Nguyen, T. T. (2018). The cost of replacing South Carolina high school principals. *Management in Education, 32*(3), 109–118.

Tran, H., & Smith, D. A. (2020a). Designing an employee experience approach to teacher retention in hard-to-staff schools. *NASSP Bulletin, 104*(2), 85–109. https://journals.sagepub.com/doi/10.1177/0192636520927092

Tran, H., & Smith, D. A. (2020b). What matters most for recruiting teachers to rural hard-to-staff districts: A mixed methods analysis of employment-related conditions. *American Journal of Education, 126*(3), 447–481.

Tran, H., & Smith, D. A. (2020c). The strategic support to thrive beyond survival model: An administrative support framework for improving student outcomes and addressing educator staffing in rural and urban high-needs schools. *Research in Educational Administration & Leadership, 5*(3), 870–919.

Tran, H., & Smith, D. A. (2021). Talent-centered education leadership: Using the employee experience to improve teacher-school relations. *Journal of Cases in Educational Leadership, 24*(1), 42–54.

Tran, H., Smith, D. A., & Fox, E. C. (2018). *Perspectives of potential and current teachers for rural teacher recruitment and retention* (Center for Innovation in Higher Education report). www.usccihe.org/s/SC-Teacher-Perspectives-on-RRI-Final-Draft-rev2.pdf

Truss, C., Soane, E., Edwards, C., Wisdom, K., Croll, A., & Burnett, J. (2006). *Working life: Employee attitudes and engagement.* CIPD.

Urick, A. (2016). The influence of typologies of school leaders on teacher retention: A multilevel latent class analysis. *Journal of Educational Administration, 54*(4), 434–468.

Walton, R. (1985, March–April). From control to commitment in the workplace. *Harvard Business Review, 53*, 77–84.

Watkins, N. (2021). Social media, employee engagement, and human resource management. *Journal of Education Human Resources, 39*(1), 75–92.

Watlington, E., Shockley, R., Guglielmino, P., & Felsher, R. (2010). The high cost of leaving: An analysis of the cost of teacher turnover. *Journal of Education Finance*, 22–37.

Weisman, E. M., & Hansen, L. E. (2008). Student teaching in urban and suburban schools: Perspectives of Latino preservice teachers. *Urban Education*, 43(6), 653–670.

Young, I. P. (2008). *The human resource function in educational administration*. Pearson Merrill/Prentice Hall.

CHAPTER 5

Selection

Henry Tran and David G. Buckman

Chapter Summary

This chapter focuses on employee hiring within the context of strategic education talent management. Modern advances in teacher selection, as well as practical and legal considerations, are emphasized to aid in preparing school leaders for the hiring process. Additionally, further insights on human resources practices such as leveraging the value of application materials, screening and interviewing analyses, teacher assignment and transfers, and research related to leadership selection and leadership succession planning will be discussed. As supplementary materials, this chapter presents case studies, discussions, and activities related to identifying and selecting talent.

Effective leaders recruit, hire, support, develop, and retain effective and caring teachers and other professional staff and form them into an educationally effective faculty.
(PSEL Standard 6a)

INTRODUCTION

One of the most important tasks of the school principal is teacher hiring (Horng et al., 2010; Norton, 2014). When principals hire high-quality teachers, those teachers have been found to be able to improve the performance of their school colleagues through positive peer effects, which will result in a school that is not only higher performing but more likely to have higher teacher retention as well (Boyd et al., 2011; Loeb et al., 2012). Moreover, hiring also represents potential

DOI: 10.4324/9781003457060-7

multimillion-dollar decisions given the severe financial penalty associated with discriminatory selection, which suggests poor hiring can have severe academic *and* financial consequences.

Unfortunately, people often underestimate the complexity of the selection process and usually rely only on job interviews and subjective "gut" reactions to evaluate candidate quality. However, these subjective-based hiring practices are often prone to biases and usually do not get at candidate job qualifications. In fact, most school districts do not include performance-based measures in their applicant screening process (Konoske-Graf et al., 2016), which begs the question, how are they identifying potentially effective candidates?

Those who rely on the status quo of a reactionary or passive way of conducting hiring often operate with the philosophy that "you never know what you get till you get it," arguing that employers cannot determine the potential effectiveness and quality of hires until *after* they have been hired. This suggests that hiring is a gamble and determined by fate. However, modern advances in selection research suggest that school employers can strategically identify the highest-caliber candidates (i.e., those most likely to stay, succeed, and grow within the school district) within their applicant pools by systematically leveraging pre-hire data during the employment process (Sajjadiani et al., 2019). The question then becomes: How might a school build its technical and human capacity to conduct more effective employee selection?

Strategic Partnership With HR for Hiring

An often-underutilized strategy to mitigate many of the aforementioned issues is a *strategic* partnership with human resources to ensure that proper preparation is provided to school leaders as they take on their hiring responsibilities. This preparation should begin with the initial development of a consensus concerning what specific qualities the ideal candidate should embody, which can be derived from a rigorous and comprehensive job analysis of the position (Tran & Bon, 2016). The preparation should then go beyond the provision of "do and don't ask" questions for legal compliance, to include how administrators can leverage the hiring process to identify the highest-quality talent available. This requires the collection of a robust set of data on candidates (e.g., past performance) to help better predict post-hire performance. The preparation is especially needed because schools rarely utilize the broad spectrum of tools that could inform more accurate employee selection (DeArmond et al., 2010), instead relying solely on traditional measures (e.g., certification status, education level) primarily because that is what has "always" been collected.

Effective selection of quality personnel to ensure alignment with the organization is critical because of the substantial costs associated with a) dismissing an ineffective teacher, which can range from $50,000 to $450,000+ (*Vergara v. California*, 2014) and b) teacher replacement due to turnover, which can potentially exceed $20,000 per teacher in larger urban settings (Barnes et al., 2007; Milanowski & Odden, 2007; Shockley et al., 2006). Even in smaller rural school settings where the overall replacement costs may be lower so, too, are the human capacity and salaries at such locales, which make repeated teacher replacement much more taxing and difficult. Beyond financial costs, replacing a teacher can further take a toll on administrators' emotional stress and time. Fortunately, a good match between an applicant and their employer can identify higher performers and increase retention rates (Jackson, 2010).

Research has long suggested the potential value of teacher candidate characteristics that are not typically considered in the hiring process. For example, half a century ago, Levin (1970) found that staffing teachers with higher verbal scores is five to ten times as cost-effective for raising student achievement test scores as paying for more experience. More recent work by Rockoff et al. (2011) found support for relying on multiple measures of candidate attributes that include the traditional data collected during hire (e.g., type of certification, teacher certification exam scores, undergraduate institution selectivity, degree and major) and non-traditional attributes (e.g., cognitive ability, feelings of self-efficacy, personality traits, college entrance scores, score on a teacher selection instrument). Using both types of information in tandem better predicts student academic achievement as a collective (12% of the variance in teacher value-added explained) as opposed to reliance on any single factor by itself (4% with only traditionally collected factors). Despite these types of findings, research has suggested principals often rate references and initial impressions (e.g., attributes such as their attire, enthusiasm, and confidence) as more influential in their assessment of applicant information than job qualification material such as work portfolios or samples (Mason & Schroeder, 2010). This seems to represent a disconnection between the empirical literature that supports "what works" versus what is often practiced. Future school leaders should make efforts to ensure their selection decisions are based on job-related predictors and that they are using the most useful set of data that they can obtain.

A principal's awareness of how to conduct proper employee selection has become more critical now than ever before. This is, in part, due to research that has found principals who spent more time on organizational management activities, such as hiring, as opposed to compliance-oriented administrative tasks or classroom monitoring experience higher student achievement, as well as higher teacher and parent ratings in their schools (Horng et al., 2010). Trendwise, in recent decades, school districts have increasingly decentralized more of their hiring decision-making down to the school-site level (Engel et al., 2018). One argument for this is that school-site personnel are more aware of local needs of the school and, therefore, can better determine whether a candidate would be a good match with the context. In addition, localized hiring increases buy-in from school-level personnel, which increases their vested interest in the success of the hiring process.

With great authority comes great responsibility, and not all principals handle the responsibility equally. DeArmond et al. (2010) examined decentralized hiring practices at ten elementary schools within a large urban district and highlighted the vast differences in how the schools approached their selection processes. Schools that relied heavily on "gut" responses typically did not have substantive benchmarks to evaluate candidate quality and mostly treated the hiring process as a perfunctory and transactional endeavor, relying solely on HR to post job advertisements on the district website, failing to do much else to proactively increase the applicant pool. They often did not have a clear vision of what the ideal candidate would look like prior to the selection process, or if the principal did have one, it was not shared among the rest of the hiring panel. On the other hand, some schools were proactive and engaged. They were internally consistent and had a clear vision of what they were looking for in a teacher before the interviews even began. This seems to suggest large discrepancies in how local schools approach hiring. Liu and Johnson (2006) concluded that decentralizing school hiring by itself does not ensure better matching with candidates, as many schools have very limited interactions with the candidates during the hiring process, with a substantive portion of schools hiring after the year has started.

Neither the school site nor HR alone can maximize the opportunities to improve the probability of making the highest-quality selection, but rather, this can be better accomplished when the two parties work collaboratively. As a result, navigating the relationship between the school site and the district remains an area worth further development. This is especially the case when they do not see or consider each other as assets in the hiring process. For instance, often school districts and collective bargaining agreements contain policies that may stymie principal authority (e.g., mandating vacancies be filled by unemployed teachers in the district without the school's approval). Consequently, employees at the school site may perceive the district office and union to be more of a hindrance than a help.

To better depict the disconnection between some HR offices and local schools during the hiring process, consider the case described in Box 5.1.

BOX 5.1: MANAGING UP

Mr. Jackson is the principal of Eisenhower High School located in Kearseville Unified School District (KUSD), the largest metropolitan school district in a small Southeastern state. KUSD houses 93 schools (51 elementary, 19 middle, and 21 high schools, and two combination schools) that support roughly 70,000 students. Student demographics include over 40,000 White, 18,000 Black, 7,000 Hispanic, 2,000 Asian, 1,000 Indigenous, and 200 multiracial/undefined students. Considering the size of the school district, Kearseville's human resources (HR) office prides itself on its efficiency and expediency of personnel matters.

For each hire, after the posting of a position for the advertisement period, the HR department provides the school-based hiring panel a list of applicants who have met their initial screening criteria and, therefore, are eligible to be interviewed by the panel. Mr. Jackson has an opening for a biology teacher. As usual, the job advertisement was posted, and the HR department screened the candidates. The assembled hiring panel received the list of eligible candidates from the HR department and was charged with analyzing the candidates' application materials and identifying which candidates should receive interview invitations. Unfortunately, the panel of schoolteachers collectively felt that the process was problematic in that school-level individuals who understand the "true" needs of the schools were not allowed to access the entire applicant pool.

Mr. Jackson is at an impasse. He considers the district HR office highly functional yet values the input and concerns of the hiring panel concerning their belief that the school-level perspective could have aided in the initial screening of applicants. The teachers on the hiring panel are not happy with the list of candidates for the biology position and feel that if they had been involved in the initial screening, they would have a candidate pool with applicants that are "better fit" to serve at Eisenhower.

Discussion Questions: As the principal, how would you address this situation? Do you comply with district policy as it is currently stated (i.e., status quo)? Do you advocate for your hiring panel to change the policy, and, if so, what exactly would you advocate for? Is there some middle ground?

Many HR procedures can be applied in the selection process. Empirical research has provided much guidance concerning how to best take advantage of these procedures. In the next few sections, some of that research and the key takeaway points for school leaders are highlighted.

APPLICATION AND PAPER CREDENTIAL ANALYSIS

The job application form itself can be used to help prescreen candidates to ensure they possess the necessary qualifications to move forward in the selection process. These qualifications should be aligned with those in the job description and care must be taken to ensure that any item that contributes information that can potentially remove applicants from the pool must be job-related.

A thorough review should be conducted with each candidate's paper credentials (e.g., resume, references, college transcriptions) before the interview begins. Some employers neglect to verify the professional references, which is problematic because unfortunately, candidates may not always be truthful in discussing their own qualifications, and failing to check the references could represent missed opportunities to either obtain more insight into the candidate's work ethic and behavior, or worse, background that may suggest the candidate is likely to put children at risk. Given that professional references have been found to be linked with teacher attendance and post-hire evaluation ratings (Bruno & Strunk, 2018; Goldhaber et al., 2017), employers should consider how to request references that will add value to the selection process in a meaningful manner.

Resumes are ubiquitously used by school employers, but recent research has provided evidence to suggest that they may provide predictive power to improve the quality of school hiring. Sajjadiani et al. (2019) converted job descriptions and titles listed on seven years of resume data from a Minneapolis school district into a measure of relevant work experience (i.e., related knowledge, skills, and abilities) to serve as a less subjective measure of "fit." This measure was found to predict applicants' retention and value-added performance evaluation post-hire. Other factors that have been reported to be critical for student learning include teacher experience, which has the strongest relationship with student achievement and behavior outcomes (e.g., reduction in absenteeism and reading outside of school) in teachers' early years but continues to be influential up to 12 years and beyond (Ladd & Sorensen, 2017). Experience information can usually be ascertained from applicant resumes. These studies suggest that school leaders can leverage much value from application and paper credential analyses to identify quality employees.

DISTRICT PRESCREENING

A strategic partnership between HR at the district office and the school site can improve the quality of the selection process. Goldhaber et al. (2017) studied and found support for the predictive validity of Spokane Public Schools teacher prescreening selection instruments on teacher value-added in student achievement and teacher retention. The prescreening process that was examined is scored in a way that is strategically aligned to the district's teacher evaluation system. The district's HR office provides value to school sites by using the hiring rubric to provide an initial screening of applicants to remove applicants with fewer than 21 points (out of 60). Then at the second stage, HR provides principals the list of applicants who have made the 21-point cut-off. At the third stage, the principal uses the information provided to decide who to offer job interviews. Assessment of the process suggests that a one standard deviation increase in the 60 points prescreening scores was associated with to .07 standard deviation increases in math and reading student achievement respectively, and a 2.5% decrease in teacher attrition. For the math finding, this equates to the difference of a student receiving an average third- or second-year teacher for their student achievement test scores as opposed to an average first-year beginning teacher.

Similarly, Bruno and Strunk (2018) assessed the prescreening assessment (known as the Multiple Measure Teacher Selection Process) conducted by the

Los Angeles Unified School District's (LAUSD) HR office and found that it was related to applicants' hire (despite the fact the principals are unaware of the actual scores and are the ones who do the eventual hiring), teachers' post-hire value-added test scores, attendance, and their evaluation ratings. Like Spokane Public Schools, LAUSD's prescreening standardized system included components such as writing samples and teacher demonstration lessons that were scored according to a rubric that was strategically linked to the district's employee performance evaluation criteria.

It makes sense that the aforementioned districts would link aspects of the selection process, such as teacher demonstration assessment, with subsequent teacher observation evaluations. Strategically speaking, the hiring process should be linked to other HR processes like evaluations to improve the chances of finding a good match between candidate and school. This is important because quality matches can have significant positive effects. For example, Jackson (2010) found that teacher's contribution to student test score growth has been found to increase after moving to a better-matched school and found that match quality explained about 10% to 40% of the teacher value-added effect.

Jacob et al. (2018) found that district-provided applicant scores based on their measures of written assessment, interviews, and sample lessons were strongly related to subsequent teacher performance yet were not heavily relied upon by school administrators in their final hiring decisions. These studies suggest that school administrators should think of HR as a resource and consider the use of all available data to make the best-informed decisions. Data-informed decision-making is routinely emphasized for students but is infrequently practiced with adults in HR decision-making. Given that the type of teachers hired can directly impact students, the process of teacher selection should hold a high degree of rigor.

WORK SAMPLES

Employers are much more susceptible to cultural bias (i.e., unable to tell the applicant is giving socially appropriate answers that the employer "wants to hear" rather than their authentic response) during the job interview than performance work samples, such as a teaching demonstration. This is because it is much easier to fake an acceptable response during an interview than to fake teaching a class when the candidate not only has to juggle demonstration of content knowledge but also pedagogical expertise. In fact, the more the demonstration mirrors the actual job, the more valid the work sample is likely to be a predictor of post-hire performance. For a teaching position, this is why it is ideal for candidates to teach a demonstration lesson in front of actual students of the hiring school during a school day. The teaching demonstration allows the hiring administrator to assess the candidate's pedagogical style, classroom management, and fit with the school.

There are many reasons why a school district may not want to implement such a realistic demonstration. For example, they may have concerns that parents will resist and feel that students are serving as guinea pigs for the district and are potentially losing valuable instructional time with a vetted teacher. Consequently, districts may decide instead to invite students to volunteer to attend the candidates' teaching demonstration after school. Because this is less realistic than a work sample, this represents a work simulation (Young, 2008). If that is not feasible, candidates may submit a video recording of their teacher auditions, as used by D.C. schools in the teacher screening process, or they may perform the teaching simulation in front of administrators and the hiring personnel. While these simulations may not be as authentic as a work sample, they are better than not having any teaching demonstration at all.

Work samples are also important because schools differ, and the strategies that are effective in another context may not be applicable in the hiring school; in fact, this is often true at the classroom level as well. Some research validates the use of work samples. For instance, Jacob et al. (2018) found D.C. public school district's application rating system, which included a component of teacher demonstration, was predictive of post-hire teacher performance. Goldhaber et al. (2017) found higher scores on teaching demonstrations were linked to higher student achievement. Likewise, Bruno and Strunk (2018) found scores on demonstration lessons to be predictive of student achievement and subsequent classroom observation ratings.

Despite its predictive power, in a nationally representative survey of school districts, Konoske-Graf et al. (2016) found only 13% of districts required applicants to perform a teaching demonstration with students and only 6% with adults. Liu and Johnson (2006) similarly found a low frequency of teaching demonstration used in the hiring process in their assessment of hiring in four states.

PRINCIPAL DATA USE WHEN MAKING HIRES

Cannata et al. (2017) noted that the large variation in principal data use during the hiring process was often within the same school district. Even among those who do not use more data-informed decision-making during the hiring process, the reasons ranged from 1) the data not being collected, 2) principals wishing they had the data and not realizing that they already have access to them, 3) districts not sharing the data with their principals, to 4) principals being aware that the data are collected but do not know how to access them. A strong collaborative relationship between HR and the school principal can mitigate a lot of these missed opportunities, by increasing opportunities for the principal to access and leverage the use of quality predictive measures. Complementarily, the school personnel can also offer HR more contextual information about the campus to refine their predictors. Unfortunately, fewer than two-thirds of school districts require a candidate to even interview with the hiring principal (Konoske-Graf et al., 2016), which suggests a potential loss of valuable matching feedback on the employer end.

THE EMPLOYMENT INTERVIEW(S)

The employment interview questions should not be randomly created, but rather they should derive from the job description of the position of focus, with the descriptions themselves generated by the job analysis (Tran & Bon, 2016). Given the technical and legal complications associated with hiring, interviewers should be provided training to conduct the task as mentioned earlier in the chapter.

BOX 5.2: WARNING – LEGAL ISSUES

Like many aspects of employee relationships, there are many laws and official guidelines that govern the selection process. They include (but are not limited to):

- *Civil Rights Act of 1964* (Title VII)
- *Age Discrimination and Employment* Act
- *Pregnancy Discrimination* Act
- *Genetic Information Nondiscrimination* Act
- *Equal Pay Act of 1963*
- Uniform Guidelines on Employee Selection Procedures, etc.

The unifying premise undergirding these laws and guidelines is the prohibition of discriminatory practices against individuals based on their protected class status (i.e., groups protected from employment discrimination such as race, sex, and religion). Employees or applicants need only show *prima facie* ("on its face" or surface rebuttable) evidence of discrimination (e.g., an interviewer remarked on the school's preference for younger candidates), then the burden of proof of discrimination shifts to the employer to demonstrate that they did not illegally discriminate. *Disparate treatment* and *disparate impact* represent two of the main anti-discrimination provisions embedded in Title VII of the federal *Civil Rights Act of 1964*.

Disparate treatment represents intentional discrimination against protected class status, such as when only women are required to answer interview questions concerning their desire to have children, with their responses affecting their probability of being hired. *Disparate impact*, on the other hand, refers to adverse action disproportionately impacting individuals from one or more protected class groups from seemingly "neutral" policies, such as when the employer systematically rejects all candidates who are determined to fit a certain personality profile according to a pre-employment test, and members of a particular racial group are disproportionately represented with this personality profile. It is important to note that according to a U.S. Supreme Court ruling, "Applying the strong-basis-in-evidence standard to Title VII gives effect to both provisions, allowing violations of one in the name of compliance with the other only in certain, narrow circumstances" (*Ricci v. DeStefano*, 2009, para 3). This seems to suggest employers should take caution against making intentional race-based hires as a mechanism to mitigate past wrongs of disparate impact, especially if it is not the "least discriminatory alternative available" consistent with the "business necessity" of the job (Title VII of the *Civil Rights Act of 1964*, 42 U.S.C. §§ 2000e).

TYPES OF INTERVIEWS

There are many interview formats that employers can use, either in isolation or in conjunction with one another. Next are several of the major different types.

In an *unstructured interview,* interviewers ask open-ended questions. The employer typically guides the interview, but the questions asked will vary across interviewee respondents, primarily based on their responses. These types of interviews represent a big legal risk because the differential questions may unfairly advantage or disadvantage certain individuals in the process, and this differential advantage may be correlated with their protected class grouping.

A *structured interview* is when applicants are each asked the same preplanned questions. With some districts, even the follow-up probes are standardized, whereas in others there is a bit more flexibility with these sub-questions. A structured interview guide can be provided to help maintain consistency, ensuring each applicant will be asked the same questions, which will increase the validity of comparisons between candidates. Structured interviews have been shown to be more valid than unstructured interviews (Dana et al., 2013; Kausel et al., 2016) and are able to predict not only student test score growth but also teacher retention (Goldhaber et al., 2017).

Behavioral interviews typically ask candidates to share their experience and focus on how applicants have previously handled situations. They are typically asked to provide examples. This is based on the theory that past performance is the best predictor of future performance and how respondents answer the questions is likely to provide insight concerning how they will address similar situations in the future.

Contrary to a behavioral interview, a *situational interview* presents hypothetical situations and inquires how applicants will respond to them. These types of questions are more appropriate than behavioral interviews if the applicant lacks the relevant experience, perhaps because they are new to the position. Situational interviews can be used in a targeted interview framework, where the questions differ depending on the applicant's experience level. Besides interviews, situational scenarios can also be presented in vignette form, in which candidates would respond via a writing sample. This has been done in the Los Angeles Unified School District.

Finally, as opposed to a one-on-one interview, some employers utilize a *panel interview*, where a group of interviewers question the applicant at the same time. Given that an educator's performance influences a variety of stakeholders (e.g., administrators, special education teachers, teachers in other grades, HR representative, parents), these individuals could be included on the interview panel. Usually, each group member will ask the interview question most relevant to their position or that focuses on the subject or domain that the interviewer has the most expertise in.

BOX 5.3: WARNING – IMPLICIT BIAS

According to the National Center for Education Statistics, in the 2015–16 school year, ethnic minorities represented 20% of all public and secondary school teachers compared to 51% of students. This is problematic, especially in light of research that suggests employers discriminate based on race (Derous et al., 2017), and there has been a lack of change in hiring discrimination for Black applicants from 1989 to 2015 (Quillian et al., 2017). Yet the research is clear that when paired with racially congruent (matched) teachers, students of color perform better on standardized academic tests (Dee, 2004; Egalite et al., 2015), have fewer disciplinary issues (Lindsay & Hart, 2017), receive higher academic expectations (Gershenson et al., 2016), are more likely to be identified as gifted (Grissom et al., 2017), and are more likely to graduate high school and enroll in college (Gershenson et al., 2018). Furthermore, teachers of color not only yield benefits for students of color but also non–students of color (Cherng & Halpin, 2016).

While overt discrimination can occur, often discriminatory practices are perpetuated by implicit biases that may be unconscious to the perpetrator. Implicit biases grow from cultural associations developed early in life. Gregory (2018) describes this form of bias as one's tendency to have differential responses to various stimuli based on the characteristics of the stimuli. In many cases, race/ethnicity, age, and gender serve as stimuli that promote bias in personnel decision-making. For example, if an individual tends to react differently to Black people as compared to White people, then this might suggest racial bias. Similarly, individuals who evaluate others based on personal or behavioral characteristics that are perceived to be associated with particular groupings or cultures (even if they do not hold true for the person being evaluated) are said to be stereotyping (e.g., women are too emotional to hold administration positions is a stereotype). Unfortunately, these biases can influence the hiring process.

When it comes to biases, one major issue in education is the misperception that juxtaposes increases in diversity with reduction in rigor and selectivity standards. For example, historically Black colleges and universities (HBCUs) may be viewed unfavorably and perceived to be less rigorous by the hiring committee than other higher education institutions. Because HBCUs educate more candidates of color, this may result in candidates of color receiving a disproportional brunt of the negative bias. Another bias may be that teachers of color are best able to work with students with disciplinary problems, and consequently, they may not be selected for a school without a large prevalence of those concerns. While the term "fit" has been used in this chapter to signify alignment between the candidate and the organization, the term has also been used in a discriminatory manner that represents exclusion based on some protected class category (e.g., a candidate is deemed ill fit because they do not physically or culturally resemble the faculty at the school).

Implicit biases can manifest in several ways in the hiring process, the most frequent of which are:

- **Stereotype bias**: When the employer makes assumptions about an individual based on their personal characteristics is stereotype bias. For example, female candidates are assumed to be less assertive than male candidates.
- **Negative emphasis**: Negative information about a candidate is weighed more heavily than favorable information. For example, a candidate's former negative teacher observation evaluation leaves a "blemish" on his record that outweighs his subsequent positive ones.
- **Halo/Horn effect**: A strong/weak point of the candidate overshadows the individual's other characteristics. For example, a candidate's nervousness during the interview is the only attribute the employer remembers about her.
- **Contrast effect:** A candidate's perceived quality is magnified or de-emphasized as a result of the sequence in which they go through the selection process. For example, a candidate who interviews after weaker candidates may appear more qualified than they actually are.
- **Similarity bias**: Candidates are preferred because they share personal characteristics with the interviewer. For example, the candidate is favored because he shares the same cultural background or alma mater as the interviewer.
- **Cultural noise bias**: Cultural noise bias occurs when interviewers are unable to detect that interviewees are providing socially acceptable responses to interview questions as opposed to authentic ones. For example, a candidate may indicate equity of learning opportunities is very important when she does not truly believe it.

Biases can manifest in the hiring process in many ways and affect the likelihood of individuals receiving a job. Biased employment decisions can influence an applicant's hire, work assignment, and even salary or wage. While conscious bias (i.e., explicit bias) can and does occur in selection and employment decisions, unconscious bias (i.e., implicit bias) may influence employment decisions, often unbeknown to the employer. This has been supported by the literature.

Although implicit biases and prejudices are difficult to control in the selection process, school districts can develop strategic practices and processes to avoid the potential of individual biases influencing selection decisions. With thorough and proper evaluations of candidates based on valid measures that adequately identify potential candidate effectiveness, employers are less likely to screen based on ambiguous and subjectively bias-laden criteria. Additional methods to control bias and ambiguity can be applied during employment interviews, such as through its structure and format.

VALIDITY AND RELIABILITY OF SELECTION INSTRUMENTS

Both the selection process and the selection itself should be assessed, not only to monitor for the ability to hire quality candidates but to mitigate the influence of bias. Employer selection should be both valid (i.e., it accurately measures what it is supposed to measure) and reliable (i.e., it is consistent). An example of an invalid screening question would be one that screens out applicants even though the content of the question has nothing to do with the job being considered for (as determined by the job analysis and job description) (Tran & Bon, 2016). Because reliability is a necessary condition of validity, we discuss in more detail the validation process.

To determine the validity of the selection process, the effectiveness of selection should be assessed via the performance of the individuals post-hire. This is known as *criterion-related validity* (Arthur et al., 2006). If the predictors from the selection process are indeed valid, they should positively correlate with the criteria measures used to judge performance success, such that better performance in the selection process should correspond to better job performance. The criteria measures can be identified through the job analysis process. This requires tracking the subsequent classroom performance of new hires, which should occur anyway. However, in many organizations that still rely on a transactional HR system, the evaluation data is in an information silo separated from the hiring data.

A strategic talent management system links the data systems to give a more complete picture to assess the effectiveness of the hiring process and how well it contributes to addressing the needs of the schools. This system should include a hiring accountability component to ensure quality hires and a professional support component for hiring managers (e.g., principals) to ensure that they are using the best information to make the best hires. Beyond performance, the system can link the selection process to other viable outcome measures including whether the hire completed their "probationary" or induction period and their retention length. The system should be streamlined and user-friendly on both the candidate and employer side, reducing cumbersome bureaucratic procedures. A strong collaborative relationship between HR and the school-site manager (e.g., the principal) is foundational for such a system.

THE TIMING OF HIRES

It is preferable to hire in advance of summer (e.g., winter or spring) to have access to a larger pool of candidates (Norton, 2014) and increase the probability of selecting a qualified individual. This is especially the case since hiring teachers after school has started has been linked to a reduction in students' math and reading achievement (Papay & Kraft, 2016), which occurs because of a disruption in the first year of teaching (when the substitute is swapped out with the late hire) and because late hire teachers are, on average, less effective at improving student achievement growth. Moreover, late-hire teachers have been found more likely to turn over as well. This is because principals that hire late often do not undergo the rigorous candidate selection process to determine potential fit but rather are hiring with the sole purpose of filling vacancies. Unfortunately, late hires most often occur at high-need schools that are underperforming academically and socioeconomically impoverished and whose students are majority-minority.

Districts can offer to help facilitate earlier hiring by providing incentives for departing teachers to provide earlier notice of their resignation, retirement, or transfer (Carver-Thomas, 2018). Districts should also expedite their internal processes and mitigate the negative impact of bureaucratic procedures that may delay hiring time (e.g., policies in which internal hires must be considered for vacancies first). Some districts hire year-round to maximize their opportunity to find the best quality candidates. However, this strategy will require more effort from some districts than others because of the size and enrollment of the district, its attractiveness, differences in timing of budget approvals, and other organizational constraints that may delay information concerning the availability of full-time equivalent (FTE) positions for the school to hire.

THE CANDIDATE EXPERIENCE

Employers, especially those in hard-to-staff contexts, must never forget that hiring is a dual-sided process. While candidates are attempting to attract employers, employers are attempting to attract potential employees. This requires consideration of the candidate's motivations and experience within the process. During the interviews conducted with candidates, rapport building is critical to help candidates feel at ease to share more about themselves. This will also help the interviewer better determine "fit."

Attunement to the candidate experience requires that communication with candidates occurs on a regular basis to provide them updates on their application status. Even if the applicant does not ultimately receive the job offer, they should be informed of this. Failing to provide professionalism and positive impression management during the selection process can hurt the district's reputation and image as a potential employer when neglected applicants share their experiences with other potential candidates. This may affect future recruitment. In fact, the candidate experience is an integral component of the total employee experience approach within Talent-Centered Education Leadership (Tran & Smith, 2020), which, when attended to, has the potential to increase employee job satisfaction, retention, and performance. After the selection process has concluded, an assessment can be conducted with the candidates to determine their evaluation of the process and provide tips on how to improve the system. Candidates should be asked about their perception of the process and whether they perceive it to be valid, fair, and equitable.

REALISTIC JOB PREVIEWS

While employers and candidates both strive to display positive attributes to put their "best foot forward," it is important for both sides to be honest about each other's strengths and limitations. For example, if a candidate does not have experience or have the skill set to perform a particular task (e.g., driving a school bus), pretending like they can do so will only cause stress and job dissatisfaction if the individual is then hired and required to immediately perform said task. Similarly, on the employer side, to increase alignment between the candidate and the employer's expectations, employers should be realistic about what the job entails and not "sugarcoat" potential negative aspects of the working conditions. Otherwise, they may be able to attract a candidate to apply for the position, but the hire may have inaccurate job expectations, which may lead to subsequent job dissatisfaction, resentment towards the employer, and an increased likelihood of turnover.

One tool employers use to provide candidates with an accurate depiction of the work environment is a realistic job preview (Tran et al., 2020). A realistic job preview might include a tour of the school where the candidate has the opportunity to see 1) a sample of its different classrooms, 2) frank descriptions of a typical work day, 3) the support teachers receive, 4) the level of autonomy teachers have, 5) the principal's management style and teacher's input on decision-making, 6) the curriculum teachers use, 7) school community members including parents to speak with (perhaps even in the absence of the hiring personnel), and 8) observations of realistic teacher working conditions (including teachers working late hours if that is how the school operates) (DeArmond et al., 2010; Liu & Johnson, 2006). This allows for clarifications concerning job expectations, which promotes better matching between candidates and schools. Like building rapport and setting the candidate at ease, a realistic job preview allows the applicant to better assess their "fit" with the school employer.

Teachers are not interchangeable, and while some pedagogical skill sets and knowledge are universally applicable across contexts, research suggests that some teachers are a better match with certain schools than others (Jackson, 2010). For example, for schools located in small rural communities, teachers are perceived to be community leaders early in their careers and must be able to navigate and engage in their relationships with the community in a much deeper capacity than in most other types of schools.

After reviewing the legality of hiring decisions and methods of addressing bias, to apply your knowledge, consider the case presented in Box 5.4.

BOX 5.4: WHEN IT'S NOT ROSY: RACE-SPECIFIC HIRING*

Ben Turner High School is in the southeastern United States and is a part of a school district that primarily serves low-income students. There are 1,347 students attending: 90% Black, 5% Non-White Hispanic, and 1% Multiracial, 2% White, and 1% "other." School staff are 62% Black, 35% White, and 3% self-identified as "other," whereas the instructional faculty consists of 84% White, 9% Black, and 7% "other." Finally, there are three White assistant principals (two females and one male) and one Black female assistant principal. You were hired last year as the new principal of the school. The district has worked with you to set the school goals of increasing the number of students enrolled in calculus and closing the math achievement gap between Black and White students, which is the largest within-school gap at 30 percentage points on standardized test assessments.

Most teachers at the school believe that rigor is antithetical to inclusion. Upper-division math teachers are complaining that you are implicitly encouraging social promotion, which they feel is unethical. As one teacher stated in a faculty meeting "We have to be realistic, not all students are going to go on to become engineers or astronauts. Many of our students will very likely end up bagging groceries at the local grocery store. Not all students want to learn and forcing them to take courses that they cannot succeed in is just a waste of everyone's time." The gateway course that is critical for how many of the students will progress in their mathematics course sequencing is Algebra 2, which currently has a teacher vacancy.

You are leading a hiring panel consisting of you and two other teachers. One teacher, Ms. Johnson, feels that the next hire should be a Black person. She indicates that a lot of the racial tension and cultural divide in the school can be addressed if the students saw more teachers who "looked like them." She shares several points to support her perspective: 1) teachers of color are severely underrepresented in the nation and especially at this school; 2) research has found that not only does having a Black teacher improve the test scores of Black students (Dee, 2004; Egalite et al., 2015) but that those students are more likely to receive higher expectations (Gershenson et al., 2016), be identified as gifted (Grissom et al., 2017), graduate high school, and enroll in college (Gershenson et al., 2018) with increasing exposure to race-matched teachers; and 3) Black teachers can serve as positive role models for Black youth. The other teacher, Mrs. Jewel, responds by saying race cannot be considered in the hiring process, as it is illegal.

Discussion Questions: You want to hire someone to help close the achievement gap. What do you do? Please rationalize and justify your responses based on ethical, legal, professional, and/or leadership frameworks.

**See Tran et al. (2020) for a similar but more detailed case study with accompanying activities.*

CLASS ASSIGNMENTS AND TRANSFERS

Class Assignments

There is evidence that teacher quality is inequitably distributed across and even within schools, where students from less advantaged backgrounds may be more likely to be placed in classrooms with ill-equipped or less effective teachers (Clotfelter et al., 2005; Feng, 2010; Kalogrides et al., 2013). Inequitable distribution of students across classrooms must be noticed and acknowledged before actions can be taken to redress the issue. In addition to the inequitable distribution of effective teachers within and across schools, research also supports the impact teacher assignment has on teacher turnover. Specifically, Donaldson and Johnson (2010) highlight that the frequency of turnover increases when teachers are assigned to hard-to-staff schools, which are typically economically impoverished and underperforming. Turnover also increases when teachers are assigned classes outside of their subject area.

In terms of class assignments within schools, Grissom et al. (2015) studied data from 2004–2013, from a large (i.e., approximately 350,000 students) district and found that experienced teachers exercised more influence on their own assignments than their less experienced counterparts and that teachers had certain student preferences in their assignments. Specifically, they found that with each ten years of experience, a teacher's class assignment was associated with a half of percentage point of fewer Black students in the teacher's classes, as well as four-tenths of a percentage point fewer number of students in poverty. Other findings indicated that greater years of teaching experience were associated with teaching classes with more students who had higher prior-year achievement scores in math and reading, fewer discipline problems, and fewer absences. From a practical perspective, this suggests a potential mechanism that sustains the inequity of the distribution of teachers, with the neediest students often receiving the less experienced teachers. In the front end of the experience level, this can be particularly problematic since research has suggested they are, on average, often less effective than more experienced teachers (Ladd & Sorensen, 2017). See Chapter 4 for a discussion on how school leaders can strategically assign teachers to counteract the aforementioned issue and improve the employee experience for new teachers, who are often more vulnerable to turnover.

When following a large sample of teachers involved in the Teach for America program (TFA), Donaldson and Johnson (2010) found that teachers' propensity to turnover via transfer or leaving the profession was differentiated by grade level and teaching assignment. Specifically, early-career elementary school teachers who were assigned to teach multiple-grade classes were at higher risk of leaving their school and transferring than elementary teachers assigned to teaching only one grade. Additionally, teachers who taught at secondary level schools were more inclined to turnover when assigned to teaching multiple subjects as compared to those assigned to teach a single subject. In terms of content areas, mathematics and social studies teachers who did not have degrees in the subject they were assigned to teach were more disposed to resign from the profession than teachers who had degrees in the specific content area they taught. This suggests that appropriate matching of personnel to teaching positions is critical for retention.

In their most current longitudinal study evaluating the assignment of teachers to high-stakes and low-stakes classrooms, Grissom et al. (2017) found that teachers with higher performance metrics (i.e., value-added scores) in both high-stakes and low-stakes classrooms were more likely to be placed in high-stakes classrooms the following year. In terms of strategic staffing, this practice impacted elementary schools, where highly effective teachers were often assigned to upper-level grades (i.e., 3–5) while less effective teachers were populated in grades that were not tested (i.e., K–2). Although this form of strategic staffing may address school accountability, the distribution of teachers can be seen as inequitable. Additionally, if the least effective teachers are the only educators teaching students during the early critical foundation period, there may be large populations of students entering grades 3–5 not meeting academic targets.

When new/early-career teachers or marginally effective teachers are systematically assigned more challenging classes (i.e., with students who need more academic support), both the student and the teachers may be negatively impacted. Some teachers may see this practice as "earning their stripes" or "a rite of passage" to which teachers' years in the field represents the dues they paid, which corresponds with higher pay and more advantageous class assignments. However, this arrangement may not represent the best working conditions for new teachers given that new teachers are more likely to turn over (Donaldson & Johnson, 2010) because of the stress of acclimating to a new job and potential poor work performance.

In sum, it is recommended that leaders equitably assign teachers classes based on their effectiveness and expertise and balance each grade with both highly effective and marginally effective teachers. Additionally, principals should consider providing marginally effective or ineffective teachers a mentor (e.g., teacher leader) and build professional learning communities to support teacher growth and effectiveness. To do so, administrators should be cognizant of the teaching demand and the abilities of all teachers, specifically those new to the profession. Assigning a challenging course load to a first-year or early-career teacher not only puts the school at risk of having the teacher transfer but may also put them at greater risk of leaving the profession altogether. Practices such as assigning teachers a single grade at the elementary level or a single subject at the secondary level can potentially increase teacher retention and effectiveness. If administrators operationalize their teacher assignment decision-making based on the instructional needs of the student population (i.e., assigning classes based on the best teacher's ability to address student instructional needs) as well as providing early-career/new teachers the necessary support to put them in positions to be successful, they may find increases in both school efficiency and academic equity. However, be warned that parents can exert much political influence on their students' class assignments, and school leaders must contend with how to respond to that in relation to their teacher assignment plans.

TRANSFER

School and district leaders assert that having autonomy in teacher placement is critical for strengthening both overall school quality and equity among schools (Cohen-Vogel & Osborne-Lampkin, 2007; Levin et al., 2005). One component of teacher placement autonomy is the power to strategically transfer teachers to different schools to address the school district's mission, meet and or exceed student achievement goals, and provide a mix of quality personnel across schools (Levin et al., 2005). Jackson (2010) notes that if districts transfer individuals to schools that match their skills and abilities, the teacher may have a more positive impact on both the students and the school, thus enhancing overall district efficiency. Indeed, earlier in this chapter, the importance and positive outcomes associated with quality teacher and school matching were discussed. For within-district transfers, the likelihood that hiring personnel can obtain the teacher's past performance information to ascertain a match is more likely because that information should be with HR.

Some caveats should be acknowledged when districts utilize their authoritative power or policy to transfer teachers. First, if a teacher is involuntarily transferred and the result of the transfer is a mismatch between student needs and the teacher's ability to address those needs, there may be no gains to district efficiency (and, in fact, things may get worse). Secondly, if the result of an involuntary transfer discourages a highly effective teacher to the point that it impacts their performance, district efficiency may again be stymied and the transfer policy becomes counterproductive. Finally, involuntarily placing teachers who have proven to be ineffective in high-performing schools can potentially increase the teachers' performance if properly supported; however, this teacher could also potentially disrupt the culture of the school and negatively impact the school's academic performance.

Lankford et al. (2002) researched Miami-Dade County Public Schools and found that the district utilized involuntary transfer policy mostly for low-performing schools. This district specifically sought to improve school student achievement by identifying and transferring low-performing teachers. The researchers found that involuntarily transferred teachers had lower value-added math achievement scores and were typically replaced with teachers with higher scores. Compared to the involuntarily transferred teachers who were moved because of ineffectiveness at lower-performing schools, their replacements were new hires who were demographically younger and less experienced teachers. Interestingly, the ineffective teachers who were involuntarily transferred demonstrated positive performance results (i.e., less absenteeism) after the move, potentially suggesting a better fit with their new school than their prior one.

As an administrator, these findings support the use of involuntary transfer, particularly when trying to remove poor-performing teachers and replace them with more effective teachers. Leaders must be strategic in their decision-making to ensure both teachers and the respective school leaders are satisfied with the moves to prevent negative outcomes. Involuntarily transferring a poor-performing teacher is great for that particular school, but what about the school they are transferred to? This can be a risky move; however, as research has shown, placing a less effective teacher in a high-performing school could benefit the teacher's performance through positive "peer effects" as described earlier in the chapter.

Contrary to involuntary transfers, voluntary transfers occur when teachers choose to relocate within the district for personal preferences. In their New York based study, Boyd et al. (2011) found that teachers with better preservice qualifications (e.g., certification exam scores and college achievement) were more likely to request a transfer to another school. Despite this, teachers with higher value-added test scores were less likely to voluntarily transfer. Loeb et al. (2012) similarly found teachers with higher value-added scores were less likely to turnover. In addition, if teachers with higher value-added scores chose to transfer, they often transferred to schools with higher school-level value-added scores rather than lower ones. It is important to note that value-added scores refer to gain scores, which means that a school can have an overall low level of achievement and still be a high value-added school. Similarly, Feng and Sass (2011), in their Florida study, found evidence indicating that the most effective teachers often transferred to schools where teachers were in the top quartile of teacher quality.

When dealing with voluntary transfers, many principals have reported experiencing restricted autonomy (Engel et al., 2018). For example, Cannata et al. (2017) indicated that because of district policy, during the district's transfer period, early vacancies are allocated to pools of internal transfers and principals are not allowed to interview external talents who may be more effective. As such, principals may have to manipulate the system by not hiring during this period and wait until job postings are communicated to the public. Districts vary in their transfer processes, and policies and collective bargaining agreements can complicate the matter. In some districts, teachers can apply to transfer without even notifying their current principal, and the receiving principal may have no authority to reject the transfer, whereas, in other districts, permission may need to be obtained by principals of both the outgoing and incoming school.

Teacher transfers can be a critical asset for schools and school systems; however, knowledgeable school leaders and HR officers must know how to best strategically leverage this tool to benefit organizational outcomes. To do so, decision-makers must have a comprehensive understanding of the school's profile. This includes having a strong understanding of 1) the student population (e.g., demographic and achievement); 2) the school's culture and climate (e.g., quantitatively or qualitatively evaluated); and 3) the teacher's individual strengths, weaknesses, and preferences (e.g., from evaluation and satisfaction assessment). Knowledge of the aforementioned school data can provide school leaders and HR officers a holistic overview to support them in making informed decisions, which can enhance school culture and climate through professional development, decrease teacher voluntary transfer or turnover, and aid in making involuntary transfer decisions that benefit both teachers and schools.

ADVANCEMENT OF TEACHERS TO ADMINISTRATORS

The selection of school leaders can be one of the most difficult HR tasks in the education environment. While much attention is often focused on teacher shortages, administrator vacancies and turnovers do not receive similar press and fanfare. The work that has been done often discusses the principal shortages across the nation, particularly in middle and high schools serving high proportions of students in poverty, majority non-White, or students for whom English is a second language (Loeb et al., 2010; Whitaker, 2001). Yet the deficit in most cases is not a function of limited numbers of individuals with the required credentials (supply), as many states credential more than enough teachers to supply leadership needs (Pounder et al., 2003; Lankford et al., 2003), but rather either many credentialed teachers choose to not pursue leadership positions (DiPaola & Tschannen-Moran, 2003; Tran, 2016; Winter et al., 2002) or the leadership candidates fail to possess the necessary knowledge, skills, and abilities to meet the demands of school leadership regardless of their licensure qualifications (i.e., a state-issued school leadership certification) (Copland, 2001).

Similarly, DeAngelis and O'Connor (2012) describe the attainment of administrative positions as an imperfect process in which some who complete administrative programs do not apply for positions, some who apply for positions do not receive job offers, and some who receive job offers decline to accept them. Their Illinois study provided insight on the topic of teacher promotion to administration and found that the majority of respondents in their study (69.3%) applied for administrative positions within two years of earning certification; however, significantly smaller percentages of the respondents received a job offer and actually made the transition into administrative work during the observed two-year time frame. Within a six-year time frame, just more than half (50.8%) of the respondents had held at least one administrative position. Another important finding was that applicants' age, as opposed to gender or race/ethnicity, was significantly related to their getting a job offer. Specifically, older applicants had lower odds of receiving a job offer than younger applicants, which may speak to potential bias and discrimination at play.

Another factor that may influence the likelihood of leader candidates receiving a job is their internal or external status. In their 2017 study, Buckman et al., analyzed the employability of teachers seeking promotion to assistant principal positions in Georgia. Promotion type was disaggregated as internally within-school, internally within-district, and external to the district. Their study concluded that internal applicants in their sample were better positioned to receive a promotion to assistant principal within their school or district than external applicants. Using a calculated employability rating for each participant, the authors concluded that advancement opportunities within a school or district were attributed to knowledge and experience obtained while working in the same or similar environment.

To evaluate the potential effectiveness of internally promoted leaders when compared to externally promoted leaders, Buckman and Tran (2018) sought to identify if there was a difference in the relationship between internally and externally promoted principals and the percentage of minimally proficient math and reading scores at their schools. In their five-year longitudinal study following a population of newly appointed Wisconsin principals (who remained in their roles for the study's duration), they found that external principals experienced more success with lower-performing students than internal principals. For example, in the area of reading, internally promoted principals had lower percentages of students categorized as minimum performers; yet, after two years, schools led by external principals experienced a percentage decrease of students identified as minimal performers, which was lower than schools led by internally promoted principals. In terms of succession planning, Buckman and Tran's (2018) research found that externally promoted principals demonstrated more progress in increasing student achievement among low performers than the internally promoted elementary principals. Although not highlighted in the described internal and external selection studies, an important factor, such as succession planning (i.e., formal or informal), may have had some influence on employer preference of internal candidates in school leader selection and the ability to better prepare for the endeavors ahead.

FORMAL AND INFORMAL SUCCESSION PLANNING

Formal succession planning is a series of intentional actions or steps taken within an organization to make certain smooth transitions occur in instances of leadership turnover. These steps include active recruitment of effective teachers from within the district, particularly those with the greatest potential to be effective leaders, as well as developing leadership pools composed of internal and external leadership candidates who have been vetted and possess the leadership qualifications that support the school's and district's mission and goals. Unfortunately, many districts fail to have formal leadership recruitment processes and rely heavily on informal processes (Lortie, 2009), such as "tapping."

Within the leadership promotion context, tapping is a process by which teachers are approached by school leaders (i.e., sponsors) to encourage them to consider making a career move towards leadership (Myung et al., 2011). Through this process, teachers are actively recruited and put on an expedited path to become an administrator by current leaders (Turner, 1960). This informal means of succession planning (i.e., sponsored mobility) is often inequitable because the likelihood of teachers being tapped is based on ambiguous criteria (that are highly susceptible to implicit bias) school leaders utilize to identify future leaders, and this form of transition to leadership is not available to all teachers. Lortie (2009) highlights that sponsored mobility is heavily used in principal selection, and approximately three out of four principals in their study acknowledged that their promotion to principal involved some sort of sponsorship.

In their study, Myung et al. (2011) found that after controlling for teaching positions, school leadership experience, leadership preparation, job satisfaction, and interest in becoming a school principal, teachers' gender and race were significant predictors of being tapped. More pointedly, male teachers were almost two times more likely to be tapped by their principals than female teachers, and Black and Hispanic teachers were 66% and 37% less likely to be tapped as compared to their White colleagues, respectively. They also found race matching to be a significant predictor of tapping, and teachers were approximately 30% more likely to be tapped if their race matched the race of their principal.

Unfortunately, these findings indicate possible accounts of implicit bias within leaders' decision to "tap" and that demographic and personal characteristics aided in leaders tapping candidates based on criteria beyond the teacher's leadership competencies. While tapping remains an informal procedure, potential discrimination associated with this practice can be prevalent enough to have legal implications. As such, schools and districts as well as state licensing agencies should be mindful of policies and practices that promote tapping and be extra vigilant to ward off potential discrimination that can ensue as a result. This requires self-reflection and awareness of biases and tapping based on objective performance-based criteria.

To address the leadership needs of schools and districts, it will likely benefit school employers to institute formal succession-planning processes instead of relying on informal tapping. To ensure that the efforts of formal succession plans are effective, they should include procedures for managing human capital, identifying associated costs to the organization, reducing staff turnover, providing professional development, informing current employees of job opportunities, and ensuring a fair process for succession (Fink & Brayman, 2006; Friedman, 1986; Rothwell, 2011; Rothwell & Poduch, 2004; Schall, 1997; Trepanier & Crenshaw,

2013). This can be approached by developing strategies to retain current leaders (Hargreaves, 2009), encouraging executive leaders to actively engage with school leaders, and most importantly creating a pool of leaders with capacity to lead in cases of an emergency or other unexpected vacancies (Rothwell, 2011).

Leadership Pools

The recruitment of effective leaders and leadership candidates should be an ongoing HR event. Ideally, districts should have at least two school leadership pools: 1) a pool consisting of assistant principals or individuals with the necessary credentials to serve as assistant principals and 2) a pool consisting of principals or individuals with the necessary credentials to serve as a principal. It is also recommended that HR offices have a vetting process that ensures that only leadership candidates with the highest potential for effectiveness are allowed entry into the pool, especially when pools are large as they often are for administrative positions. By doing so, this pool can serve as value-added to school- and district-level administrations during times of turnover.

Leadership Cohorts

Given the bias that can be associated with "tapping," Kanter (1993) associates this form of sponsored mobility with homosocial reproduction (i.e., a practice where leaders tend to establish sponsorship ties with teachers with whom they share demographic characteristics). School districts can curtail this practice through formalized succession planning. For example, "contest," or sometimes identified as "tournament," mobility is a more egalitarian form of social mobility that allows each individual an opportunity to compete for elite status in a company or organization. In this case, the competition or tournament would be an opportunity for entry into the district's leadership cohort, which would provide professional learning and put them on the "fast track" to a leadership position. To formalize the practice, school districts would allow multiple teachers throughout the school district to self-identify and apply to the leadership cohort, and selection into the cohort would be based on objective performance-based criteria.

As noted by Young (2008), "the effectiveness and the efficiency of any public school district depends largely on the quality of its workforce yesterday, today, and tomorrow" (p. 130). Therefore, with the establishment of leadership pools with candidates who hold the credentials to serve as school leaders as well as leadership cohorts with teachers being groomed to serve as future leaders, school districts are better able to address leadership succession and have developed a viable principal pipeline of quality leaders. In addition to a formalized succession plan, HR officers must maintain efforts to increase leader satisfaction by providing support and professional learning and by taking further measures to reduce turnover by remaining competitive with salaries and benefits.

Learning Activities

Discussion Questions:

1. It is important to acknowledge that not all schools have the ability to be equally selective, as some schools are more disadvantaged than other schools, given their lack of attractiveness to prospective teachers because of factors such as lack of community wealth and "hard-to-staff" locations. Are such districts able to benefit from more strategic selection, and if so, how?
2. When only Hispanic candidates are asked to provide evidence to demonstrate their competency, while other candidates' responses are taken at face value, would that put the employer at risk for disparate treatment, disparate impact, or neither? Why?
3. How might an employer mitigate the cultural noise bias and identify when an applicant is providing a socially acceptable response rather than an authentic one?
4. As an elementary school principal, you have to replace ten teacher vacancies in a single year. Build a hiring plan to recruit and select the most able candidates. How would you ensure a match between school needs and candidate qualities? How would you design the plan to support the goal of enhancing the diversity of your teaching staff? How would you leverage district HR resources to strengthen the plan?

CONCLUSION

Employers often shy away from employment assessments and tests, erring on the side of caution because of concerns that they may be invalid, yet many of the most commonly used metrics for hiring provide no better information.

Ultimately, data are meant to inform, not direct, administrative decision-making. The data can help provide guidance on how to select the most promising candidate, but they do not (and should not) entirely replace human judgment. Remember, the data are only tools. However, when they are used strategically and effectively, they have the potential to substantively improve HR practices. It is ultimately up to the administrator to use them.

Summary of Key Points

- It is important for the school site and the HR office to collaborate to maximize the opportunities to improve the probability of making the highest-quality selection. Valid predictors of post-hire performance can be collected pre-hire to support data-informed employment decisions.
- Implicit biases and prejudices are difficult to control in the selection process; however, school districts can develop strategic practices and processes to avoid the potential of individual biases influencing selection decisions. By

conducting proper evaluations of candidates, employers are less likely to screen based on ambiguous and subjectively biased criteria.

- It is recommended, when developing teacher assignments, that leaders equitably assign teachers classes based on their effectiveness and balance each grade with both highly effective and marginally effective teachers. Principals should also consider providing marginally effective or ineffective teachers a mentor to support teacher growth and effectiveness.
- Teacher transfers can be a critical asset for schools and school systems; however, knowledgeable school leaders and HR officers must know how to best strategically leverage this tool to benefit organizational outcomes.
- When developing an effective formal succession plan, plans should include procedures for managing personnel human capital, identifying costs to the organization, reducing staff turnover, providing professional development, and informing current employees of job opportunities.

This chapter was co-written with Dr. David G. Buckman.[1]

NOTE

1 Dr. David Buckman is an Associate dean for partnerships in the College of Education at the university of West of Georgia. He completed his Doctor of Philosophy degree in the Educational Leadership and Policies Department at the University of South Carolina. In addition, he also received an Ed.S. in Educational Leadership from the University of South Carolina, a M.Ed. in Educational Leadership from the University of South Carolina, and a B.S. in Physical Education from the University of South Carolina. He has professional experience in South Carolina's public school system serving as a teacher, coach, and school administrator. His primary research area is school human resources practices and school finance issues in K- 12 educational environments. Dr. Buckman serves as the Chair of the Editorial Board at the *Journal of Education Human Resources*. His research can be found in other prominent academic journals, such as the *Journal of Educational Administration and Leadership & Policy in Schools.*

REFERENCES

Arthur Jr, W., Bell, S. T., Villado, A. J., & Doverspike, D. (2006). The use of person-organization fit in employment decision making: An assessment of its criterion-related validity. *Journal of Applied Psychology, 91*(4), 786.

Barnes, G., Crowe, E., & Schaefer, B. (2007). *The cost of teacher turnover in five school districts: A pilot study.* National Commission on Teaching and America's Future.

Boyd, D., Lankford, H., Loeb, S., Ronfeldt, M., & Wyckoff, J. (2011). The role of teacher quality in retention and hiring: Using applications to transfer to uncover preferences of teachers and schools. *Journal of Policy Analysis and Management, 30*(1), 88–110.

Bruno, P., & Strunk, K. O. (2018). *Making the cut: The effectiveness of teacher screening and hiring in the Los Angeles Unified School District* (Working Paper 184). National Center for Analysis of Longitudinal Data in Education Research (CALDER).

Buckman, D. G., Johnson, A. D., & Alexander, D. L. (2017). Internal vs. external promotion: Advancement of teachers to administrators. *Journal of Educational Administration, 56*(1), 33–49.

Buckman, D. G., & Tran, H. (2018). Internal and external principal hiring and minimal student achievement: A 5-year cohort model. *International Journal of Educational Leadership Preparation, 13*(1), 1–18.

Cannata, M., Rubin, M., Goldring, E., Grissom, J. A., Neumerski, C. M., Drake, T. A., & Schuermann, P. (2017). Using teacher effectiveness data for information-rich hiring. *Educational Administration Quarterly, 53*(2), 180–222.

Carver-Thomas, D. (2018). *Diversifying the teaching profession: How to recruit and retain teachers of color.* Learning Policy Institute.

Cherng, H.-Y. S., & Halpin, P. F. (2016). The importance of minority teachers: Student perceptions of minority versus White teachers. *Educational Researcher, 45*(7), 407–420.

Clotfelter, C. T., Ladd, H. F., & Vigdor, J. (2005). Who teaches whom? Race and the distribution of novice teachers. *Economics of Education Review, 24*(4), 377–392.

Cohen-Vogel, L., & Osborne-Lampkin, L. (2007). Allocating quality: Collective bargaining agreements and administrative discretion over teacher assignment. *Educational Administration Quarterly, 43*, 433–461.

Copland, M. A. (2001). The myth of the superprincipal. *Phi Delta Kappan, 82*, 528–533.

Dana, J., Dawes, R., & Peterson, N. (2013). Belief in the unstructured interview: The persistence of an illusion. *Judgment and Decision Making, 8*(5), 512–520.

DeAngelis, K. J., & O'Connor, N. K. (2012). Examining the pipeline into educational administration: An analysis of applications and job offers. *Educational Administration Quarterly, 48*(3), 468–505.

DeArmond, M., Gross, B., & Goldhaber, D. (2010). Is it better to be good or lucky? Decentralized teacher selection in 10 elementary schools. *Educational Administration Quarterly, 46*(3), 322–362.

Dee, T. (2004). Teachers, race and student achievement in a randomized experiment. *The Review of Economics and Statistics, 86*(1), 195–210.

Derous, E., Pepermans, R., & Ryan, A. M. (2017). Ethnic discrimination during résumé screening: Interactive effects of applicants' ethnic salience with job context. *Human Relations, 70*(7), 860–882.

DiPaola, M., & Tschannen-Moran, M. (2003). The principalship at a crossroads: A study of the conditions and concerns of principals. *National Association of Secondary School Principals Bulletin, 87*(643), 43–65.

Donaldson, M. L., & Johnson, S. M. (2010). The price of misassignment: The role of teaching assignments in Teach for America teachers' exit from low income schools and the teaching profession. *Educational Evaluation and Policy Analysis, 32*(2), 299–323.

Egalite, A. J., Kisida, B., & Winters, M. A. (2015). Representation in the classroom: The effect of own-race teachers on student achievement. *Economics of Education Review, 45*, 44–52.

Engel, M., Cannata, M., & Curran, F. C. (2018). Principal influence in teacher hiring: Documenting decentralization over time. *Journal of Educational Administration, 56*(3), 277–296.

Feng, L. (2010). Hire today, gone tomorrow: New teacher classroom assignments and teacher mobility. *Education Finance and Policy, 5*(3), 278–316.

Feng, L., & Sass, T. (2011). *Teacher quality and teacher mobility* (Working Paper 57). National Center for Analysis of Longitudinal Data in Education Research.

Fink, D., & Brayman, C. (2006). School leadership succession and the challenges of change. *Educational Administration Quarterly, 42*(1), 62–89.

Friedman, S. D. (1986). Succession system in large corporations: Characteristics and correlates of performance. *Human Resource Management, 25,* 191–213.

Gershenson, S., Hart, C., Hyman, J., Lindsay, C., & Papageorge, N. W. (2018). *The long-run impacts of same-race teachers* (No. w25254). National Bureau of Economic Research.

Gershenson, S., Holt, S. B., & Papageorge, N. W. (2016). Who believes in me? The effect of student–teacher demographic match on teacher expectations. *Economics of Education Review, 52,* 209–224.

Goldhaber, D., Grout, C., & Huntington-Klein, N. (2017). Screen twice, cut once: Assessing the predictive validity of applicant selection tools. *Education Finance and Policy, 12*(2), 197–223.

Gregory, M. (2018). An implicit bias primer. *Journal of Social Policy & the Law, 25*(1), 27–58.

Grissom, J. A., Kalogrides, D., & Loeb, S. (2015). The micropolitics of educational inequality: The case of teacher-student assignments. *Peabody Journal of Education, 90*(5), 601–614.

Grissom, J. A., Kalogrides, D., & Loeb, S. (2017). Strategic staffing? How performance pressures affect the distribution of teachers within schools and resulting student achievement. *American Educational Research Journal, 54*(6), 1079–1116.

Hargreaves, A. (2009). Leadership succession and sustainable improvement. *School Administrator, 66*(11), 10–14.

Horng, E. L., Klasik, D., & Loeb, S. (2010). Principal's time use and school effectiveness. *American Journal of Education, 116*(4), 491–523.

Jackson, C. K. (2010). *Match quality, worker productivity, and worker mobility: Direct evidence from teachers* (Working Paper No. 15990). National Bureau of Economic Research.

Jacob, B. A., Rockoff, J. E., Taylor, E. S., Lindy, B., & Rosen, R. (2018). Teacher applicant hiring and teacher performance: Evidence from DC public schools. *Journal of Public Economics, 166,* 81–97.

Kalogrides, D., Loeb, S., & B′eteille, T. (2013). Systematic sorting teacher characteristics and class assignments. *Sociology of Education, 86*(2), 103–123.

Kanter, R. (1993). *Men and women of the corporation.* Basic Books.

Kausel, E. E., Culbertson, S. S., & Madrid, H. P. (2016). Overconfidence in personnel selection: When and why unstructured interview information can hurt hiring decisions. *Organizational Behavior and Human Decision Processes, 137,* 27–44.

Konoske-Graf, A., Partelow, L., & Benner, M. (2016). To attract great teachers, school districts must improve their human capital systems. *Center for American Progress,* 1–30. www.americanprogress.org/issues/education-k-12/reports/2016/12/22/295574/to-attract-great-teachers-school-districts-must-improve-their-human-capital-systems/

Ladd, H. F., & Sorensen, L. C. (2017). Returns to teacher experience: Student achievement and motivation in middle school. *Education Finance and Policy, 12*(2), 241–279.

Lankford, H., Loeb, S., & Wyckoff, J. (2002). Teacher sorting and the plight of urban schools: A descriptive analysis. *Educational Evaluation and Policy Analysis, 24*(1), 37–62.

Lankford, R. H., O'Connell, R. W., & Wyckoff, J. H. (2003). *Our next generation: School leadership in New York State*. New York State Education Department.

Levin, H. M. (1970). A cost-effectiveness analysis of teacher selection. *Journal of Human Resources*, 24–33.

Levin, J., Mulhern, J., & Schunck, J. (2005). *Unintended consequences: The case for reforming the staffing rules in urban teachers union contracts*. The New Teacher Project.

Lindsay, C. A., & Hart, C. M. (2017). Exposure to same-race teachers and student disciplinary outcomes for Black students in North Carolina. *Educational Evaluation and Policy Analysis, 39*(3), 485–510.

Liu, E., & Johnson, S. M. (2006). New teachers' experiences of hiring: Late, rushed, and information-poor. *Educational Administration Quarterly, 42*(3), 324–360.

Loeb, S., Kalogrides, D., & Béteille, T. (2012). Effective schools: Teacher hiring, assignment, development, and retention. *Education Finance and Policy, 7*(3), 269–304.

Loeb, S., Kalogrides, D., & Horng, E. H. (2010). Principal preferences and the uneven distribution of principals across schools. *Educational Evaluation and Policy Analysis, 32*, 205–229.

Lortie, D. (2009). *School principal – managing in public*. University of Chicago Press.

Mason, R., & Schroeder, M. (2010). Principal hiring practices: Toward a reduction of uncertainty. *Clearing House, 83*(5), 186–193. https://doi.org/10.1080/00098650903583727

Milanowski, A., & Odden, A. (2007). *A new approach to the cost of teacher turnover*. School Finance Redesign Project, Center on Reinventing Public Education.

Myung, J., Loeb, S., & Horng, E. (2011). Tapping the principal pipeline: Identifying talent for future school leadership in the absence of formal succession management programs. *Educational Administration Quarterly, 47*(5), 695–727.

Norton, M. S. (2014). *The principal as human resources leader: A guide to exemplary practices for personnel administration*. Routledge.

Papay, J. P., & Kraft, M. A. (2016). The productivity costs of inefficient hiring practices: Evidence from late teacher hiring. *Journal of Policy Analysis and Management, 35*(4), 791–817.

Pounder, D. G., Galvin, P., & Shepherd, P. (2003). An analysis of the United States educational administrator shortage. *Australian Journal of Education, 47*, 133–146.

Quillian, L., Pager, D., Hexel, O., & Midtbøen, A. H. (2017). Meta-analysis of field experiments shows no change in racial discrimination in hiring over time. *Proceedings of the National Academy of Sciences, 114*(41), 10870–10875.

Ricci v. DeStefano, 557 U.S. 557 (2009).

Rockoff, J. E., Jacob, B. A., Kane, T. J., & Staiger, D. O. (2011). Can you recognize an effective teacher when you recruit one? *Education Finance and Policy, 6*(1), 43–74.

Rothwell, W. J. (2011). Replacement planning: A starting point for succession planning and talent management. *International Journal of Training and Development, 15*, 87–99.

Rothwell, W. J., & Poduch, S. (2004). Introducing technical (not managerial) succession planning. *Public Personnel Management, 33*, 405–419.

Sajjadiani, S., Sojourner, A. J., Kammeyer-Mueller, J. D., & Mykerezi, E. (2019). Using machine learning to translate applicant work history into predictors of performance and turnover. *Journal of Applied Psychology, 104*(10), 1207.

Schall, E. (1997). Public-sector succession: A strategic approach to sustaining innovation. *Public Administration Review, 57,* 4–10.

Shockley, R., Guglielmino, P., & Watlington, E. J. (2006). *A national crisis in teacher education: What are the costs?* Pearson Education.

Tran, H. (2016). The South Carolina principal applicant pool: Are principal preparation students ready to take lead. *Teacher Education Journal: 2016 Edition.* www.scateonline.org/pdfs/Journal.Final.2016.pdf

Tran, H., & Bon, S. C. (2016). Principal quality and selection: Including multiple stakeholders' perspectives. *Journal of School Public Relations, 37*(1), 56–79.

Tran, H., Buckman, D. G., & Johnson, A. (2020). Using the hiring process to improve the cultural responsiveness of schools. *Journal of Cases in Educational Leadership, 23*(2), 70–84.

Tran, H., Hardie, S., Gause, S., Moyi, P., & Ylimaki, R. (2020). Leveraging the perspectives of rural educators to develop realistic job previews for rural teacher recruitment and retention. *Rural Educator, 41*(2), 31–46.

Tran, H., & Smith, D. A. (2020). Designing an employee experience approach to teacher retention in hard-to-staff schools. *NASSP Bulletin, 104*(2), 85–109.

Trepanier, S., & Crenshaw, J. T. (2013). Succession planning: A call to action for nurse executives. *Journal of Nursing Management, 21,* 980–985.

Turner, R. H. (1960). Sponsored and contest mobility and the school system. *American Sociological Review,* 855–867.

Vergara v. California (2014). Case No.: BC484642. http://studentsmatter.org/wpcontent/uploads/2014/06/Tenative-Decision.pdf

Whitaker, K. (2001). Where are the principal candidates? Perceptions of superintendents. *NASSP Bulletin, 85*(625), 82–92.

Winter, P. A., Rinehart, J. S., & Muñoz, M. A. (2002). Principal recruitment: An empirical evaluation of a school district's internal pool of principal certified personnel. *Journal of Personnel Evaluation in Education, 16*(2), 129–141.

Young, I. P. (2008). *The human resource function in educational administration* (9th ed.). Pearson Merrill/Prentice Hall.

PART 3

Building Human Capacity

CHAPTER 6

Induction

Chapter Summary

This chapter introduces research-based practices for effective induction of new teachers. Induction encompasses a variety of activities designed to promote the efficacy and confidence of new teachers in order to build an engaged and productive staff. The teaching profession is characterized by high rates of early turnover, and induction is designed to provide a lifeline to new teachers to strengthen teaching practices, build support networks, reduce turnover, and improve student achievement. The term "induction" encompasses a broad range of activities including orientation, mentoring, formal training and support, and reductions or modifications to the work assignments for new employees, including supports for both novice and experienced teachers who are new to the school. The chapter provides practical considerations regarding the design and structure of induction activities, including the role of peers, principals, district administrators, and state policymakers in building effective induction supports. The chapter includes case examples and activities related to the design of mentoring and induction programs.

Effective leaders plan for and manage staff turnover and succession, providing opportunities for effective induction and mentoring of new personnel.

(PSEL Standard 6b)

DOI: 10.4324/9781003457060-9

INTRODUCTION

After an employee is hired, *orientation* helps to shape the new employee's ability to participate fully and feel welcomed, comfortable, and confident in their new position. Orientation is the first step in actualizing and engaging the capacity of new employees who have been carefully screened and selected for their knowledge, skills, and abilities. It provides new employees with an understanding of how to access tools and supports and lays out basic expectations and norms of behavior. Orientation is typically short in duration and occurs after an individual is hired but before they begin the main work of the job. In contrast, induction or onboarding are longer-term, job-embedded supports that are addressed later in the chapter.

Policy handbooks provide important information to new employees about district or school policies. However, orientation needs to go further to address both written and unwritten rules. Providing early answers to questions that make new teachers avoid gaffes with other employees include: "What time should I arrive in the morning, and when should I expect to be able to leave in the afternoon? What activities am I expected to participate in? Is there a protocol for getting students to the lunchroom? What do I do if a piece of equipment doesn't work? What if I have security concerns? Which bathroom should I use? Where should I park? How does the copy machine work? How does the library work?" And since it would be impossible to anticipate all the questions a new employee might have, "Who do I talk to if I need help or advice?"

Orientation can help an employee quickly become "one of us" by explaining how "most people" operate in the organization. Alternatively, in a carefully managed change process, orientation may be designed to teach new employees desirable behaviors that are not currently the norm, to leverage new employees in support of bringing more desirable habits into the workplace and thereby begin to shift school or district cultural norms (e.g., creating a more inclusive environment that has traditionally only welcomed certain groups of people). Whether to become one of us or begin to change who we are, being intentional about orienting new employees to the work supports their transition and enables them to get quicker traction in becoming familiar with the written and unwritten rules of the new school.

A web presence is a terrific way to communicate important resources and make them available to new employees. It also provides a recruitment tool for prospective teachers who may be considering applying to the district. Resources like these help to onboard new employees to the mission, vision, values, norms, goals, and rules of the organization; celebrate new membership in the school; and acknowledge the importance and challenge of making a successful transition into the school community (Caldwell & Peters, 2018; Johnson & Senges, 2010; Zink & Curran, 2018).

New employees are susceptible to information overload as there is a lot of complex knowledge that needs to be communicated and taken in over a short period of time. Too much information can be as much of a problem as too little in the induction process (Caldwell & Peters, 2018). Finding the right balance can be challenging. Perhaps that is why many school districts have focused on mentoring as a major component of induction support. The mentor can help to manage the information flow and reinforce essential messages to the new employee.

In addition to orientation to the school and district, information needs to be communicated to new employees about the work itself. New teachers need an opportunity to learn from their peers, fill in gaps in their understanding, observe what others are doing, and receive feedback and support to hone their skills and shape their own practice. Induction (analogous to onboarding in noneducation sectors) is a broad term that encompasses orientation but also includes a variety of activities designed to support new teacher success and build capacity and confidence. Table 6.1 provides a menu of forms of induction, beginning with orientation.

Mentoring is a major component of most induction programs (Wechsler et al., 2010). Assigning a mentor is a popular option because of the deep multilayered (e.g., relational, pedagogical, and content) support mentors can provide for new teachers. The mentor can provide advice and answer questions in a nonjudgmental context. The quality of the mentoring experience is influenced by mentor training, release time for mentoring activities, the relationship between the mentor and new teacher, the broader context of the school, and the proximity of the new teacher and mentor, which can provide opportunities for chance conversations throughout the day.

In addition to the formally assigned mentor, other faculty and staff can provide important support. Schools that take collective responsibility for the success of the new teacher provide support in teacher team meetings, collaboration during planning times, opportunities to observe other teachers in their classrooms, and sharing of expertise with the new teacher. A study of induction programs in Illinois found that collective responsibility for the new teacher – as demonstrated by their collaboration with other teachers (not just the mentor), invitations to observe other classrooms, and shared problem-solving – was one of the most important sources of support for new teachers (Wechsler et al., 2010). These activities break down the isolating nature of schools as organizations. Teachers

Table 6.1 Forms of Induction

Orientation
Mentoring
Faculty Collaboration
Meetings With Supervisors
Reduced Workloads
Less Challenging Work Assignments
Extra Classroom Assistance
Developmental Workshops

Source: Ingersoll and Strong (2011)

have many opportunities to interact with their students, but often new teachers especially feel isolated from other adults in the building and have a difficult time integrating themselves into the fabric of the school. When schools take collective responsibility for the new teacher, they can quickly break down the isolation and help the new teacher feel welcomed into a new professional community.

The principal plays an important role in the induction process by meeting with new teachers, observing their classrooms, providing structures and supports, and holding the mentor and others accountable for providing support to ensure the new teacher's success. Principal support can also include shaping the new teacher's work to support success by providing reduced workloads, less challenging work assignments, extra classroom assistance, and/or developmental workshops for the new teacher. Districts can provide further opportunities by allowing new teachers to build networks with other new teachers as part of a formal district induction program.

BOX 6.1: LEADING ONBOARDING PRACTICES IN THE PRIVATE SECTOR

Corporate organizations employ a variety of effective onboarding practices for new employees. These practices vary greatly based on the size and mission of the company. Here are two example employers that offer corporate onboarding practices that could potentially be leveraged by school employers.

L'Oreal has thousands of employees worldwide. In 2017, L'Oreal developed the Fit Culture App, "a one-of-a-kind mobile app that helps newcomers in decoding, understanding and mastering the company culture." The app, through texts, videos, employee testimonials, as well as quizzes, games, and real-life missions, aims to give new employees the "keys to succeed in full alignment with company values such as multiculturalism, diversity and inclusion." Newcomers are encouraged to use the app five to ten minutes a day for a month to earn points and eventually become true "#CultureGurus." The app provides a fun self-competition to encourage employees to get to know the organization. The Fit Culture App is used as part of the 18–24 month onboarding system that runs from mentoring to ensuring that employees experience the company's products. Some sites even offer geographic adjustment support. For example, in L'Oreal's Miami office, current employees help new employees learn how to live in a new place: neighborhoods to rent in, cars to buy, cellphone prices, and more.

At *Google,* managers are emailed when they get a new employee, and they are tasked with the following:

- Discussing roles and responsibilities
- Matching the new hire with a peer buddy

- Helping the new hire build a social network
- Setting up employee onboarding check-ins once a month for the new hire's first six months
- Encouraging open dialogue

Given these corporate onboarding practices, consider:

- How might these companies' onboarding practices translate to a school building?
- What onboarding practices might be useful to integrate at your school?
- What are the challenges and opportunities of adapting their corporate onboarding practices for a school setting?
- How can you leverage these onboarding practices to create a more welcoming and inclusive environment?

Source: Johnson and Senges (2010); www.loreal.com/en/press-release/hr-and-diversity/loral-launches-fit-culture-app-a-custommade-app-to-welcome-new-employees/

WHY DOES IT MATTER? THE IMPORTANCE OF INDUCTION PROGRAMMING

Effective induction provides the building blocks to improve employee satisfaction, retention, commitment, and performance (Bauer & Erdogan, 2011). Induction can support these outcomes by building and reinforcing compliance, clarification, culture, and connection. *Compliance* is an understanding of the basic rules and policies of the organization. *Clarification* provides the employee with an understanding of the job in all of its complexity and what the expectations are related to the position. *Culture* is the opportunity for the employee to learn the formal and informal organizational norms. *Connection* is the chance for new employees to make new and lasting interpersonal relationships and provide an opportunity for the new employee to become familiar with networks important to their success (Bauer, 2010).

Induction is often seen as the transition between teacher preparation and independent teaching practice. The underlying theory of action for induction is that teaching is highly complex, and teacher preparation programs rarely provide sufficient training for new teachers to be fully prepared to take on a classroom by themselves, so a good portion of teacher learning occurs after the teacher enters the classroom. Induction provides that additional support to ensure that the teacher is fully prepared to teach when in the field (Ingersoll & Strong, 2011), and the evidence suggests that induction supports in the first year of teaching are associated with reduced teacher migration and attrition (Ronfeldt & McQueen, 2017).

SATISFACTION AND RETENTION

While the importance of retention was addressed in Chapters 2 and 3, we provide more context in this chapter to expand on that discussion. To start, turnover in teaching is high compared to other professions with similar education and training requirements. It is not only a major contributor to teacher shortages (Carver-Thomas & Darling-Hammond, 2017; Ingersoll, 2001; Ingersoll & Smith, 2003) but also to the disparity in the quality of education and educational outcomes across schools (Carver-Thomas & Darling-Hammond, 2017; Smith & Ingersoll, 2004). Analyses of turnover data have led scholars to conclude that teacher shortages are caused by high rates of turnover of new teachers rather than actual shortages in the supply of individuals going into teaching (Carver-Thomas & Darling-Hammond, 2017; Ingersoll & Strong, 2011). In addition, teacher turnover has a measurable negative effect on student achievement (Ronfeldt et al., 2013). Teacher turnover means that there are more inexperienced (and therefore, on average, lower quality, since teachers tend to become better with experience) teachers. Because teacher turnover is not evenly distributed across schools (Ronfeldt et al., 2013), high-poverty schools are more adversely impacted. In these schools, turnover undermines opportunities to build and sustain teaching capacity, strong and cohesive school cultures, and strong school-community relationships. The high rate of teacher turnover means that one in five teachers in the US are in their first three years on the job (Goldrick, 2016).

Nationally, about 8% of teachers leave the profession each year, contributing to about 90% of the demand for new teachers. Overall annual teacher turnover rates (due to leaving the profession or moving to a new school) are highest in the South (at 16.7%) and lowest in the Northeast (10.3%). These differences are thought to be attributed to the better pay and working conditions for teachers in the Northeast. Turnover rates are higher for math and science teachers, special education teachers, and English-language learner and foreign language teachers (Carver-Thomas & Darling-Hammond, 2017).

Turnover is higher for schools with high concentrations of poverty (50% higher). Schools with the highest concentrations of students of color have turnover rates 70% higher than average (Carver-Thomas & Darling-Hammond, 2017; Ronfeldt et al., 2013).

Two-thirds of new teacher attrition is attributable to job dissatisfaction or pursuit of a better job or career (Ingersoll & Smith, 2003). Research across a variety of studies suggests induction programs may mitigate some of this attrition, as they have been found to positively impact teacher job satisfaction, teacher performance, and student achievement. Specifically, Smith and Ingersoll's (2004) analysis of the 1999 Schools and Staffing Survey data showed that having a mentor who has expertise in your field reduced the likelihood of turnover after the first year by 30%. Having common planning time with other teachers reduced the risk of leaving by 43% and of moving to another school by 25%. Participation in an external cohort of teachers reduced the likelihood of leaving by 33% but slightly increased the likelihood of moving to another school, although neither effect was statistically significant. Having a teacher's aide in the classroom reduced the likelihood of moving by 41% but did not affect the rate of turnover due to leaving the profession. Most of the schools that provided induction support, provided multiple types of support, compounding the positive effects on retention.

COMMITMENT AND PERFORMANCE

Clearly, induction is a leadership tool that can have a dramatic impact on teacher retention and, in turn, school quality. Comprehensive, multiyear induction programs accelerate the professional growth of new teachers, reduce the rate of new teacher attrition, provide a stronger return on states' and school districts' investment, and improve student learning.

While the evidence on the relationship between induction program design and teacher commitment and performance is not definitive, there is evidence that teachers feel that access to a mentor has a large impact on their effectiveness as a teacher and positively impacts their commitment to remaining in the profession (Behrstock-Sherratt et al., 2014).

DESIGNING EFFECTIVE INDUCTION PROGRAMS

Thus far, we have focused on defining the components of induction and explained why providing careful attention to new teacher induction is important for satisfaction, retention, commitment, and performance. Before turning to details regarding the design of an effective induction program, it is worth stepping back to consider the broader context of the school as a workplace. As we discussed in Chapters 2 and 3, research on teacher turnover suggests that the working conditions of a school are an important factor in teacher satisfaction and commitment (Johnson et al., 2012).

While induction programs can help teachers transition to a new school, they do little to change the core features of the school organization. If a school is not a good place to work, carefully informing teachers about the nuances of the school's culture is unlikely to meaningfully improve teacher satisfaction or commitment and, therefore, is unlikely to impact teacher retention and performance. While not the primary focus of this chapter, leaders interested in providing new teachers a strong foundation for success need to begin by attending to the broader conditions of work. While induction has positive impacts on teacher satisfaction and performance, by far the most important predictor of teacher retention is school context (Wechsler et al., 2010; Ingersoll & Strong, 2011). Specifically, induction works best when it builds on foundational features of good schools such as providing clear goals and a sense of purpose, offering regular and meaningful opportunities for teacher evaluation and feedback, establishing policies and procedures for effectively managing student behavior, giving opportunities for peer collaboration that minimize the professional isolation of teachers, and facilitating opportunities for meaningful teacher involvement in decision-making (Halverson & Kelley, 2017; Rosenholtz, 1989; Toropova et al., 2019).

We turn next to examine the role of the principal, the district, and the state in designing and supporting effective induction processes. While we view induction as primarily the responsibility of the principal, there are opportunities for borrowing strength from the district- and state-level policy to help fund, shape, and extend induction opportunities for new teachers.

BOX 6.2: WHEN IT'S NOT ROSY: UNPLEASANT EXPERIENCE DISSIPATES ENTHUSIASM

Sarah Carpenter had just completed her training at Medford Academy, a small private women's college in the Midwest. Sarah was especially motivated by the social justice components of the curriculum in her teacher training program, and she looked forward to her first teaching job when she would put her skills to work in a diverse, low-income urban elementary school. After interviewing and receiving multiple offers, she chose King Elementary School. The principal of King was young and charismatic, and Sarah looked forward to learning from her experienced colleagues and making a difference for her students.

Sarah spent the week before school started in a largely empty building, with limited interaction with other teachers. Two days before classes were to start, Sarah's car was broken into while parked in the school parking lot. Although sympathetic, the other teachers she spoke with did not seem surprised and instead shared their own horror stories about their experiences at King.

Sarah tried to make an appointment with the principal, but he seemed busy with parents and students and had little time to talk to her. Her students and their parents were invited to come to meet her before school started. She stood in the hall to welcome her students, but few came. As she pulled together materials for the first week of class, she realized that she did not know how to use the copy machine. Some of her textbooks were missing, and there were not enough books for all the students in her class.

She checked with the other teachers in fourth grade to see if they could collaborate during a common planning time, but they all had different prep periods. Her class had 28 students, including 10 identified with special needs. When she interviewed, the principal had suggested that she would have a special education teacher with her to help in the classroom, but the school was short-staffed, and she would have to figure out how to address the student's needs on her own. The year had not even started, and Sarah felt her optimism wane.

Discussion Questions: If you were the principal at King Elementary and learned of Sarah's experience, what leadership moves would you make to change the experience for Sarah and other new teachers at King Elementary? Please rationalize and justify your response based on ethical, legal, professional, and/or leadership frameworks.

PRINCIPAL'S ROLE

As the formal building-level leader, the principal is in a unique position to shape the onboarding experience by designing working conditions and induction support for new teachers. Through these leverage points, they play a primary role in building an effective induction experience. We focus here on the ways in which principals impact induction through *direct supervision, work design, staffing,* and *professional development.*

1. The principal supports induction through *direct supervision.* From conversations in the interview stage through the first days on the job, the principal provides important context for the new teacher about what to expect and what is expected of them. The principal provides both substantive and symbolic guidance. Making a point of meeting with the new teacher on their first day, stopping by their classroom regularly, and taking the time to see how things are going let the employee know that they are valued. These actions also provide an opportunity for the new teachers to get their questions answered and problems resolved quickly. One induction study found that the principal's role was as important as the mentor's role in shaping the teacher experience. The primary role of the principal was to reinforce the new teacher's sense of competence by showing, through their interactions, that they trusted the new teacher's professional judgment (Bickmore & Bickmore, 2010).
   How frequently the principal comes into the teacher's classroom to observe and what they talk about provides not-so-subtle cues about what aspects of the work are important and deserve attention. Important to note are what questions does the principal ask and what do their conversations with teachers focus on. Is it instruction? Student learning and collaboration? Student behavior? Social justice? Through these interactions, the principal acts as a potter, carefully shaping the cultural understanding and expectations for teacher work (Deal & Peterson, 1990).
2. The principal also shapes induction through attention to *the design of work.* The early experiences of teachers shape their decisions about whether to commit to staying in the same school and/or whether to stay in the profession. Important work design factors include providing structured opportunities for faculty collaborations so teachers do not feel isolated. The principal has

a responsibility to both structure the day to provide collaborative planning time and provide leadership (goals, facilitation training, agenda setting, and accountability) to ensure that the collaborative time effectively contributes to teacher growth, collaboration, and improvement.

In addition to attending to the structure of work for all teachers, work design for novice teachers may require attention to the specific working conditions of the individual teacher. The learning curve for a new teacher is very high. In some districts, seniority rules drive teaching assignments, and beginning teachers get the teaching assignments that no one else wants. These conditions almost ensure failure for anyone but the most talented and motivated. Paying attention to the level of challenge can help the new teacher master the curriculum and build classroom management and instructional skills. Allowing new teachers to have smaller class sizes, reduced workloads, and/or less challenging work assignments can provide important induction support to enable a new teacher to experience success and develop a sense of self-efficacy. Even ensuring that beginning teachers have the materials they need and a classroom located near peers who can support their success can all contribute to reducing turnover and facilitating their success.

Similarly, if resources are available, new teachers might receive additional assistance, such as the placement of a special education teacher or paraprofessional in their classrooms, who can provide support to scaffold student learning.

3. The principal shapes induction through *staffing decisions*, such as defining mentor roles, matching mentors to new employees, goal-setting and supervision of mentors, and allocating resources to ensure that mentors have sufficient time available to work with new employees. The important role of mentors was discussed previously, but we reiterate it here to emphasize the importance of the principal's role in staffing and supervising the mentoring process. The principal is responsible for establishing clear goals and expectations for mentors and overseeing the mentoring process to ensure that assigned mentors are providing regular and meaningful mentoring support for new teachers. Research suggests that mentors tend not to focus on teaching culturally or linguistically diverse students. By helping to establish expectations for the mentoring experience, principals can overcome limitations of typical mentoring programs by explicitly focusing attention on teaching diverse learners as a goal of the mentoring experience.

   Often when we think of mentoring, we focus on the important dyadic relationship between a mentor and mentee. But research on effective mentoring suggests that schools that have built a shared and collective responsibility for new teachers as a cultural norm provide much more effective mentoring support. By shaping teacher expectations for shared responsibility, principals can help to build a community of support for the new teacher.
4. The principal shapes induction by providing opportunities for *professional training and development*. Even if the school is unable to offer customized

targeted professional development opportunities for new teachers, the principal can still identify important developmental workshop opportunities for new teachers to learn specific pedagogical approaches or curricula that the school or district has adopted. Often, professional development opportunities are widely available during textbook adoption or school improvement process implementation, but they may be less available for the new teacher who comes into the school community after others have already been trained. The principal and the mentor can work together to identify training opportunities to bring the new teacher up to speed on behavioral or instructional models that they need to know to be successful in that particular school environment. These opportunities may include connections to professional networks outside of the school (Wechsler et al., 2010).

Together, these types of opportunities help new teachers understand and implement behavioral, curricular, or pedagogical models. Beyond that initial training, the principal should identify resources to support the ongoing professional development of teachers beyond their initial entry into the school community. These opportunities might involve finding these teachers a collaborative partner who could provide them ongoing support and professional community, providing them opportunities to become mentors themselves, or developing their leadership experiences by providing them some leadership opportunities (e.g., becoming a department chair).

We cannot overstate the importance of the principal's role in shaping the induction experience. Whether a principal carefully and intentionally shapes their leadership to support an effective induction or is drawn into other activities and ignores these responsibilities, they will play an important role in framing a new teacher's understanding of what it means to be a teacher in their school. Failure to carefully frame these experiences is a significant lost opportunity, as new teachers may fill in their own knowledge gaps with assumptions that negatively reshape the school's culture, instructional norms, and staff collaboration or isolation. Proactive attention to these factors will provide a stronger foundation for building an effective culture and making the hiring process an opportunity to strengthen positive cultural norms rather than weaken them.

Ideally, induction support should be designed to address the challenges that teachers face early in their careers or their placements in a particular school. The challenges facing each teacher depend, in part, on their specific teaching assignment. For example, new special education teachers may have concerns related to teaching practice, collaboration with other teachers, manageability of the workload, isolation, a lack of high-quality curricular materials, and their ability to master complex legal issues (Billingsley & The IRIS Center, n.d.).

There are many ways an induction program can be structured. Wechsler et al. (2010) describe one type of induction program which supports regular interaction between mentors (who are full-time teachers) and mentees by providing the pairs 1.5 hours of mandatory release time every other week. Each mentor/mentee pair determines how to use the time. New teachers described the variety of activities they engaged in during this time, including teaching their own class and being observed by their mentors, observing their mentor conduct a demonstration lesson in the new teacher's classroom, observing their mentors teaching in the mentor's classroom, and observing other teachers in the school or in other district schools. A substitute teacher is available to make the release time possible, and release time across mentor/mentee pairs in a school is coordinated by a staff member at the school. This flexible setup enables each mentor/mentee pair to request a release time that may vary from week to week so they can observe different class periods or subject areas. Combined with prep periods, the release time creates valuable time for new teachers and their mentors to observe one another in the classroom and to focus new teacher support on real-time classroom situations.

DISTRICT'S ROLE

While the principal has a significant opportunity to understand and establish the conditions of work for the new teacher, the district has an opportunity to leverage resources to support the cohort of new teachers or new employees across the district. The district's role can include providing a common experience for new employees to the district by allocating resources to schools for mentoring and professional development. The district can bring in experts to support new teachers, provide incentives to leverage existing experts within the school for support, and advance district-level goals through professional development, such as training to minimize the disparate impact of behavioral policies, advance curricular goals, and promote quality instruction as defined by the district. The district may also have sufficient resources to develop materials to support new employees and connect teachers to the community.

A good example of the kinds of resources that a district might provide to orient new employees can be found on the Denver Public Schools website, which provides resources to support new employees. The website includes links to human resource policies and paperwork that needs to be completed, information about compensation and benefits, employee wellness materials, district curriculum frameworks, and social supports to help new teachers settle into life in Denver. The site details what to do before you start, in your first 30 days, your first year, and beyond your first year as a Denver Public Schools employee.[1]

STATE ROLE

The clear evidence that shows a strong and consistent relationship between teacher induction and teacher retention and performance has prompted interest by states in policies that promote effective induction practices. By 2016, 24 states had policies requiring some type of induction support for new teachers (Goldrick, 2016). State programs illustrate the multiple and sometimes competing goals of induction programs, which can include teacher socialization, adjustment, development, and assessment (Ingersoll & Strong, 2011).

Many states also tie mentoring to licensure. In these states, typically mentors must provide positive evaluations of new teachers for a provisional license to be converted to a standard teacher license. Thus, the goal of many state programs includes both supporting teachers to reduce turnover and counseling out low performers.

BOX 6.3: STATE SUPPORT FOR NEW TEACHER INDUCTION PROGRAMS

The New Teacher Center identifies the characteristics of high-quality state induction support for new teachers. These include:

1. **Educators served**: All beginning teachers should receive induction support during their first two years in the profession.
2. **Mentor quality**: Mentors should be identified through a rigorous selection process, with foundational training and ongoing professional development.
3. **Program standards**: The state should adopt formal program standards that guide the design of mentoring and induction programs.
4. **Funding**: The state should dedicate funding for mentor programs.
5. **Educator certification/licensure**: The state should require participation in a mentoring program in order to move from an initial educator license.
6. **Program evaluation**: The state should maintain a regular process of evaluation of induction programs.
7. **Teaching conditions**: The state should adopt standards for and assess school conditions and require attention to these conditions in school improvement plans. (Adapted from Goldrick, 2016)

Discussion Questions: Does your state have a teacher induction policy? What impact does the policy have on the practice of mentoring and induction? As an administrator, how could you design school or district practices in conjunction with this policy to strengthen teacher induction in your district?

Learning Activities

Discussion Questions:

1. If you were to design a comprehensive induction program, what would it look like? How would you design for high quality and accountability? What aspects of new teacher induction can be generically designed to apply to all teachers, and what aspects need to be tailored to the needs of the specific teacher?
2. If you were hiring a new teacher with a cultural identity that was not shared by anyone else in the school, what features of the induction experience would you pay particular attention to in order to facilitate a positive experience for the new teacher?
3. Special education teachers have particular challenges in making a positive transition into a new school. What aspects of the special educator position contribute to making the transition challenging, and what could you do as a principal to improve the experience for special education teachers?

BOX 6.4: CASE EXAMPLE – IMPLEMENTING ORIENTATION PROCEDURES AT THE SCHOOL LEVEL

Riverview High School (RHS) is in the northeast region of the United States and enrolls 1,934 students: 21% Asian; 15% Black; 46% Non-White Hispanic; 16% White; and 2% other. Seventy-four percent of students are classified as low-income. With this large student body, there are 275 staff members at the school including 150 teachers. As your second year as the principal of RHS is coming up, one of your priorities is to reduce teacher turnover. You know that effective teacher onboarding and orientation can make a difference for teacher retention and thus you reflect on the past year and turn your attention to the first few weeks of the upcoming school year.

RHS, like many high-poverty schools, has the highest teacher turnover in the district, losing 20% and 23% of first-year teachers in the past two years, respectively. You have observed over the past two years that many of the veteran teachers in the building are reluctant to help the new teachers navigate their first year at a new school because there has been such a high turnover rate. Further, many of the veteran teachers resist changing their curriculum plans and are wary of new, hypothetically untested, ideas from beginning teachers. Making matters additionally difficult for new teachers in RHS is the fact that they are historically assigned to teach the more challenging lower-level courses. They are rarely assigned any honors, AP, or IB courses and are instead teaching standard- and remedial-level courses.

You have 30 new teachers entering your building this year. Twenty-two are brand new to teaching and eight have teaching experience in other districts. All 30 teachers have been required to attend the 4-day orientation provided by the district, where the teachers worked on preparing for the first week of school, setting high expectations for students, and beginning to teach a standards-based curriculum. At the end of the 4-day district orientation, the 30 new teachers will be coming to RHS for a day-long school-based orientation before all teachers report for teacher workdays the following week.

Discussion Questions: What will you emphasize during this day-long orientation for the new teachers? Further, knowing that effective orientation and onboarding (induction) extends beyond the initial one-day orientation, what programs and procedures will you implement throughout the school year to ensure that new teacher turnover is reduced at RHS?

CONCLUSION

Turnover of new teachers is higher than in most other professions. Turnover is higher in low-income and high-poverty schools, impacting the quality of teaching and the ability of teachers to establish stable relationships with students over time (Carver-Thomas & Darling-Hammond, 2017). Principals can reduce teacher turnover, improve new teacher effectiveness, and shape the culture of the school by providing high-quality induction support for new teachers and staff.

Summary of Key Points

- Orientation helps to shape new employees' experience by making them feel welcomed, comfortable, and confident in their new roles. Orientation provides an opportunity for a new employee to learn how to access tools and supports and lays out basic expectations for norms of behavior.
- Mentoring is a major component of induction support for new teachers. Mentors provide advice and answer questions in a nonjudgmental manner.
- The principal plays a primary role in building an effective induction experience by designing working conditions and induction supports for new teachers. Principals shape induction through their direct supervision of new employees, by designing work in ways that enable collaboration and support for new teachers, by assigning new teachers with manageable workloads and realistic teaching assignments, and by ensuring that new teachers have the professional development they need to learn key features of the school's approach to curriculum, instruction, behavioral management, and collaboration with other teachers.

- Induction can be designed to acclimate new employees to the existing organizational culture or to help orient new employees to desirable behaviors that are not currently the norm, to promote positive changes to school or district cultural norms.

NOTE

1 See http://thecommons.dpsk12.org/Page/2215

REFERENCES

Bauer, T. N. (2010). *Onboarding new employees: Maximizing success.* The SHRM Foundation's Effective Practice Guideline Series. www.shrm.org/about/foundation/products/Pages/OnboardingEPG.aspx.

Bauer, T. N., & Erdogan, B. (2011). Organizational socialization: The effective onboarding of new employees. In S. Zedeck (Ed.), *APA handbooks in psychology. APA handbook of industrial and organizational psychology, Vol. 3. Maintaining, expanding, and contracting the organization* (pp. 51–64). American Psychological Association. http://dx.doi.org/10.1037/12171-002

Behrstock-Sherratt, E., Bassett, K., Olson, D., & Jacques, C. (2014). *From good to great: Exemplary teachers share perspectives on increasing teacher effectiveness across the career continuum.* Center on Great Teachers and Leaders.

Bickmore, D. L., & Bickmore, S. T. (2010). A multifaceted approach to teacher induction. *Teaching and Teacher Education, 26*(4), 1006–1014.

Billingsley, B., & The IRIS Center. (n.d.). *Beginning teacher support.* http://iris.peabody.vanderbilt.edu/wp-content/uploads/pdf_case_studies/ics_begtch.pdf

Caldwell, C., & Peters, R. (2018). New employee onboarding – psychological contracts and ethical perspectives. *Journal of Management Development, 37*(1), 27–39.

Carver-Thomas, D., & Darling-Hammond, L. (2017). *Teacher turnover: Why it matters and what we can do about it.* Learning Policy Institute.

Deal, T. E., & Peterson, K. D. (1990). *The principal's role in shaping school culture.* US Department of Education, Office of Educational Research and Improvement.

Goldrick, L. (2016). *Support from the start: A 50-state review of policies on new educator induction.* New Teacher Center.

Halverson, R., & Kelley, C. (2017). *Mapping leadership: The tasks that matter for improving teaching and learning in schools.* Jossey-Bass.

Ingersoll, R. M. (2001). Teacher turnover and teacher shortages: An organizational analysis. *American Educational Research Journal, 38*(3), 499–534.

Ingersoll, R. M., & Smith, T. M. (2003). The wrong solution to the teacher shortage. *Educational Leadership, 60*(8), 30–33.

Ingersoll, R. M., & Strong, M. (2011). The impact of induction and mentoring programs for beginning teachers: A critical review of the research. *Review of Educational Research, 81*(2), 201–233.

Johnson, M., & Senges, M. (2010). Learning to be a programmer in a complex organization. *Journal of Workplace Learning, 22*(3), 180–194.

Johnson, S. M., Kraft, M., & Papay, J. P. (2012). How context matters in high-need schools: The effects of teachers' working conditions on their professional satisfaction and their students' achievement. *Teachers College Record, 114*(10), 1–39.

Ronfeldt, M., Loeb, S., & Wyckoff, J. (2013). How teacher turnover harms student achievement. *American Educational Research Journal, 50*(1), 4–36.

Ronfeldt, M., & McQueen, K. (2017). Does new teacher induction really improve retention? *Journal of Teacher Education, 68*(4), 394–410.

Rosenholtz, S. (1989). Workplace conditions that affect teacher quality and commitment: Implications for teacher induction programs. *The Elementary School Journal, 89*(4), 421–439. www.jstor.org.ezproxy.library.wisc.edu/stable/1001780

Smith, T. M., & Ingersoll, R. M. (2004). What are the effects of induction and mentoring on beginning teacher turnover? *American Educational Research Journal, 41*(3, Fall), 681–714.

Toropova, A., Myrberg, E., & Johansson, S. (2019). Teacher job satisfaction: The importance of school working conditions and teacher characteristics. *Educational Review, 73*(1). https://doi.org/10.1080/00131911.2019.1705247

Wechsler, M. E., Caspary, K., Humphrey, D. C., & Matsko, K. K. (2010). *Examining the effects of new teacher induction*. SRI International.

Zink, H. R., & Curran, J. D. (2018). Building a research onboarding program in a pediatric hospital: Filling the orientation gap with onboarding and just-in-time education. *Journal of Research Administration, 49*(2), 109–132.

CHAPTER 7

Professional Development and Coaching

Chapter Summary

Investing in employee knowledge and skill development is a core feature of Talent-Centered Education Leadership. The development of highly qualified teachers requires intentional, data-informed, supportive, and strategic leadership in schools. This chapter introduces the design and implementation of professional development and coaching supports to build teacher skills and strengthen and focus teaching and learning. Research on teacher development has shown the importance of embedding learning opportunities for teachers in the structure of their work. Here, we examine the design of formal, programmatic professional development and coaching as important elements of Talent-Centered Education Leadership. This chapter provides practical considerations regarding the design and structure of professional development and coaching, including case examples, activities, and discussion questions.

Effective leaders develop teachers' and staff members' professional knowledge, skills, and practice through differentiated opportunities for learning and growth, guided by understanding of professional and adult learning and development.

(PSEL Standard 6c)

DOI: 10.4324/9781003457060-10

INTRODUCTION

Professional development and coaching are core elements of inclusive talent management in a Talent-Centered Education Leadership (TCEL) approach. The term *professional development* describes "learning opportunities that engage educators' creative and reflective capacities to strengthen their practice" (Bredeson & Johansson, 2000, p. 387). Here, we refer to professional development as formal, organized activities targeting groups of teachers that are designed to improve instructional or leadership practice. Coaching describes hands-on, in-class support for individual teachers to model and provide feedback to improve teaching practice. TCEL views professional growth and fulfillment of individual employees as the building blocks of a successful organization. In Chapter 6, we examined mentoring and induction as ways to introduce new employees to the organization and provide them with the support they need to make a successful transition into the school or the profession. In this chapter, we examine professional development as a mechanism for providing broad support for employee knowledge and skill development and coaching as a mechanism to support individual teachers in building knowledge and skills for more effective instruction. Chapter 8 provides an examination of the role of school and district leadership in fostering communities of practice among teachers, which provide opportunities for ongoing job-embedded teacher development. Together, mentoring and induction, professional development and coaching, and communities of practice provide foundational practices to promote a positive employee experience and to build teacher capacity and effectiveness.

Professional development and coaching provide opportunities for growth and development throughout the teaching career to address skill gaps and enable teachers to build a sense of teaching efficacy associated with success in the classroom. In addition, teaching is a career that has limited opportunities for career growth within the classroom, and professional development and coaching provide mechanisms to support continuous learning that is associated with a fulfilling career. Professional development and coaching allow teachers to grow in their existing practice as well as to test out new approaches.

As we highlighted in Chapter 1, schools can only succeed if teachers are well-trained and well-supported and are viewed as critical organizational assets. Thus far, we have provided information about how to build structures and supports to attract and retain effective teachers, create a world-class work experience to foster high-quality teacher work, and facilitate the transition of new teachers into the school through carefully designed onboarding and orientation programming.

But preservice training and induction is just the beginning. Throughout their careers, the best teachers continue to learn and refine their craft. In addition to the value of honing teaching skills, continuous teacher learning provides opportunities for teacher leadership development and models the importance of continuous learning and risk-taking as teachers work to improve their practice. In this way, they model for students and peers a willingness to continue to invest in their own learning and take risks to improve. Professional development and coaching strengthen teacher capacity by providing opportunities for teachers to continue to learn and grow.

PROFESSIONAL DEVELOPMENT

Historically, professional development for teachers included opportunities to attend conferences, lectures, book studies, and hands-on training during staff meetings. Researchers studying the effectiveness of professional development found that while teachers often enjoyed opportunities to step outside their classrooms and learn new techniques, once they went back to their classrooms, this new knowledge rarely translated into changes in teaching practice (Darling-Hammond et al., 2017). Often, attending a professional development session sparked new ideas and energized teachers, but back in the classroom, there was limited time and support to try out new techniques and no one to hold them accountable for implementing new methods (Guskey, 2002).

Professional development can only improve teaching practice if teachers use the information they receive. Over time, a recognition of the importance of implementing new ideas into classroom practice led to changes in the design and evaluation of professional development programs. Instead of judging the professional development based on how inspired or satisfied teachers felt when they left the program, researchers recommend focusing on the impact of the professional development on classroom practice and improved student learning.

This research helped to shift the landscape of teacher professional development from "sit and get" programming to more long-term, job-embedded professional learning, rooted in practical application. Traditional teacher professional development programs were delivered in the form of workshops, seminars, conferences, or courses (Ono & Ferreira, 2010). Researchers have been critical of these methods as "being brief, fragmented, incoherent encounters that are decontextualized and isolated from real classroom situations" (Ono & Ferreira, 2010, p. 60). Further, 30 years ago, Linda Darling-Hammond observed that professional development needed to go beyond merely supporting teachers to acquire new knowledge or skills. She and other scholars have argued for professional development that provides opportunities for teachers to reflect on their teaching practices and to build new beliefs about content-based pedagogy and student learning (Darling-Hammond & McLaughlin, 1995).

In a review of 35 research studies that noted a link between professional development, teaching practices, and student outcomes, Darling-Hammond et al. (2017) found that successful programs shared specific design features, which are shown in Table 7.1.

These features, combined with opportunities for teachers to participate in professional learning communities, provided a strong and sustained opportunity for growth and development.

Table 7.1 Characteristics of High-Quality Professional Development Programs

Are Content-Focused
Incorporate Active Learning
Support Collaboration
Use Reflection
Are Sustained in Duration

Source: Darling-Hammond et al. (2017)

As it emerged through intensive study of professional development programs, this concept of teacher professional development represented a significant shift towards professional development as a long-term, job-embedded process that involves regular opportunities for teacher learning, reflection, and growth. The shift was so profound that scholars described it as a "new paradigm" of professional development (Villegas-Reimers, 2003; Cochran-Smith & Lytle, 2001; Walling & Lewis, 2000).

BOX 7.1: TEACHER PROFESSIONAL DEVELOPMENT

In 2004, Heather Hill and Deborah Ball conducted an evaluation of the California Mathematics Professional Development Institutes, a professional development program focused on how to teach math, in which teachers participated in 40 to 120 hours of training over the summer and an additional 80 hours of follow-up during the school year. Teachers received a $1,500 stipend for participating in the training. The training focused on in-depth teaching of a math topic (such as long division) in the morning and discussion of the relationship of that topic to teaching practice and standards in the afternoon, including specific activities teachers could use to teach that topic in their classroom. The focus enabled teachers to learn both math content and math pedagogy. Hill and Ball developed an instrument to assess teachers' knowledge of math content and math pedagogy before and after the training and found that professional development with this approach and duration can effectively increase teachers' math pedagogical content knowledge. The authors noted that a key challenge in evaluating professional development is having instruments that can directly assess teacher learning (Hill & Ball, 2004).

Discussion Questions: Consider a professional development program you have participated in. What features of the program were consistent with the design features described by Hill and Ball? How would you directly assess your learning or changes in practice resulting from the training?

New approaches to professional development provide a greater emphasis on viewing teachers as reflective practitioners who make informed professional choices. With this emphasis on reflective practice, teachers are positioned as active participants in their own learning and growth (Girvan et al., 2016).

Professional development can have a profound impact on the practice of teachers who participate, but the effects of professional development can also extend beyond the participating teachers. Teams of teachers within a school also benefit from the enhanced expertise of one of their members, as teachers who have participated in professional learning opportunities bring that knowledge back to discussions within their teacher teams and in conversations with colleagues. Researchers who studied teachers who participated in an intensive professional development experience in writing found significant spillover effects, with teacher colleagues learning from those who participated in the training. In fact, the spillover effects on teaching practice were sometimes as large as the direct effects of participation (Sun et al., 2013)!

THE PRINCIPAL'S ROLE IN PROMOTING TEACHER LEARNING

The importance of high-quality professional development as a mechanism for talent development and talent management has been well-established. The best professional development is designed as a part of the larger organizational system. As the leader of that system, the principal plays a central role in designing high-quality professional development opportunities. Bredeson (2003) uses the metaphor of architecture to highlight the critical importance of attention to professional development design elements. Bredeson notes that:

> High-quality professional development: (1) focuses on teachers as central to student learning, yet includes all other members of the school community; (2) focuses on individual, collegial, and organizational improvement; (3) respects and nurtures the intellectual and leadership capacity of teachers, principals, and others, in the school community; (4) reflects the best available research and practice in teaching, learning, and leadership; (5) enables teachers to develop further expertise in subject content, teaching strategies, uses of technologies, and other essential elements in teaching to high standards; (6) promotes continuous inquiry and improvement embedded in the daily life of schools; (7) is planned collaboratively by those who will participate in and facilitate that development; (8) requires substantial time and other resources; (9) is driven by a coherent long-term plan; (10) is evaluated ultimately on the basis of its impact on teacher effectiveness and student learning, and this assessment guides subsequent professional development efforts.
>
> (Bredeson, 2002, p. 665)

Principals and their leadership teams are in a unique position to leverage school-level data to assess the professional development needs of teachers. By examining student learning data with a leadership or data team, the principal can lead an assessment of what the data suggest about teacher learning needs in areas where students are not progressing as much as should be desired or expected. As the lead teacher evaluator, principals can leverage their understanding of teaching practice across the school to identify areas where teachers could use support to improve their practice. The principal is also positioned to understand and assess the needs of newer teachers, who may enter the school after other teachers have all received training around school or district curricular initiatives or may need training to more fully develop specific aspects of their knowledge and skills to perform effectively.

For professional development to meaningfully impact student learning, it needs to be integrated with the instructional design and curriculum; designed based on data analysis about the learning needs of students and on the knowledge and skill gaps of teachers; and integrated with evaluation systems for teachers and students. In designing professional development opportunities, the principal should actively seek information to understand existing levels of knowledge and skill to determine which teachers need which specific types of developmental support to move the school forward. Professional development activities can be targeted towards stages of the teacher's career or to levels of skill development. Teachers who are experts in important elements of practice could be identified to lead professional development for other teachers in the school. The opportunity to lead professional learning activities is also an important opportunity for teacher leadership development.

A perpetual challenge in schools is the limited amount of "student-free" time teachers have so that they can focus on their own learning needs. Darling-Hammond (1995) suggests that principals should take advantage of opportunities to weave professional development into multiple aspects of school routines. She argues that "everything that goes on in school presents an opportunity for professional development." For example, faculty meetings can be utilized as an opportunity to engage faculty members in examination of their own students' work and their curriculum plans. Other typically mundane or tedious tasks "such as student assignments or the creation of a master schedule, contain opportunities to reflect on norms, assumptions about practice, and organizational goals."

Leveraging existing meetings for teacher learning signals to teachers the importance of continuous learning as a core value of the school's culture. The principal can also communicate a culture of learning by modeling their own learning, joining as an active participant in schoolwide professional development activities (Halverson & Kelley, 2017).

STATE AND DISTRICT ROLES IN PROMOTING TEACHER LEARNING

States and school districts are also responsible for creating "the conditions in schools through which teachers can become experts at teaching the curriculum they are using and adapting instruction to the needs of their particular students"

(Wiener & Pimentel, 2017, p. 2). Structures that support teacher learning include clear and consistent curriculum standards and aligned assessments. Assessment outcomes need to be regularly examined to identify gaps in student learning at the school and classroom levels. Teachers need to have the time and resources to collaboratively assess student learning outcomes at a fine-grained level so that they can identify gaps in student understanding and backward map to determine professional learning opportunities needed to address the learning needs of teachers that are critical for closing those gaps.

It takes consistent leadership direction to enable a school to operate as an effective learning organization (Senge, 2006). The curriculum and aligned assessment need to be in place long enough to be able to evaluate student performance on the standards underlying the curriculum. Teachers then adjust their teaching to address student learning gaps. If students are unable to improve performance after teachers have honed their teaching practice, there may be a need for focused professional development to address teacher knowledge and skill gaps that are contributing to student learning gaps. The new professional development needs to be provided consistently over time, with opportunities for teachers to try out new approaches and test whether the new methods lead to improved student learning outcomes. The district can support teacher professional learning by consistently holding principals accountable for student learning outcomes and by providing resources (e.g., teacher time, training opportunities) to support teacher professional learning. Wiener and Pimentel (2017) describe an improvement cycle in which curriculum can be integrated with teacher professional learning. Teachers can begin this improvement cycle by creating "engaging learning environments" and delivering high-quality instruction. Assessment provides information to identify student learning needs. The assessment information informs the design of professional learning and focuses instructional improvement efforts. Teachers leverage assessment information and professional learning opportunities to continuously fine-tune their teaching craft. In this way, curriculum and assessment help to continuously inform and shape professional learning opportunities and instructional design efforts.

Another obvious pathway to assessing teacher learning needs is through teacher performance evaluation. As we discuss in Chapter 9, unfortunately, teacher performance evaluation often lacks the rigor, consistency, and focus needed to meaningfully inform teacher professional learning. However, evaluation systems can be important potential sources of information and feedback for teachers to focus their efforts to improve instructional practice and to school and district leaders to provide system-level information to inform professional development.

Teacher evaluation typically focuses on the individual teacher, but if evaluation processes are rigorous, standards-based, and have strong inter-rater reliability, they could be used to identify consistent areas of growth across teachers to inform investment and design of professional development opportunities. In a study of the role of teacher evaluation in promoting teacher learning, Maslow and Kelley (2012) describe a district that leveraged teacher evaluation data to inform professional development. The district invested heavily in evaluator training and studied evaluation data as an important source of information to promote school improvement. In that district, teachers identified district-sponsored professional development as their most valuable source of professional learning. In other districts, district-sponsored professional development was largely viewed as a waste of time because it failed to acknowledge and build on teacher learning needs and existing teacher expertise.

The need to extend the learning in professional development programming to the classroom has led some districts to expand support for teacher learning to more individualized, classroom-based support. Next, we turn to coaching as an individualized approach to supporting teacher learning.

COACHING

Coaching is an evidence-based practice that can improve teaching quality and student learning (Blazar & Kraft, 2015; Desimone & Pak, 2017; Kraft & Blazar, 2017). While professional development programs typically serve groups of teachers, coaching provides an opportunity for teachers to work one-on-one with an expert instructor who can observe, model lessons, and provide feedback to improve teaching practice. Coaches may also play a role in more systemic change by working with teams of teachers, whole schools, or districts to support teachers in implementing new curricula or instructional practices to support reform efforts (Hopkins et al., 2017).

Models of coaching for teachers include instructional coaching, content-focused coaching, and cognitive coaching. Instructional coaching is the broadest of the three approaches, focusing on behavior, content, instruction, and formative assessment (Knight, 2018). Content-focused coaching examines student learning in a particular subject area and the teacher's lesson plans, instructional strategies, and methods to influence learning in that subject. Cognitive coaching assumes that teacher thought patterns shape instruction, so the coaching focuses on revealing and then changing or disrupting thought patterns to change teaching practice. All three types of coaching typically use a three-stage cycle, including a pre-lesson conference, lesson observation, and post-lesson conference (Bengo, 2016).

BOX 7.1: KEY QUESTION

Think about a time that you have been coached (this could occur in a variety of settings). Was your coach effective or ineffective and why? What leadership qualities did this coach demonstrate? How can these attributes be translated to instructional coaching?

Research on coaching in mathematics (Knight et al., 2016; Obara, 2010; Hull et al., 2009) has shown that effective coaches are expert teachers with excellent "communication skills, leadership skills, pedagogical content knowledge, content knowledge, [and] curriculum knowledge" and ability to work with adults (Bengo, 2016, p. 89).

CONDITIONS FOR SUCCESS AND COACHING CHALLENGES

At its best, instructional coaching is a partnership between teacher and coach. The teacher and coach need to have a strong trust relationship in order for the teacher to be willing to take risks and share vulnerabilities. Because it is important that the teacher is a willing participant, many coaches take a humanistic approach to working with teachers. They first spend time building strong positive relationships with teachers, then they seek volunteers willing to work with them, and gradually, as the word spreads through the school, more teachers step up and volunteer to be coached. The ability to build positive working relationships with teachers is clearly an important skill of an instructional coach (Devine et al., 2013).

This model of coaching enables the teacher to determine the focus of coaching sessions in collaboration with the coach so that the coaching sessions focus on areas of practical concern to the teacher. As a TCEL practice, the ability of teachers to determine the focus of the coaching sessions is a strength. Enabling teachers to work on issues of concern to them is likely to motivate engagement with the coach, enhance teacher efficacy, and make teachers feel more valued by their employer.

But this model of coaching is not always possible. For instance, the district may have invested in coaching because it wants to speed up and ensure high-quality implementation of new standards or curricular reforms. The district may want coaches to proactively address specific challenges that have been identified with achievement, such as the success of English-language learners, or disparities in student access or achievement. Coaches may also be assigned to teachers who have been identified to be struggling with their performance in the classroom. In these situations, it is critical that there is a clear established expectation that teachers will work with the coach and that the exchange between teacher and coach will remain confidential. In these examples, an effective coach will establish clear parameters for the focus of their work with teachers while working to be responsive to teacher learning needs. Researchers have documented examples of instructional coaches successfully working with entire school faculties to implement curricular reforms (Gibbons et al., 2017).

Because of the importance of trust in the coaching relationship, the research literature typically recommends that coaches not have a supervisory role over the teachers they are coaching; otherwise, the teacher might be reluctant to be open with areas of strengths and needed support. In this model, the principal and the coach agree that the coach will be able to work with teachers in confidence and not be asked to provide details to inform performance evaluations of teachers (Mette et al., 2017), which will hopefully spur more candid dialogue between the coach and teacher.

Coaching is an effective way of embedding professional learning into teachers' daily practice. However, coaches need time to successfully work with teachers. Studies have found that instructional coaches spend large proportions of their time on administrative or logistical tasks, such as attending meetings, administering assessments, or substitute teaching, resulting in a lack of time for coaching to work directly with teachers on issues of instruction (Campbell & Griffin, 2017; Kane & Rosenquist, 2019; Knight & van Nieuwerburgh, 2012). Principals and coaches need to have a clear plan and clear understanding of how the coaches will spend their time, and this time should be protected for working directly with teachers.

BOX 7.2: WHEN IT'S NOT ROSY: ROUGH SAILING FOR THE NEW COACH

Concerned about the lack of success for their English-language learners, the Midtown School District hired Sandy Jones, a successful teacher from a nearby district, to serve as an instructional coach for Northeast High School. She has been tasked with working with teachers to support improvements in instruction, particularly with English-language learners, who make up 12% of the Northeast High population. The principal introduced Sandy to the staff but made it clear to the teachers that it was up to them (i.e., voluntary) if they wanted to work with her. Three months into the year, no expectations have been established for teachers to work with the coach. In addition, the principal has left Sandy to her own devices and has not talked to her about her role as coach or how it connects to the broader goals of the school. Sandy has tried to talk to teachers in their teacher teams and before and after school, and she has invited them through email to reach out to her for coaching support, but so far, the teachers have shown limited interest. Sandy is hopeful that her colleagues will show some interest soon, but she spends most of her time reviewing literature on best practices in ELL instruction.

Discussion Questions: How would you rewrite the introduction of the instructional coach to the school to set her up for success? Why might the principal not want to advocate for the new coach? Should the principal or district require teacher participation? Why or why not? Please rationalize and justify your response based on ethical, legal, professional, and/or leadership frameworks.

THE PRINCIPAL'S ROLE IN FACILITATING COACHING SUCCESS

As we have discussed, to be effective, coaching requires a high level of trust. The teacher needs to be willing to be vulnerable in letting the coach into their professional space, sharing their concerns about their teaching practice. They need to trust the coach to maintain confidentiality. They need to believe in the coach's expertise and abilities.

The principal can play an important role in establishing the conditions for success by:

- *Including teacher voice in coaching implementation*: Ensuring that teachers have a voice in what coaching looks like at the school level can make coaching practices more effective and can also prevent future conflict and misunderstandings. What do teachers want to gain from coaching? What coaching model works best for them? It would also be beneficial for the coaches and the principals to be on the same page from the beginning and for principals to share power with coaches by treating them as partners. Once the principal and coach have established a partnership, they should present their initial vision of the coaching model to the staff, then give teachers the opportunity to offer feedback and help them refine their vision:

  > If the principal and coach take the time to engage teachers in the design of the coaching work, they are likely to find that teachers are not only more amenable to coaching, but that teachers can help them refine the plan.
  >
  > (West, 2017, p. 315)

- *Fostering a continuous learning environment:* For any professional development or coaching model to be effective, school leaders must foster a school culture that is conducive to taking risks and to continuous learning:

  > Coaching requires teachers to be willing to open themselves to critique and recognize personal weaknesses. This openness on the part of teachers is facilitated both by a school culture committed to continuous improvement and by strong relational trust among administrators and staff members.
  >
  > (Kraft et al., 2018, p. 574)

  One way to encourage this school culture is by modeling: Principals and coaches who are learners take public risks (West, 2017). This may include volunteering to teach a class using a new technique and asking teachers for their feedback. Coaches must not only exhibit the ability to work with and teach teachers but also demonstrate that they have ability *as* teachers and show that they are unafraid to take the same risks that they are asking of the teachers. Modeling can build trust among staff members in that teachers are not the only ones who are asked to take risks. In a school with a culture of continuous learning, *all* parties are continuously learning and growing.

- *Establishing a full-school culture of learning and growing*: This atmosphere of continuous development can also alleviate issues that may arise from teachers perceiving that they are receiving coaching for "remedial" purposes. When this culture is in place, all teachers become more accustomed to receiving feedback and learning from coaching rather than feeling that they have done something wrong to "need" coaching. If coaching is integrated into many aspects of the school, it can be leveraged to meet varying needs as they arise.
- *Ensuring relevancy and cohesion:* Coaching and professional development should be integrated into the school in many ways. First of all, these opportunities should have clear and direct links with classroom practice. The greater relevance that professional development has to teachers' in-classroom practice, the more potentially effective it will be. Further, principals should ensure that professional development opportunities are cohesive with other similar opportunities as well as making sure these sessions support the overall school vision and mission. There is a danger in providing disparate professional development opportunities for teachers, in that it may become overwhelming for teachers and create a lack of coherence within the school. Consistent messaging is essential to improving teacher practice.

  Teachers should also be provided the opportunity to adapt what they have learned to their specific contexts (Girvan et al., 2016). Coaching is one way to encourage teachers to apply new skills in their classrooms. Additionally, coaching and professional development can be integrated into the school through grade-level teams. Having coaches work with grade-level teams is one way to encourage collective learning. Coaches working with teams of teachers can help to encourage consistency of instructional practices based on the coach's messaging.

  Consistent messaging and communication are all the more important when coaches are from outside the building and are district-assigned. Principals must clearly communicate with coaches to establish clear expectations as well as communicate with teachers to set expectations. Principals should not only rely on district-appointed coaches to provide teachers with the PD they need; additional supports, with consistent messaging, should be provided to help teachers improve instructional practices.

Learning Activities

Discussion Questions:

1. If you were to design professional development programming for your school, what would it look like? What characteristics would you be sure to include in order to design for success? How would you measure success?
2. What are three ways you could design professional development opportunities to address the needs and skill levels of all your teachers – from the least experienced or skilled teacher to those who are highly experienced or highly skilled?

3. Coaches are typically positioned as intermediaries who support teachers in a nonevaluative manner as opposed to administrators who have authority to formally supervise teachers. How do administrators effectively navigate their relationship with both coaches and teachers in order to improve teaching practices and raise student achievement?
4. Should you require coaching or let teachers decide if they want to be coached? How can you require coaching for remediation and intervention without stigmatizing being coached as a punishment or remediation activity?
5. Professional development also matters for coaches, principals, and district leaders: How would professional development for coaches, principals, and district leaders look different than professional development for teachers? Are there elements that would remain the same? What qualities make any level of professional development successful?

CONCLUSION

Professional development and coaching are important design features of a learning organization. Evidence-based professional development is content-focused, incorporates active learning, supports teacher collaboration, uses reflection, and is of a sustained duration. The best professional development is job-embedded; it enables teachers to apply what they learn in the classroom, problem-solve with other teachers, or work with a coach to refine new practices. Coaching provides opportunities to work with an expert instructor one-on-one to improve classroom practice or implement new approaches. Coaches can support remediation, but the coach needs to be able to establish a strong positive working relationship with the teacher to be most effective.

Summary of Key Points

- Professional development and coaching provide opportunities for growth and development throughout the teaching career to address skill gaps and to enable teachers to build a sense of teaching efficacy associated with success in the classroom.
- Professional development design has evolved towards a long-term, job-embedded process that involves regular opportunities for teacher learning, reflection, and growth.
- States and districts are important partners in professional development. By establishing clear standards, aligned assessments, and accountability systems that are high-quality and stable over time, state and district policymakers provide clear targets against which to design and measure the success of professional development in improving teaching practice.
- Coaching is an evidence-based practice that can improve teaching quality and student learning. While professional development programs typically

serve larger groups of teachers, coaching provides an opportunity for teachers to work one-on-one with an expert instructor who can observe, model lessons, and provide feedback to improve teaching practice.
- The principal plays an important role in building a shared understanding in the school about the role of the instructional coach, setting expectations for participation in coaching, and ensuring that the coach's time is preserved for coaching and not siphoned away to other activities in the school.

REFERENCES

Bengo, P. (2016). Secondary mathematics coaching: The components of effective mathematics coaching and implications. *Teaching and Teacher Education, 60,* 88–96.

Blazar, D., & Kraft, M. A. (2015). Exploring mechanisms of effective teacher coaching: A tale of two cohorts from a randomized experiment. *Educational Evaluation and Policy Analysis, 37*(4), 542–566.

Bredeson, P. V. (2002). The architecture of professional development: Materials, messages and meaning. *International Journal of Educational Research, 37*(8), 661–675.

Bredeson, P. V. (2003). *Designs for learning: A new architecture for professional development in schools.* Corwin Press.

Bredeson, P. V., & Johansson, O. (2000). The school principal's role in teacher professional development. *Journal of In-Service Education, 26*(2), 385–401.

Campbell, P. F., & Griffin, M. J. (2017). Reflections on the promise and complexity of mathematics coaching. *The Journal of Mathematical Behavior, 46,* 163–176.

Cochran-Smith, M., & Lytle, S. L. (2001). Beyond certainty: Taking an inquiry stance on practice. In *Teachers caught in the action: Professional development that matters* (pp. 45–58). Teachers College Press.

Darling-Hammond, L. (1995). Changing conceptions of teaching and teacher development. *Teacher Education Quarterly,* 9–26.

Darling-Hammond, L., Hyler, M. E., & Gardner, M. (2017). *Effective teacher professional development.* Learning Policy Institute.

Darling-Hammond, L., & McLaughlin, M. W. (1995). Policies that support professional development in an era of reform. *Phi Delta Kappan, 76*(8), 597–604.

Desimone, L. M., & Pak, K. (2017). Instructional coaching as high-quality professional development. *Theory into Practice, 56*(1), 3–12.

Devine, M., Houssemand, C., & Meyers, R. (2013). Instructional coaching for teachers: A strategy to implement new practices in the classrooms. *Procedia-Social and Behavioral Sciences, 93,* 1126–1130.

Gibbons, L. K., Kazemi, E., & Lewis, R. M. (2017). Developing collective capacity to improve mathematics instruction: Coaching as a lever for school-wide improvement. *The Journal of Mathematical Behavior, 46,* 231–250.

Girvan, C., Conneely, C., & Tangney, B. (2016). Extending experiential learning in teacher professional development. *Teaching and Teacher Education, 58,* 129–139.

Guskey, T. R. (2002). Does it make a difference? Evaluating professional development. *Educational Leadership, 59*(6), 45.

Halverson, R., & Kelley, C. (2017). *Mapping leadership: The tasks that matter for improving teaching and learning in schools.* Jossey-Bass.

Hill, H. C., & Ball, D. L. (2004). Learning mathematics for teaching: Results from California's mathematics professional development institutes. *Journal for Research in Mathematics Education*, 330–351.

Hopkins, M., Ozimek, D., & Sweet, T. M. (2017). Mathematics coaching and instructional reform: Individual and collective change. *The Journal of Mathematical Behavior, 46*, 215–230.

Hull, T. H., Balka, D. S., & Miles, R. H. (2009). *A guide to mathematics coaching: Processes for increasing student achievement*. SAGE.

Kane, B. D., & Rosenquist, B. (2019). Relationships between instructional coaches' time use and district-and school-level policies and expectations. *American Educational Research Journal, 56*(5), 1718–1768.

Knight, D. S., Hock, M., & Knight, J. (2016). Designing instructional coaching. *Instructional-Design Theories and Models: A Learner-Centered Paradigm of Education, 4*, 269–286.

Knight, J. (2018). Coaching to improve teaching: Using the instructional coaching model. In *Coaching in education* (pp. 93–113). Routledge.

Knight, J., & van Nieuwerburgh, C. (2012). Instructional coaching: A focus on practice. *Coaching: An International Journal of Theory, Research and Practice, 5*(2), 100–112.

Kraft, M. A., & Blazar, D. (2017). Individualized coaching to improve teacher practice across grades and subjects: New experimental evidence. *Educational Policy, 31*(7), 1033–1068.

Kraft, M. A., Blazar, D., & Hogan, D. (2018). The effect of teacher coaching on instruction and achievement: A meta-analysis of the causal evidence. *Review of Educational Research, 88*(4), 547–588.

Maslow, V. J., & Kelley, C. J. (2012). Does evaluation advance teaching practice? The effects of performance evaluation on teaching quality and system change in large diverse high schools. *Journal of School Leadership, 22*(3), 600–632.

Mette, I. M., Range, B. G., Anderson, J., Hvidston, D. J., Nieuwenhuizen, L., & Doty, J. (2017). The wicked problem of the intersection between supervision and evaluation. *International Electronic Journal of Elementary Education, 9*(3), 709–724. www.iejee.com/index.php/IEJEE/article/view/185

Obara, S. (2010). Mathematics coaching: A new kind of professional development. *Teacher Development, 14*(2), 241–251.

Ono, Y., & Ferreira, J. (2010). A case study of continuing teacher professional development through lesson study in South Africa. *South African Journal of Education, 30*(1).

Senge, P. M. (2006). *The fifth discipline: The art and practice of the learning organization*. Currency.

Sun, M., Penuel, W. R., Frank, K. A., Gallagher, H. A., & Youngs, P. (2013). Shaping professional development to promote the diffusion of instructional expertise among teachers. *Educational Evaluation and Policy Analysis, 35*(3), 344–369.

Villegas-Reimers, E. (2003). *Teacher professional development: An international review of the literature*. International Institute for Educational Planning.

Walling, B., & Lewis, M. (2000). Development of professional identity among professional development school preservice teachers: Longitudinal and comparative analysis. *Action in Teacher Education, 22*(suppl. 2), 65–72.

West, L. (2017). Principal and coach as partners. *The Journal of Mathematical Behavior, 46*, 313–320.

Wiener, R., & Pimentel, S. (2017). *Practice what you teach: Connecting curriculum & professional learning in schools*. Aspen Institute.

CHAPTER 8

Communities of Practice

Chapter Summary

This chapter reviews the rich history of research that examines the importance of teacher social relationships and opportunities for collective problem-solving as mechanisms that support teacher learning and improve student achievement outcomes. The chapter draws on research, practice, and theory related to communities of practice and teacher social networks to inform the management of schools and provide guidance to current and aspiring school leaders. The chapter also provides case study examples and discussion questions for readers to consider.

> *Effective leaders foster continuous improvement of individual and collective instructional capacity to achieve outcomes envisioned for each student.*
>
> (PSEL Standard 6d)

INTRODUCTION

Teaching is a complex task, and despite the siloed nature of schools, teachers greatly benefit from opportunities for collaboration with their colleagues. In the 1990s, researchers identified *professional community* as an important feature of high-performing and successfully restructuring schools (Bryk et al., 1999; DuFour & Eaker, 1998; Hord, 1997; Louis, 2006; Louis & Marks, 1998; Newmann & Associates, 1996; Rosenholtz, 1991). We use Bryk et al.'s (1999) definition of professional community "to refer to schools in which interaction

DOI: 10.4324/9781003457060-11

among teachers is frequent and teachers' actions are governed by shared norms focused on the practice and improvement of teaching and learning" (p. 753).

Schools exhibiting professional community are characterized by teachers working together to address problems of practice through:

- "reflective dialogue among teachers about instructional practices and student learning;"
- "deprivatization of practice in which teachers observe each others' practices" and problem solve together; and
- "peer collaboration in which teachers engage in actual shared work."

(Bryk et al., 1999, p. 753)

DuFour and Eaker (1998) brought attention to the ways that principals and district leaders can build and support *professional learning communities* (PLCs) among teachers in their schools. DuFour recommended structuring teacher time to support collaborative teams of teachers organized around grade level or content area. The teams were designed to have a *shared purpose* focused on high academic expectations for students; a *shared mission* of creating the structures and cultures to support student learning; *collective commitment* to the goals of supporting student learning; and *shared goals* around specific indicators of student learning to support progress monitoring (see DuFour, 2004; DuFour & DuFour, 2013).

In short, PLCs break down silos and provide opportunities for teachers to build shared pedagogical content knowledge, analyze student work, and strengthen teaching practice. The next section examines the rich body of theoretical and empirical evidence to support the importance of professional learning communities and to explain why they yield so much potential to advance teacher and student learning.

THEORETICAL FOUNDATIONS OF PROFESSIONAL COMMUNITY

Two theoretical traditions provide support for the power of professional communities and their important role in knowledge development and production in schools. Thus, we turn to an introduction to social capital theory and sociocultural theory.

Social Capital Theory

Social capital theory was introduced by two distinct scholars – James Coleman and Pierre Bourdieu – at about the same time, with different origin stories, but quite similar meanings. James Coleman developed the idea of social capital by drawing from economic and sociological theories to posit social capital as a third category of capital in addition to physical and human capital. To Coleman, social capital exists in the relationships between people that facilitate action. In essence, relationship networks reduce transaction costs and provide access to exchanges of information, resources, and trust that promote both human and physical capital. Social capital provides a mechanism for agency by enabling an individual to build or be a part of relationship networks that facilitate capital formation (Coleman, 1988).

Bourdieu's slightly different approach emphasizes the inequitable playing field that can arise from unequal access to relationship networks and the cultural capital that supports the development of these relationships (Bourdieu, 1986).

Applying social capital theory to teacher development, within the context of a school organization, by facilitating the development of relationships between educators, leaders enhance opportunities for problem-solving and information and resource sharing, which, in turn, facilitates teacher learning and improvement of instructional practice.

Research affirms the positive relationship between teacher social interaction and teacher learning and student achievement. Recent advances in social network theory and social network analysis have enriched our understanding of how teacher social interactions in schools support teacher innovation, motivation, problem-solving, reform implementation (Blanc et al., 2010; Daly et al., 2014), and ultimately, student achievement (Lomos et al., 2011; Louis & Marks, 1998; Penuel et al., 2009).

Sociocultural Learning Theory

Sociocultural learning theory was introduced by Lev Vygotsky in the 1930s. Vygotsky drew from psychological and sociological theories to develop ideas about how people learn. Specifically, sociocultural learning theory posits that cognition occurs in a specific social and historical context. Individuals interact with others to socially negotiate meaning. Knowledge construction does not occur in the mind, but instead, it occurs through social interactions, particularly between more and less knowledgeable individuals. Vygotsky introduced the concept of the zone of proximal development, which is the space between what a learner can do without assistance versus in collaboration with more capable peers. To Vygotsky, meaning is derived from experience, and each individual develops their own sense of meaning from an act while explaining it to others (Vygotsky, 1978).

Sociocultural learning theory and social capital theory both suggest that the opportunity for teachers to work together to discuss problems of practice provides an essential tool for teacher learning. By teaching others, teachers make meaning of their teaching practice and provide rich opportunities for other teachers to learn and grow. By developing strong trust relationships with their peers, teachers build social capital that they can draw on to promote their own human capital. Clearly, there are strong theoretical foundations and emerging empirical research to support the importance of fostering strong relationships among teachers in a school to promote teacher learning. In the next section, we turn to research by Etienne Wenger and his colleagues, who provide guidance on how to foster communities of practice to facilitate teacher learning and growth (Lave & Wenger, 1991; Wenger, 1998).

COMMUNITIES OF PRACTICE

Communities of practice (COP) are characterized by three structural elements: first, they are grounded in a *practice*, which is situated in a specific social, cultural, and historical context that gives it meaning. Second, members come together to constitute a *community* that forms around a shared interest. Third, the members share expertise in a particular professional or knowledge *domain*. Members of the community interact, problem-solve, and learn together. They build expertise and resources that enable them to solve or address shared problems of practice (see https://wenger-traynor.com; Lave & Wenger, 1991; Wenger, 1998; Wenger et al., 2002).

While communities of practice exist across many domains, they represent a familiar organizational form in education as teams of teachers come together in many schools to share ideas and work together to solve problems of practice. Data teams, grade-level teams, subject-area teams, and leadership teams all represent examples of efforts to formalize communities of practice in schools.

BOX 8.1: COMMUNITY OF PRACTICE EXAMPLE

Midtown Middle School's fourth-grade math teachers (the community) represent a community of practice with expertise in mathematics education (the domain) and meet together weekly to strengthen the curriculum. For the next several meetings, they are working on developing curricula around word problems (the practice) in order to advance student achievement on the state math test.

Discussion Questions: Can you identify one or more communities of practice in which you are a member? Are they part of a formal organizational structure (such as an academic department), or did they emerge organically from a shared desire to advance a practice? How are they structured? Who participates? How has membership in the community of practice enhanced your work?

Communities of practice emerge out of a desire by like-minded individuals to address a particular problem of practice. Participation in the COP helps to advance the practice, but it also can have a profound impact on members of the community. In researching COPs, Wenger (1998) found that participants built expertise and confidence through shared *learning*. As a result of their work together, they found deeper *meaning* in their work as a member of the community. And over time, they formed a personal *identity* around membership in the COP.

As a Talent-Centered Education Leadership practice, creating opportunities for teachers to engage in COPs can support their development as professionals and can promote a strong attachment to the school community, as teachers are motivated by finding deeper meaning in the work. Ultimately, they may come to link their personal identity to their membership in the COP. Because communities of practice help to build personal commitment to the work and offer a rich opportunity to engage in learning with others, they are an important Talent-Centered Education Leadership practice. Principals should consider how to leverage the power of COPs in their schools. In the next section, we consider what role the principal should play in fostering COPs.

BOX 8.2: KNOWLEDGE COMMUNITIES AT STATE FARM INSURANCE

Like many private companies, State Farm Insurance began to pay close attention to knowledge management (KM) in the 1990s and decided to develop a network of communities of practice (CP) to better capture and share knowledge within the organization. By building a network of communities of practice and supporting them with information management technology, the company hoped to maintain better access to knowledge when it was needed and to prevent the loss of knowledge and institutional memory associated with employee turnover. Hemmasi and Csanda (2009) studied the communities of practice to assess their impact on job performance and employee satisfaction. As Hemmasi and Csanda (2009) describe,

> State Farm is the largest property and casualty insurance company in the United States and operates in a decentralized structure with 13 zone offices, more than 300 claim offices and contact centers, and 17,000 agents. Recognizing the need for better knowledge sharing and connectivity among these decentralized offices and processing centers, State Farm launched a KM initiative. The centerpiece of this initiative has been the formation of a network of communities of practice with a focus on inducing a greater quantity and quality of intentional collaboration and accelerating the transfer of best practices throughout the organization through the CP network.
>
> (p. 264)

The results of their study show that State Farm employees perceived that participation in a community of practice contributed to enhanced performance through increased access to "the ideas, knowledge, and best practices shared among community members" (Hemmasi and Csanda, 2009, p. 274). The greatest challenge experienced was in finding time for participation in community activities. As members found value in the activities, they made time for participation, which highlights the importance of making sure the community's activities are relevant to the job.

The Principal's Role in Fostering Communities of Practice

Communities of practice can emerge on their own if teachers have a good relationship with their colleagues, are willing to deprivatize practice, and have time to connect either during the school day or before or after school to work on the practice. But because it can be difficult in the context of the school day for teachers to find the time for communities of practice to emerge organically, school leaders can cultivate opportunities for collective problem-solving by creating shared planning time and developing teacher teams to foster collective problem-solving. School leaders can help to shape the focus of problem-setting by working to establish a clear shared mission, vision, and goals for instructional improvement, by creating shared planning time to foster teacher interaction, and by building teacher skills at facilitation so they can effectively lead team meetings.

Principals and department chairs play important leadership roles in establishing the conditions for the success of communities of practice. As Printy (2008) explains,

> Principals who communicate clear vision, support teachers, and buffer them from outside influences – conditions that encourage teachers toward productive learning – positively affect teachers' participation in communities of practice
>
> (p. 211)

> Principals contribute importantly to teachers' social relations and learning when they establish a school vision that can serve as a guide for teachers' joint work, extend support for teachers' efforts, and protect teachers from external interference
>
> (p. 215).

> Strong departmental leaders who communicate expectations, establish goals, secure resources, carry out plans, and promote innovation encourage other teachers toward full community participation
>
> (p. 215).

Wahlstrom and Louis (2008) also identified the importance of shared leadership in professional communities: "Teachers have to *learn* how to successfully interact and it requires initiatives from both teachers and principals to create conditions for rich dialogue about improvement" (p. 463, emphasis in original).

BOX 8.3: TOOLS AND PROTOCOLS FOR EXAMINING PRACTICE

Building an engaged community of practice often requires breaking down established professional norms and building new ones. It also requires a high level of trust and willingness to be vulnerable to colleagues. Teachers may need training, or the school may choose to provide professional support to facilitate deep discussions about teaching practice. Two sources of support for engaging in deep conversations about teacher and student work include resources provided by the National School Reform Faculty[1] and by the Authentic Intellectual Work (AIW) Institute.[2]

The National School Reform Faculty (NSRF) supports the establishment of Critical Friends Groups, a community of practice facilitated by trained coaches in which conversations are guided by protocols that structure and focus conversations and put in place guardrails to ensure that participants feel safe and supported as they engage in critical conversations about practice. The protocols typically include structured questions to guide conversation. Many of the protocols are available to download from the NSRF website.[3]

The AIW Institute grew out of research by Fred Newmann and his colleagues at the University of Wisconsin-Madison. The AIW Institute provides professional consultation and support as well as standards and scoring criteria that can be applied to student work to assess the extent to which the curriculum and assignments support students in engaging in high-quality, rigorous intellectual work. Two books by Newmann, King, and Carmichael (*Authentic Intellectual Work: Improving Teaching for Rigorous Learning*, 2015; and *Teaching for Authentic Intellectual Work: Standards and Scoring Criteria for Teachers' Tasks, Student Performance, and Instruction*, 2009) define authentic intellectual work and provide standards and rubrics that teachers can use to evaluate instruction and student work. These tools can be used to structure teacher conversations and support meaningful critiques of curriculum, pedagogy, and student work.

Discussion Questions: Consider a time that you engaged with others to solve a problem of practice. What kinds of support or conditions needed to be in place to create the conditions for a meaningful, engaged, and collaborative conversation about the work? What challenges did you face, and how did you overcome them?

In addition to leveraging resources from organizations like the National School Reform Faculty and the AIW Institute (see Box 8.3), principals can provide leadership to support communities of practice in their schools. Some specific examples of support that principals can provide include:

- *Establishing a collaborative vision and goals:* The principal should work with teachers and the school community to establish a clear collaborative vision and goals to guide the work occurring in the school, including in communities of practice. Collaborative measurable goals, such as *at least 95% of our students will graduate on time each year,* can help professional communities in the school stay focused on the big picture while also creating space for work towards more immediate goals (Huffman, 2003).
- *Building trust:* The principal should work to provide opportunities for teachers to build trust within their PLCs. Deep improvements in practice require teachers to make themselves vulnerable by sharing their own challenges and participating in conversations to set uncharted directions for improvement. Principals should pay close attention to the dynamics within communities of practice to ensure that teachers feel comfortable and safe sharing challenges and building new futures.
- *Structuring time and providing access to tools:* Principals should provide time in the form of structured opportunities for teachers to meet and work together (both time and space to meet) and resources such as professional learning opportunities, training in facilitation skills, and resources to support critical assessment of teaching and learning in the community of practice (see, e.g., Bryk et al., 1999; Coburn, 2001; Wahlstrom & Louis, 2008).

  One tool that may be helpful is a template for meeting agendas that the community of practice completes at each meeting. This template could provide space for agenda items, decision points, and follow-up, along with identifying who will be responsible for action beyond the meeting. Another helpful tool could provide a suggested time frame for agendas that clearly identify specific objectives at upcoming meetings. For instance, the time frame may suggest that next meeting the teams establish outcome goals for students and in the following meeting they work on developing and identifying common assessments. School leaders must balance providing suggestions and requirements while also allowing teachers the freedom to continue to be the experts in their own communities.
- *Holding communities accountable through artifacts:* School leaders can set requirements for submission of "artifacts" that each community must complete to ensure that communities of practice are making progress and are working towards a common vision of student success. These artifacts may include group norms, essential outcomes, SMART goals (Doran et al., 1981), common assessments, student data, differentiated lesson plans, or meeting minutes.
- *Assessing progress:* Principals can support communities of practice by holding them accountable for processes and progress. For example, the National School Reform Faculty has a survey to assess progress that asks teachers to self-assess five elements of professional community: reflective dialogue, deprivatization of practice, collective focus on student learning, collaboration, and shared norms and values. They also assess human resources and structural support for the community.[4]

BOX 8.4: WHEN IT'S NOT ROSY: DATA-INFORMED IMPROVEMENT

Shaundra Rhymes has accepted a position as the new principal of Nathan Chen Elementary School (ES). She knows from conversations with friends in the district that Chen Elementary has suffered from low expectations for students as well as low achievement. She was excited to bring her experience with PLCs to the school. However, in her initial conversations with the leadership team, she learned that the school already has PLCs in place. The previous principal worked to reorganize the school schedule to provide collaborative planning time. But the leadership team feels that the learning communities are not very effective. Teachers spend time together, but the conversations are not well-directed and often the teams meet and then release themselves back to their own classrooms to catch up on planning.

Worse yet, the previous principal tried to mobilize the school to adopt a new math curriculum, but the PLCs effectively blocked implementation. Only the kindergarten team actually worked to implement the new curriculum. Principal Rhymes turns to consider how to kick-off the year to get things moving in a better direction.

Discussion Questions: What additional data should Principal Rhymes collect to assess the effectiveness of the existing PLCs? What feedback and indicators could help guide her assessment? If her additional data collection confirms the concerns of the leadership team, what should Principal Rhymes do? Build a three-month plan to improve the effectiveness of PLCs at Chen Elementary. Please rationalize and justify your response based on ethical, legal, professional, and leadership frameworks.

CHALLENGES FOR LEADERS

School leaders must grapple with unknown outcomes of PLCs. While PLCs can often be intended to foster school change or help implement a new policy, the outcomes of PLCs may not always be what is expected or desired.

As teachers work together, they begin to build shared understandings and use a common language to discuss problems of practice. PLCs shape collective sensemaking and thereby influence how teachers interpret and respond to new policies. These communities can mobilize teacher knowledge and move schools forward. But the dynamics of the community can also impede reform. In a study of reading reform, Coburn (2001) found that professional communities of teachers developed shared language and understandings that shaped their interpretation of new content standards. Ultimately, the teacher learning communities collectively interpreted the policy, decided whether they would engage or ignore it, and shaped how and whether they would take up the reform in their classrooms. The learning communities served a gatekeeping function, in which teachers interpreted the new policy together and assessed whether it should be taken up. The teachers' prior work together helped to shape consensus within the group about whether the new curriculum standards were appropriate for their grade level or too challenging for their students and whether it was comprehensible, manageable, or unmanageable. When teachers decided that the policy passed this gatekeeping function, teacher learning communities examined the technical and practical details of the policy and worked together to figure out how best to implement it.

Depending on the dynamics of the specific team, communities of practice support innovation and reform, or they can serve to undermine it. As Printy (2008) notes:

> It is important to acknowledge that communities of practice, which have the potential for productive change and innovation, are just as likely to perpetuate stereotypes, prejudice, and staid or destructive practices (Orr, 1996; Wenger, 1998). Particularly where the community is tightly bonded as a result of shared values, learning is likely to confirm the "rightness of existing thought and action" rather than open collective or individual practices to inspection and modification.
>
> (Knight, 2002, p. 233)

School leaders can mitigate these negative effects by maintaining an active leadership presence in the school's professional learning communities. Principals, assistant principals, department chairs, and instructional coaches can attend or rotate through professional learning communities and pay attention to the potential for detrimental shifts in practice or culture. The principal can leverage professional development opportunities to build shared values and keep the potential for the development of destructive cultures or practices in check.

School leaders must also understand that PLCs are not the only way in which teachers will engage in collective sensemaking. It is important to allow space and time for teachers to still engage in their own informal professional communities. Craig's (2009) study brought forth the idea that when enforcing PLCs, teachers may feel forced to walk "the administrative party line and being accountable to that line" (p. 614) as opposed to feeling empowered to utilize the knowledge they already possess in a way that is beneficial to them. When outcome requirements are part of PLCs, it is important to co-develop outcomes with teachers, in a way that is important to them. Forcing requirements upon teachers without having teacher voice in creating the requirements can lead to resentment, nonexistent buy-in, and/or a lack of trust between teachers and administrators. For PLCs to be fruitful and productive, it is important to create and implement shared expectations and requirements.

In isolation, teachers in learning communities will try to make sense of new policies themselves. Principals can and should play an important role in helping to build collective understanding to support this sensemaking process.

Learning Activities

Discussion Questions:

1. In what ways are communities of practice a strategic human resources management tool? What outcomes do they produce that are desired by school employers?
2. How will you know if a community of practice is successful? By what measures should a community of practice be judged or supported?
3. Setting aside time for teachers to participate in communities of practice can be tough. How will you ensure this time is available on a regular basis? What are the trade-offs for creating time for teacher collaboration by taking away individual planning time, creating shorter days for students, or setting aside whole workdays within the year? How will you balance the need for collaborative planning time with other important time demands? How will this decision be made?
4. What should you hold your communities of practice accountable for? How much of their time should be self-directed versus having their agenda set by the principal?
5. How would you balance the need for teachers to self-identify what their community of practice focuses on (based on their own insights and observations) versus providing them leadership-directed assignments that will advance the goals of the school?

CONCLUSION

The opportunity to collaborate with others is an important contributor to workplace satisfaction. When teachers are provided the opportunity – including the time and the guidance – to collaborate with one another, they may be more likely to stay and grow in the school and in the profession. Ultimately, organizing communities of practice for teachers can be a powerful tool for teachers' professional development, for student success, and for retaining strong teachers.

Summary of Key Points

- Communities of practice emerge when a group of individuals who share expertise in a particular *domain,* come together to form a *community* to work on shared problem-solving, and advance their *practice.*
- Participation in a community of practice supports teacher *learning,* helps to create deeper *meaning* in the work, and helps to shape the teacher's professional *identity.*

- Participation in communities of practice, such as PLCs in schools, strengthens professional efficacy, supports knowledge-sharing and problem-solving, reduces the loss of implicit knowledge caused by turnover, and improves satisfaction and retention.
- Communities of practice build shared understandings, which can promote effective implementation of reform, but can also impede reform when the learning community serves as a gatekeeper, filtering out reforms that are inconsistent with the community's professional norms and beliefs.
- Principals can support the development and effectiveness of professional communities by building a clear shared vision across teachers in the school, structuring collaborative planning time, building trust, holding communities accountable, and assessing progress.

NOTES

1 nsrfharmony.org
2 aiwinstitute.org
3 https://nsrfharmony.org
4 See www.nsrfharmony.org/wp-content/uploads/2017/10/plc_survey_0.pdf

REFERENCES

Blanc, S., Christman, J. B., Liu, R., Mitchell, C., Travers, E., & Bulkley, K. E. (2010). Learning to learn from data: Benchmarks and instructional communities. *Peabody Journal of Education, 85*(2), 205–225.

Bourdieu, P. (1986). The forms of capital. In J. G. Richardson (Ed.), *Handbook of theory and research for the sociology of education*. Greenwood.

Bryk, A., Camburn, E., & Louis, K. S. (1999). Professional community in Chicago elementary schools: Facilitating factors and organizational consequences. *Educational Administration Quarterly, 35*(5), 751–781.

Coburn, C. E. (2001). Collective sensemaking about reading: How teachers mediate reading policy in their professional communities. *Educational Evaluation and Policy Analysis, 23*(2), 145–170.

Coleman, J. S. (1988). Social capital in the creation of human capital. *American Journal of Sociology, 94* (Supplement: Organizations and Institutions: Sociological and Economic Approaches to the Analysis of Social Structure), S95–S120. www.jstor.org/stable/2780243

Craig, C. J. (2009). Research in the midst of organized school reform: Versions of teacher community in tension. *American Educational Research Journal, 46*(2), 598–619.

Daly, A. J., Moolenaar, N. M., Der-Martirosian, C., & Liou, Y. H. (2014). Accessing capital resources: Investigating the effects of teacher human and social capital on student achievement. *Teachers College Record, 116*(7), 1–42.

Doran, G., Miller, A., & Cunningham, J. (1981). There's a S.M.A.R.T. way to write management goals and objectives. *Management Review, 70*(11), 35–36.

DuFour, R. (2004). What is a "professional learning community"? *Educational Leadership, 61*(8), 6–11.

DuFour, R., & DuFour, R. (2013). *Learning by doing: A handbook for professional learning communities at work TM*. Solution Tree Press.

DuFour, R., & Eaker, R. (1998). *Professional learning communities at work: Best practices for enhancing student achievement*. Solution Tree Press.

Hemmasi, M., & Csanda, C. M. (2009). The effectiveness of communities of practice: An empirical study. *Journal of Managerial Issues*, 262–279.

Hord, S. M. (1997). *Professional learning communities: Communities of continuous inquiry and improvement*. Southwest Educational Development Lab.

Huffman, J. B., & Hipp, K. K. (2003). *Reculturing schools as professional learning communities*. R&L Education.

Knight, P. (2002). A systemic approach to professional development: Learning as practice. *Teaching and Teacher Education, 18*(3), 229–241.

Lave, J., & Wenger, E. (1991). *Situated learning: Legitimate peripheral participation*. Cambridge University Press. https://doi.org/10.1017/CBO9780511815355

Lomos, C., Hofman, R. H., & Bosker, R. J. (2011). Professional communities and student achievement–a meta-analysis. *School Effectiveness and School Improvement, 22*(2), 121–148.

Louis, K. S. (2006). Changing the culture of schools: Professional community, organizational learning, and trust. *Journal of School Leadership, 16*(5), 477–489.

Louis, K. S., & Marks, H. M. (1998). Does professional community affect the classroom? Teachers' work and student experiences in restructuring schools. *American Journal of Education, 106*(4), 532–575. www.jstor.org/stable/1085627

Newmann, F. M., & Associates. (1996). *Authentic achievement: Restructuring schools for intellectual quality*. Jossey-Bass.

Newmann, F. M., King, M. B., & Carmichael, T. (2009). *Teaching for authentic intellectual work: Standards and scoring criteria for teachers' tasks, student performance, and instruction*. Tasora Books.

Newmann, F. M., King, M. B., & Carmichael, T. (2015). *Authentic intellectual work: Improving teaching for rigorous learning*. Corwin Press.

Orr, J. (1996). *Talking about machines: An ethnography of a modern job*. Cornell University Press.

Penuel, W., Riel, M., Krause, A., & Frank, K. (2009). Analyzing teachers' professional interactions in a school as social capital: A social network approach. *Teachers College Record, 111*(1), 124–163.

Printy, S. M. (2008). Leadership for teacher learning: A community of practice perspective. *Educational Administration Quarterly, 44*(2), 187–226.

Rosenholtz, S. J. (1991). *Teachers' workplace: The social organization of schools*. Teachers College Press.

Vygotsky, L. S. (1978). *Vygotsky and education: Instructional implications and applications of sociohistorical psychology* (L. C. Moll, Ed.). Cambridge University Press. (Original work published 1933)

Wahlstrom, K. L., & Louis, K. S. (2008). How teachers experience principal leadership: The roles of professional community, trust, efficacy, and shared responsibility. *Educational Administration Quarterly, 44*(4), 458–495.

Wenger, E. (1998). *Communities of practice: Learning, meaning, and identity*. Cambridge University Press.

Wenger, E., McDermott, R. A., & Snyder, W. (2002). *Cultivating communities of practice: A guide to managing knowledge*. Harvard Business Press.

CHAPTER 9

Performance Appraisal

Chapter Summary

This chapter reviews the literature on teacher and principal evaluation and examines the role that principals can play in leveraging teacher evaluation as a mechanism to improve teacher quality. The chapter draws on research, practice, and theory related to evaluation to provide guidance to current and aspiring school leaders. It also provides case study examples and discussion questions for readers to consider.

Effective leaders deliver actionable feedback about instruction and other professional practice through valid, research-anchored systems of supervision and evaluation to support the development of teachers' and staff members' knowledge, skills, and practice.

(PSEL Standard 6e)

INTRODUCTION

Given the focus and emphasis on talent, performance evaluations are critical for Talent-Centered Education Leadership. The two most common functions of evaluation include performance accountability and feedback to support professional growth and development (Milanowski, 2017; Tran & Bon, 2015). Unfortunately, these dual purposes commonly conflict, and in many organizations, one purpose often takes precedence over the other. If used strategically, evaluation can provide an opportunity for the school or district to develop a clear shared definition of good teaching and provide guidance to help teachers achieve that vision.

DOI: 10.4324/9781003457060-12

Evaluation models, such as the Danielson Framework, are designed to provide an opportunity for teacher engagement around the development of a shared understanding of performance expectations and rubrics to support the evaluation of teaching practice with opportunities to provide teachers with feedback for performance improvement (Danielson, 2007).

HR-developed evaluation rubrics have served as valuable tools for principals to help them focus on what matters when conducting performance evaluations, supporting teacher development and reducing subjectivity in the process (Neumerski et al., 2018). Working with the district, structured rubrics can be developed to enhance the predictive validity of the evaluation process towards outcomes that are valued by the school community. The district office can also train principals on how to communicate the mechanics of assessment scores so that the principals can clearly explain to teachers how their scores were calculated in order to create transparency (and therefore trust) in the process. A clear plan for how teachers should respond to the evaluation can lend itself to the provision of meaningful feedback for teachers. Even when accounting for school characteristics and teacher working conditions, teachers are more satisfied when they perceive their evaluation experiences to be more supportive (especially when they feel their evaluations have resulted in positive changes in practice) (Ford et al., 2018).

A HISTORY OF TEACHER EVALUATION IN THE US

Unfortunately, it is largely acknowledged that the teacher evaluation system has historically not achieved effective accountability or promoted professional growth in the classroom. In many schools, evaluation was sporadic and often did not occur for many teachers (Kraft & Gilmour, 2017). If feedback was provided, it was often not meaningful, direct, or actionable. A seminal report by Weisberg et al. (2009) on teacher evaluations performed across multiple states found almost nonexistent differences in teacher ratings (i.e., more than 94–99% rated satisfactory) and the majority of surveyed teachers noted their evaluation did not identify professional growth areas (and fewer than half of those that did found the support useful for their development). Consequently, poor teaching performance was not adequately addressed.

Despite advancements in teacher evaluation in the late 1990s through the development of the National Board for Professional Teaching Standards (Kelley, 1999) and the Danielson Framework for Teaching (Danielson, 2007), concerns about the state of teacher evaluation persisted among policymakers. The federal government allocated $4.35 billion in Race to the Top program funding and waivers from the *No Child Left Behind* Act. In order to participate, states had to agree to adopt more rigorous statewide teacher evaluation systems that included the use of structured classroom observation rubrics and student standardized achievement test scores as components of new state teacher evaluation systems. These efforts resulted in almost universal adoption of new teacher evaluation across the nation. The new evaluation systems incorporated the use of student standardized test scores to calculate the test score value added by the teacher.

The systems varied across the US in their efforts to provide formative feedback for teacher learning versus high-stakes accountability, but the reforms ultimately promoted a sense of disempowerment and demoralization for many teachers. In response, in New York, "parents, teachers, and students organized in opposition to state exams and the way exam scores are used to penalize under-performing schools" (Williamson, 2018, para 1). As a result of the public resistance to the teacher education reforms, Value-added models (VAM) were later de-emphasized in the teacher evaluation provisions in the *Every Students Succeeds* Act *(ESSA)*.[1] Accountability-oriented policymakers and reformers were disappointed to find that there was no substantive change in the percentage of *ineffective* or *not proficient* teachers identified and counseled out as a result of the evaluation reforms (Doherty & Jacobs, 2015; Kraft & Gilmour, 2017; Sartain & Steinberg, 2016; Walsh et al., 2017). Overall, while 45 states required some linkage of student test scores to educator evaluations, the National Council on Teacher Quality's (2019) latest report on the state of teacher and principal evaluations shows that over half of the states in the nation have since dropped that requirement.

PRINCIPALS' ABILITY TO DISTINGUISH THE PERFORMANCE OF TEACHERS

Despite the general lack of differentiation between performance ratings for teachers, research shows that principals are able to make distinctions between high- and low-performing teachers. Grissom and Loeb (2017) compared principal evaluation of teachers for high-stakes personnel evaluation (for the district office) and low-stakes evaluation (just for the researchers). They found that principals were more likely to identify ineffective teachers in private to the researchers as compared to for the district office in a formal evaluation. Kraft and Gilmour's (2017) work found a similar pattern in that principals rated three times as many teachers as proficient than they believed were present in their schools. In fact, principals' personal identification of their most and least effective teachers has been found to correspond with teachers who produce the largest and smallest value-added test score gains although identification for the middle performers was less precise (Jacob & Lefgre, 2008).

If principals have the ability to differentiate between the performances of teachers, then why has this consistently not been reflected in the resulting performance evaluation? Kraft and Gilmour (2017) interviewed principals and discovered several barriers that they faced in providing negative feedback to underperforming teachers. These barriers included a lack of time to sufficiently document unsatisfactory ratings, being uncomfortable having challenging conversations about performance with underperforming teachers, concerns that the rating might negatively affect the teacher's career, inability to provide needed support or replace the teacher, concerns about the impact on teacher morale, and concerns that it would be too difficult to force the teacher out and attempting to do so would just destroy the relationship between the principal and the underperforming teacher.

Strategic talent management of faculty and staff in the school could address many of these barriers. For example, one way to address the capacity issue for principals is to distribute the leadership responsibilities so that other administrators or teacher leaders take on evaluator roles. This is particularly helpful when you can select administrators or other teacher leaders who are experts in areas in which the principal is not well-versed. Another area of leverage for school principals is having the due diligence to carefully observe and screen out teachers before they achieve tenure or increase efforts to hire teachers who would be receptive and responsive to receiving improvement feedback (Reinhorn & Johnson, 2014). The key is for principals to consider how to best maximize the potential of the school's talent through tools such as performance evaluations.

EVALUATION METHODS

The teacher evaluation models adopted by most states typically included three main methods of evaluation: value-added models, teacher observations, and student learning objectives (SLOs). Each of these methods will be discussed in the following sections.

Value-Added Models

Value-added models (VAMs) were designed in an effort to leverage student learning gains as a measure of teacher or school performance (Meyer, 1997). VAMs attempt to isolate individual teachers' contributions towards students' achievement test score growth, accounting for contextual factors such as student background. They do this by establishing a baseline for comparison, statistically projecting student performance on standardized exams based on their prior performance. This baseline is then compared with students' actual performance in the teacher's classroom, with the score gap being the degree of "value-added." Some models account for demographic backgrounds such as student poverty status, while others do not, based on the assumption that accounting for prior performance will capture the effect of poverty on test score outcomes (Chetty et al., 2014). The individual "value-added" scores averaged across all students for a given teacher in a given class represent that teacher's value-added.

While value-added models have the appearance of being far less subjective than other measures of teacher performance (e.g., teacher observations), VAMs have their limitations. The American Statistical Association (ASA) (2014), the American Educational Research Association (2015), and the Board on Testing and Assessment (BOTA) of the National Research Council of the National Academy of Sciences (BOTA, 2009) each put out independent statements that expressed caution against the use of VAMs for high-stakes personnel decisions (e.g., teacher compensation, hiring, evaluation, tenure, and dismissal).

Some of the most salient concerns with VAMs include:

- VAM scores cannot be readily calculated for many teachers, for example, for teachers who teach subjects not measured by standardized tests; teachers without prior student test scores (e.g., first-year teachers or teachers who transfer schools); or teachers who regularly share students with other teachers (e.g., special education, differentiated curriculum, or team teaching).
- VAM scores are derived from tests designed to directly measure student, not teacher, performance. Student scores are affected by external factors (e.g., curriculum, student background, how students were sorted to teachers, influences of other teachers including from prior years/semesters, student attendance, summer reading loss, after-school tutoring, parental engagement), and VAM estimates have been found to be biased against teachers who work with low-performing and other marginalized groups of students.
- VAMs are sensitive to model specifications, and the ratings may be highly unstable from one year to the next.
- VAM scores are not available until it is too late for the teacher to use the score as feedback to improve instruction. The calculation of VAMs is also typically very complex, making it very difficult for teachers to feel they have control over their VAM scores or to know what they would need to do to improve their scores.

(American Statistical Association, 2014; Baker et al., 2010; Campbell & Ronfeldt, 2018; Derrington & Campbell, 2018; Jackson & Bruegmann, 2009; Pressley et al., 2018; Schochet & Chiang, 2010)

Given the bias associated with VAM scores, some suggest that they should be adjusted for student and teacher characteristics to more accurately and fairly identify teacher performance. However, Milanowski (2017) suggests that whether adjustment should be made to the scores depends on the purpose of the evaluation. For example, if the purpose of the evaluation is for teacher development, adjustments will make it harder to determine areas of improvement for the teacher or may influence them to be less adaptive to the needs of their student population. Not only will doing so make the rating score less transparent than it probably already is, but it ignores that in reality, you cannot just statistically adjust away the external factors associated with certain types of students that affect their learning in the classroom. However, if VAM is used for accountability purposes, then the adjustments will provide fairer (although still imperfect) teacher assessments.

Despite their weaknesses, some argue that test score–based teacher evaluations have value and should not be dismissed altogether in the teacher evaluation process. Specifically, teachers' VAMs seem to explain at least some of the teacher's contribution to student test score gains (between 1–14% according to ASA's review of VAM research; American Statistical Association, 2014) and have been linked with numerous other positive student outcomes such as students' future college attendance, salaries, and lower likelihood of being a teenage parent (Chetty et al., 2014). Proponents of VAMs argue that they are a more accurate predictor of student learning than any other available evaluation instrument and that not using VAM would mean we are not using the best available tools we have to evaluate teachers. In short, they argue that an imperfect tool is better than an inferior tool or no tool at all.

How Should VAMs Be Used?

If VAMs are to be used, ASA (2014) recommends that they serve as an information tool for development purposes by allowing teachers to see how their students performed relative to other students with similar prior test scores and that teachers are provided information concerning the precision, assumptions, and limitations associated with the model used. This is particularly relevant because it has been reported that teachers often receive VAM scores without any explanation from their principals (Pressley et al., 2018). This can result in teachers losing trust in their principal's programmatic knowledge and discounting the entire process altogether, rendering the entire activity a waste of time. If teachers are going to be evaluated based on a metric score, an explanation should be provided concerning all that goes into it, how test scores are linked to their specific evaluation, and what their VAM score means. If used, VAMs should represent a piece of the overall teacher evaluation, corroborated with another basis of evidence (Milanowski, 2017).

TEACHER OBSERVATIONS

Classroom observations have evolved alongside other teacher-evaluation reform efforts. Because the teacher evaluation process often has at least some degree of subjectivity, teachers may be concerned that they will be evaluated unfairly (Marsh et al., 2017). Training in evaluation can ensure consistency of ratings and provide support for evaluators to ensure that they are conducting consistent, high-quality evaluations with feedback to support teacher performance improvement. Professional development can help evaluators provide the requisite coaching, mentorship, and engagement skills that are critical for communicating the process effectively to stakeholders, conducting the proper documentation, and engaging in meaningful evaluations that lead to reflective growth (Sartain et al., 2011). Unfortunately, training is often not provided, or if so, it is frequently superficial and focuses only on the logistical process of implementation (e.g., length of observations, how many should be done) as opposed to the content of evaluation and how to assess performance (Reid, 2018). In these types of instances, one way to gain that knowledge is to engage with a network of other principals to help one another navigate performance assessment and better make data-informed decisions with the collected performance data.

The use of multiple highly structured classroom observations in the evaluation process has been found to be linked with improvement in teacher effectiveness (Steinberg & Sartain, 2015; Taylor & Tyler, 2012), most likely a result of the feedback provided as well as the time and opportunity for meaningful reflection and conversation on instruction. While principals may often find themselves busy in a myriad of different tasks or "fires that need to be put out," they must never forget that ultimately, what goes on in the classroom is the heart and purpose of the school. Principals should match teachers with evaluators who have expertise in their teaching area, can provide coaching, and model exemplary practices (Reinhorn & Johnson, 2014).

Shifting from a perspective of "how effective is a teacher" to an explanation of "how is a teacher effective" (Kraft & Gilmour, 2017, p. 243) can better identify areas of strengths and improvements in the evaluation process and can be less contentious during feedback conversations, given that it can be framed in a way that presumes teacher competence, inquiring for examples to merely substantiate it. The evaluator should facilitate structured post-observation conferences with the evaluated teacher and come to the meeting with notes and ratings (if appropriate in the school/district) for feedback, reflection, and discussion.

Classroom observations should be accompanied by careful documentation to evidence teacher performance across multiple domains (e.g., pacing, student engagement, classroom management, instructional delivery, and content). This documentation has often included "scripting," a process that attempts to chronicle the direct quotes of students and teachers to capture their interactions. Structured rubrics with more detailed criteria for a range of teacher performance levels across teaching dimensions have replaced simple observational checklists that merely capture whether satisfactory behaviors were exhibited. The provision of ongoing detailed feedback throughout the year to develop and improve classroom teaching and the increased presence of the principal in the classroom has become an expectation (Sartain & Steinberg, 2016).

Challenges with teacher observation evaluation that principals should be aware of and work to mitigate include:

- The tension for principals between investing in substantive, sustained, and frequent observations in the classroom and the impact to other leadership activities. This may be a particular concern in smaller districts, with fewer opportunities for other administrators to fill in as needed to make time for teacher observations.
- The need to balance ratings from classroom observations with other evaluation evidence, such as value-added models, which may produce dissimilar results.
- The variety of factors unrelated to teacher performance that routinely affect teacher observation ratings, including the timing of the observation (e.g., the day before break, on a day with a major distraction such as an ambulance or fire drill), the demographic makeup of the class (e.g., more challenged learners

or students with behavioral disabilities may act out during the observation), the extent to which the sample of classroom practice is representative of typical teaching practice (versus a "dog and pony show"), and the effect of any preconceived principal attitudes towards the teacher, which increase the likelihood of confirmation bias.

- Failure on the part of the principal to embrace evaluation as a meaningful and authentic process.
- Inability to navigate post-observation conference meetings, without the evaluated teacher taking critical feedback personally, especially if the norm of the school culture has been to avoid any type of criticism (Milanowski, 2017; Neumerski et al., 2018).

When used correctly, structured observation rubrics can be helpful as they can clarify expectations by communicating performance standards, potentially reduce subjectivity, and serve as a useful tool to offer specific feedback in the evaluation process. Some districts have invested significantly in evaluator training and have leveraged evaluation as part of a broader strategy to create a shared definition of effective teaching across the organization and build teacher capacity. These districts have worked to increase the reliability of evaluations to leverage evaluation systems for teacher performance improvement or to advance performance pay systems that reward teachers, in part, based on their evaluation scores (Halverson et al., 2004). For example, some districts make teacher knowledge and skill-based pay increases (such as for taking graduate classes or participating in district professional development programs) contingent on meeting expectations in the evaluation system (Kelley, 2000). Research suggests that in districts that have invested in evaluator training, observations using the Danielson Framework are correlated with value-added student learning (Gallagher, 2004; Milanowski, 2004). In these districts, teachers were heavily involved in the design of the evaluation rubrics, and the model of teaching was broadly understood by teachers. One district used the information from the evaluation districtwide to determine future professional development programming in order to build teacher knowledge and skills around areas that routinely received lower ratings (Maslow & Kelley, 2012). Districts that operate with Talent-Centered Education Leadership make evaluation a priority, selecting and training principals that have strong pedagogical content knowledge (Nelson & Sassi, 2000) and leveraging that knowledge for effective teacher feedback.

How Should Teacher Observations Be Used?

Conducting in-depth observations for each teacher can be time-consuming, which may result in principals feeling like they are giving up on their other duties in order to add on the performance of valid teacher evaluations. One way to mitigate this is to identify areas of overlap with the different duties and align them so that the principals use the process to enhance other aspects of their job responsibilities including provision of feedback for teacher development, an integral component of their work as instructional leaders (Derrington & Campbell, 2018).

The use of multiple observers (as opposed to just a single observer) can also help capture nuances and different aspects of a teacher's performance and allow for better detection of differences between teacher performances (Doherty & Jacobs, 2015). It can also mitigate the likelihood of biases from individual evaluators unduly influencing teacher ratings (Campbell & Ronfeldt, 2018) and reduce the contention concerning the subjectivity associated with only one observer's ratings.

Discussion Questions: When conducting observations, especially with more seasoned teachers, principals might have concerns that their observation and associated feedback may be interpreted as interference that stifles the autonomy of teachers (especially when the school culture has historically emphasized teacher autonomy). If teaching is an art, could there not be multiple ways to achieve success? How might you resolve these potentially conflicting perspectives?

Discussion Questions: Should principals give teachers advance notice of when they will be observing them? Why or why not?

BOX 9.1: WARNING – EVALUATION BIAS

There is evidence to suggest that teacher observation ratings can be biased against teachers teaching low-achieving, Black, Hispanic, and male students, even accounting for teachers' VAM scores (Campbell & Ronfeldt, 2018; Steinberg & Garrett, 2016). Part of this may be a result of how school administrators sort and assign students to teachers. For example, if students with low academic abilities are systematically assigned to particular types of teachers (e.g., inexperienced teachers who have less seniority "bumping" privileges), those teachers may be systematically rated lower when evaluators observe weaker academic performance in those classrooms. Similarly, if teachers are more likely to teach Black and Hispanic students, then their evaluations may be more negatively affected by factors outside of teacher performance. Male teachers have also been found more likely to receive lower ratings than female teachers (Campbell & Ronfeldt, 2018).

Because of the strong relationships that can develop between school administrators and teachers, personal bias can also affect evaluation ratings. It can be hard to distinguish someone who is a great person from someone who is a great teacher because, while those things can often align, they are not synonymous. Furthermore, evaluations can be complicated by the additional information administrators have on employees. For example, if the teacher is being rated on their classroom performance, then should the fact that the teacher is always willing to volunteer for extra-curricular duties, such as serving as the chaperone for school dances, be considered in that evaluation?

Should two teachers who are underperforming be rated equally if one shows more motivation and potential to improve than the other?

These are decisions that evaluators must make, and they should be guided by the purpose of the evaluation as outlined by the school and/or district.

STUDENT LEARNING OBJECTIVES

Because standardized test scores do not exist for the subject areas and grade levels taught by most teachers, many districts rely on the use of student learning objectives (SLOs) to incorporate student achievement in teacher evaluations. Teachers, often in collaboration with the evaluator, set individual student learning goals at the beginning of the evaluation period and review the extent to which those goals were achieved at the end of the period. Often, local (e.g., teacher-, school-, or district-developed) tests are used to assess student learning.

Given that SLOs are relatively new when compared with other forms of teacher evaluation measures, the research on examining their efficacy is relatively scant. However, like with other evaluation measures, SLOs have both strengths and weaknesses. One major strength of SLOs is that they are student-focused while allowing for teachers to have the flexibility to identify the learning outcomes that are relevant to them. This can function as a mechanism to recognize teacher expertise and encourage teacher engagement by allowing them to focus on what they deem important. In theory, SLOs could accommodate a broader range of artifacts for assessment, such as student portfolios and projects, to help capture different dimensions of teaching.

Unfortunately, according to Doherty and Jacobs' (2015) comprehensive review of evaluation systems across the nation, "more often than not, SLOs are turning out to be not very meaningful measures of teacher performance. Part of the issue is whether teachers have the knowledge and data to set appropriate student achievement goals" (p. 17). Teachers can benefit from training on data-informed decision-making and setting meaningful goals. Because teachers help set the standard for their own evaluation, a major weakness of the SLOs is that they can provide the incentive for setting the bar low, which, of course, translates to lower student expectations and results in associated negative consequences (e.g., student internalization of low expectations affecting their motivation and self-esteem). The evaluator, often the principal, is critical here because they are not only a collaborator in setting the area of focus but also a negotiator to ensure that the process is rigorous and meaningful. A principal who treats the process as merely a check in the box of a list of things to do may be tempted to allow teachers to set low standards and might even actively encourage it. Therefore, it is important that the evaluator holds high standards and maintains the integrity of the process.

Many of the same principles associated with and recommendations made for other measures apply to SLOs. For example, principals who lack subject-matter expertise in the subject that the teacher is being evaluated in would benefit from enlisting the support of teacher evaluators with the subject-matter background and professional credibility. In addition, SLOs can provide the structure, time, and space for the intentional planning and reflection that is the foundation of growth. One tool principals can utilize is providing teachers with time to conduct regular (e.g., weekly) journaling and discussion to reflect on their teaching strategies and the progress of their students (Marsh et al., 2017). These support structures may yield the additional benefit of strengthening communities of practice within the school.

OTHER EVALUATIVE MEASURES

Because of the limitations associated with each of the aforementioned evaluation methods, it has been increasingly recommended that multiple measures of performance be used to evaluate teachers. This could include blending evaluative measures such as teacher observations, test score growth, feedback surveys, student and parent surveys, and portfolio projects in the teacher evaluation process. This is particularly advantageous because each of the current measures is associated with its own strengths and weaknesses and often addresses different components of the broader construct of "teacher performance." Multiple measures allow for the increased likelihood of capturing the full range of performances required for a teacher to be effective.

BOX 9.2: PERFORMANCE FEEDBACK SHOULD BE STRENGTHS-BASED

Remember the last time you received performance feedback from your supervisor as part of an evaluation process. If you are like most people, you probably didn't look forward to the conversation, and it may have made you feel uncomfortable. It is difficult to give performance feedback, and it is difficult to receive it.

Most evaluators would assume that you need to be honest and that both negative and positive feedback can improve employee performance. Employees who receive negative feedback should respond by working to address their weaknesses, and employees who receive positive feedback should respond by continuing those behaviors, right? Surprisingly, research by Kluger and DeNisi on performance feedback has shown that about a third of the time, highly critical feedback actually causes performance to decline, and negative feedback does not have the expected effect of causing improvement in performance (Kluger & DeNisi, 1998).

The research on the unintended negative effects of performance feedback highlights the importance of evaluator training and, in particular, the importance of focusing on strengths-based feedback to employees. Aguinis et al. (2012) provide nine recommendations growing out of the research literature for delivering feedback using a strengths-based approach:

1. Focus on the ways in which employee strengths are producing positive results.
2. Connect negative feedback to employee knowledge and skills, which can change through training.
3. Build on employee talents even when addressing weaknesses; if needed, revise the job so the employee has the ability to succeed.
4. Familiarize yourself with the employee's knowledge, skills, and talents as well as the job requirements and work context. Feedback should connect to these realities.
5. Provide feedback in a private setting.
6. Give at least three pieces of positive feedback for every one piece of negative feedback.
7. Be specific and connect feedback to concrete evidence.
8. Explain how the employee's work has an impact at various levels of the organization.
9. Create an employee development plan and check on their progress in a specified time period.

Care must be taken to ensure that the multiple measures do not unduly influence each other. For example, when principals are told to intentionally match teacher observation ratings to student growth scores, this reduces the amount of independent information that is being offered by each (Hazi, 2017). The forced correlation negates the benefit of having multiple measures of performance in the first place.

BUY-IN

Despite recent reform efforts that aim at standardizing the evaluation process and removing much of the discretion related to establishing evaluations away from principals, principals have always played a critical role in the implementation of evaluation processes. In fact, how they treat the process communicates whether there is internal accountability (within the school) for substantive performance improvements or whether school actions are merely a superficial response to externally imposed accountability (Derrington & Campbell, 2018). This, of course, has a trickle-down effect and influences the extent to which teachers will buy into the process.

Donaldson and Woulfin (2018) presented a typology of discretionary activities that principals can perform in response to the district evaluation process. These range from (but are not limited to) minor adjustments to practices (*tinkering*) and integrating evaluation activities with other duties and practices (*hybridizing*), to making decisions to skew the results in a positive direction, such as observing teachers only when they are with specific students in order to benefit teachers/the school in the evaluation process (*gaming*). Depending on how these activities are carried out, many of them have the potential to enhance or dull the potential benefit of the evaluation process. For example, sometimes principals have to adjust the policy to better fit their local environment, which can be beneficial if those adjustments can provide a more meaningful development experience for teachers. However, implementation of the process may not be followed correctly (e.g., fewer observations made than required) because of the lack of available time to do so, which would hurt the validity and rigor of the evaluations. This all suggests that even with a highly prescriptive evaluation process provided by the district, principals are often able to exercise a great deal of discretion that can potentially change the course of the evaluation outcomes. Consequently, thought should be put into how the principal plans to implement the process.

Even if meaningful and actionable feedback is provided to teachers, it is of little use if the teachers do not acknowledge and make changes in response to the feedback. One important prerequisite of increasing the likelihood of that occurring is ensuring that there is a foundation of trust between the evaluator and the teachers. This requires that the evaluator (often the principal) works to reduce the vulnerability of the evaluated teachers, putting them at ease by engaging them in ways that demonstrate relational and task-oriented trust (e.g., the evaluator knows what they are talking about and the feedback is sound and could lead to improvement), both of which comprise the overarching faculty trust that is correlated with positive school climate and student achievement (Bryk & Schneider, 2002; Tschannen-Moran & Gareis, 2015). For principals, that means exhibiting honesty, valuing relationships, and empowering teachers by including them in the decision-making process (Leis & Rimm-Kaufman, 2015), which reduces mistrust and helps create the teacher buy-in necessary for the evaluation process to be successful.

Relatedly, the management of teachers' perception of control over their performance results is critical. When they do not feel they have complete ability to influence the outcomes of their evaluation, they will be more likely to feel anxiety and stress and less likely to buy into the evaluation (Pressley et al., 2018). The perception of invalidity of the performance assessment from the evaluated teachers will likely result in a lack of engagement and commitment to any feedback received from it. Therefore, school employers should work to mitigate these sentiments. One way to do this is to include teacher voices and participation in the development, design, or modification of the standards and criteria for evaluation.

While the importance of developing relationship trust and camaraderie with the faculty is important, it becomes much more difficult to deal with employee performance-based "problems" when administrators have become or were close friends with their faculty and staff prior to their promotion. This is not to say that principals should not have close relationships with their employees, as teachers are more willing to buy into the evaluation process if they trust the principal. However, it is important to realize that when the lines between a professional and personal relationship are blurred, the professional relationships become more personal, and consequently, actions taken by the administrator can be perceived through that lens by others. Principals who occupy that space walk a very fine line between the two worlds.

BOX 9.3: MANAGING UP

Many principals are unable to fully leverage the power of teacher evaluations because they do not feel they have the skill set to do so. Consequently, principals should communicate this to HR/the district office so they can be provided the requisite support (e.g., teacher observation training, test score interpretation) needed to ensure the school is a thriving learning organization in service of student support. Working with the district, structured rubrics can be developed to enhance the predictive validity of the evaluation process towards outcomes that are valued by both the school and the district. The district may want to adopt a framework for teaching that provides foundational conversations about effective teaching that lay the foundation for a more effective evaluation system. The district office can also train principals on how to communicate the mechanics of assessment scores so that the principals can clearly explain to teachers how their scores were calculated in order to create transparency (and therefore trust) in the process.

STRATEGIC RETENTION: TEACHER EVALUATIONS AND TURNOVER

There is some evidence to suggest that teacher evaluation reforms are linked with the departures of lower-rated teachers and subsequent replacement with higher-rated ones. In an examination of the consequences of the Chicago-based teacher evaluation systems reform pilot, Sartain and Steinberg (2016) found no impact on overall teacher turnover, except for the lowest-performing teachers, especially those without tenure. While some principals activated the dismissal process, teachers often left on their own before the conclusion of the process. Similarly, Kraft and Gilmour (2017) spoke to several principals who planned to use their newly reformed and more stringent evaluation systems to dismiss teachers but often reported that the low-rated teachers would depart before the dismissal would take place. Rockoff et al. (2012) also found that principals' use of teacher performance data in the evaluation process was associated with higher turnover of lower-rated teachers and small gains in student test scores.

Indeed, performance feedback was often found to influence teachers' affective reactions to their workplace. For instance, in their study on a newly implemented teacher evaluation system, Koedel et al. (2017) provided strong evidence that linked teacher evaluation ratings and teachers' workplace satisfaction, that is, higher-rated teachers were more satisfied with their work as compared to teachers with lower ratings. Conversely, low evaluation ratings (to the point of near threats of dismissal) have been linked with the turnover of the lower-performing teachers and performance improvement of those that remain (Dee & Wyckoff, 2015). And consistent with studies mentioned earlier, the departing low-performing teachers were replaced with higher-performing ones (Adnot et al., 2017). Results from these studies provide evidence to suggest that the evaluation process can not only be used to improve the performance of existing employees but also to strategically retain them, in that lower-rated employees can be motivated to leave and be replaced with higher-performing ones. While this can yield benefits for the school, administrators should be critically self-conscious of potential biases they may have that would result in differential retention of teachers based on factors outside of validated work performance.

CONFRONTING PERFORMANCE PROBLEMS

Data collection during the evaluation and subsequent feedback process can be potentially helpful with improving teacher performance. Furthermore, in the event that the performance does not improve to a satisfactory level, the documentation can show that the employer has tried their best to support the employee before deciding to move forward with more drastic action (e.g., dismissal). This is preferable to the often-applied approach of not documenting the process until there is a "problem," and when the employer realizes they would like to move forward with dismissal, the administrators begin to rapidly build a paper trail to *document* the employee to termination. This raises lots of red flags for the employee and may be deemed unfavorable in court if other employees with similar performance issues are not documented. Just like teachers expect administrative enforcement of student disciplinary policies, they also expect the same with employee discipline.

Employers should develop, nurture, support, and actively communicate with (which includes listening to) their employees. However, when an employee does not have the best interest of the organization at heart and is not demonstrating substantive progress towards improvement, then that employee needs to be removed. If you have never interacted with a "problem" employee and you consider yourself a hard worker, it may be difficult to believe that some employees will flat out not do their jobs, resist efforts towards change, and/or actively sabotage the organization. As an administrator, you will likely meet all different types of employees from "star" performers who invest all their time and effort on the job, to good and average workers who perform their jobs competently, to those who are downright "incompetent" for the position. Of course, honest efforts to communicate, understand, and engage with "problem" employees should be attempted. Demonstrating the value of positive peer effects, Papay et al. (2016) found that partnering low-performing teachers with high-performing teachers was linked to an improvement of the low-performing teachers' performance ratings. Consequently, that partnership may help struggling employees improve.

However, if these efforts fail, the employer may need to move towards dismissal. While one may mistake this to be misaligned with the tenants of a Talent-Centered Education Leadership, it is actually not because retaining an employee who is underperforming and willfully dismissive can damage the overall morale of other teachers in the school. Indeed, when hardworking teachers have to carry the instructional burden of their underperforming colleagues, they tend not to be satisfied (Shields et al., 2001). The bottom line is, hard workers expect professionalism from their colleagues and will have negative reactions to their work context if their colleagues refuse to perform their job duties and face no consequences as a result.

BOX 9.4: WHEN IT'S NOT ROSY: DOCUMENTING FOR DISMISSAL

Because of the dismissal process for ineffective teachers is often perceived to be too cumbersome, specifically as it relates to length (often years, that can be extended with appeals and challenges); cost (hundreds of thousands of dollars per teacher); and procedures (e.g., multiple observations, pre-requirement to place teachers on improvement plan), many school employers opt not to move forward with taking action to release teachers they deem ineffective (Griffith & McDougald, 2016). Furthermore, the process can be even more challenging in certain contexts (e.g., depending on collective bargaining agreements, local laws).

This all suggests that it is imperative for districts to vet teachers carefully and proactively address concerns as they arise before tenure status is granted. However, even after a teacher has achieved tenure, it does not mean the teacher cannot be dismissed if they are found to be ineffective or have violated serious school or district behavioral policies. Tenure status does not provide immunity from consequences for workplace violations or underperformance, rather it legally grants teachers due process to ensure they cannot be arbitrarily and unfairly dismissed and presumes the teacher does not warrant dismissal until sufficient evidence and documentation presented in a fair hearing suggest otherwise. It often focuses on providing the teacher in question an opportunity to improve. These processes must be followed if employers wish to move forward with the employment dismissal of a tenured teacher in a traditional public school setting.

Districts that do not engage in the dismissal proceedings when they know the teacher is ineffective beyond improvement or behaviorally problematic are doing a disservice to not only the students they teach (which represents an ethical issue) but also the colleagues who teach beside them (because those teachers will likely have to work harder to "pick up the slack"). Indeed, teachers do perceive performance differences between their colleagues. In a nationally representative poll, teachers rated 12% of their colleagues in their local schools as "unsatisfactory" (Education Next, 2018). Ignoring the problem is the opposite of Talent-Centered Education Leadership, as it completely neglects the performance aspect of the talent.

Integral to initiating the dismissal process is effective documentation and engaging in difficult conversations with the struggling teacher. Even before dismissal, these activities may either spur teachers to improve their performance or lead them to voluntarily exit the organization on their own (Grissom & Bartanen, 2019). The conversation may also lead to the realization that the teacher may be a better fit in a different school or working in a different capacity (e.g., as a tutor or support specialist), which would result in the teacher being transferred to a position that better fits their skill set.

While documentation is key, many managers and leaders are unfamiliar and uncomfortable with how to produce high-quality documentation in the performance counseling/dismissal process. Given this, the assignment here is to write a letter about a teacher who is failing to perform to expectations or has repeatedly violated district policy (e.g., attendance) that will result in reprimand. The letter will be kept in the employee file. You can create a hypothetical scenario for a teacher to base your content on, or you can think back to a teacher you know who has recently underperformed or violated district policy and reference their situation under a pseudonym in this letter.

Your letter should include:

- Specific date of the incident(s)
- Detail about underperformance or violation (such as missed deadlines)
- Clear identification of the expectation that was unmet or the policy that was violated (and the acknowledgement that the teacher was aware of these prior to write-up)
- Include both perspectives by allowing the employee the opportunity to provide a written response
- Identify any consequences if repeated behavior should occur
- Describe the impact of the behavior

- Avoid subjective commentary that is not germane to the performance issue or violation
- Connect the performance issue or violation to prior related warnings or disciplinary actions
- Prepare a document with the expectation that a third party (e.g., a judge) will review it

DUE PROCESS

Due process in education exists because of the historical mistreatment of teachers and capricious employer decision-making that negatively affected their livelihoods. With due process, covered employees are protected from the denial of their property rights (e.g., their job, their pay) without a legitimate cause and are provided a hearing before an impartial forum to determine the legitimacy of any negative employment actions against them. These protections for teachers include job protection from unreasonable demands of their employers, such as changing student grades solely because of parental pressure.

Essentially, due process asks school employers "What is the process that is due?" (Looney, 2014) for employees that they are considering placing on disciplinary action up to, and including, dismissal. Employers must ensure that the appropriate process (as determined by state law, district policy, and collective bargaining contracts, among other factors) is followed in the correct manner and form. This process usually includes components such as hearings, time-sensitive notifications, opportunities for employee response, consideration of employee process rights, and involvement of the school board.

In order to avoid overturn of dismissal decisions or potential lawsuits, the termination decision should be both substantively and procedurally sound (Young, 2008). In order for the decision to be deemed substantively sound, there should be a legitimate reason for the dismissal and accompanying evidence to support it (e.g., the employee willfully violated an employment policy that has severe consequences for student safety and there exists evidence to substantiate this). Procedurally sound means that the process was completed properly (e.g., an employee was given proper notification of the potential dismissal and an opportunity to tell their side of the story).

BOX 9.5: WHEN IT'S NOT ROSY – FOLLOW-UP CASE STUDY

One of the teachers that you recently hired has been underperforming and you plan to rate her as such. Your assistant principal is concerned that if you rate that teacher as "not proficient" or "needs improvement," then the teacher will leave and the school will not be able to easily replace her because it struggles with recruiting and retaining teachers.

Discussion Questions: Given these concerns, would you still rate the teacher "not proficient"? How can you maximize the probability that the teacher works on their areas of improvement, without giving up on the school (i.e., quitting) altogether? Please rationalize and justify your response based on ethical, legal, professional, and/or leadership frameworks.

The nonprofit education news organization The 74 analyzed disciplinary records of New York teachers who were terminated from their employment over a 16-month time period in 2015 and 2016 (Cantor, 2018a, 2018b). The problematic issues they found included escalating absences; claims brought forth against administrators for harassment, discrimination, or creating a "hostile work environment" when administrators enforce performance standards or work policies; active refusal of professional support or improvement assistance; lying; failing to work while receiving compensation for the work; physical violence; sexual abuse; not performing work duties (e.g., grading assignments); escalating aggression towards administrators; actively engaging in insubordination; and repeatedly making claims of being the target of conspiracies and lies upon receipt of negative evaluations/disciplinary notices. Many of these issues can be quite stress-inducing for principals. For example, many often toss the words *harassment* and *hostile work environment* around, without fully understanding their meaning. From a legal perspective, the terms do not just connote a bother or an unhappy work environment. Administrators who are not clear on the definition may second-guess their own actions or let fear dictate how they will respond. According to the U.S. Equal Employment Opportunity Commission (n.d), harassment is

> unwelcome conduct that is based on race, color, religion, sex (including pregnancy), national origin, age (40 or older), disability or genetic information. Harassment becomes unlawful where 1) enduring the offensive conduct becomes a condition of continued employment, or 2) the conduct is severe or pervasive enough to create a work environment that a reasonable person would consider intimidating, hostile, or abusive. Anti-discrimination laws also prohibit harassment against individuals in retaliation for filing a discrimination charge, testifying, or participating in any way in an investigation, proceeding, or lawsuit under these laws; or opposing employment practices that they reasonably believe discriminate against individuals, in violation of these laws.

> Petty slights, annoyances, and isolated incidents (unless extremely serious) will not rise to the level of illegality. To be unlawful, the conduct must create a work environment that would be intimidating, hostile, or offensive to reasonable people.
>
> (para 2–3)

Illegal hostile work environments perpetuate harassment in that they are typically discriminatory (i.e., related to protected class status as mentioned in the quote), pervasive, severe (i.e., results in harm, humiliation, or unreasonably interferes with job performance), and unwelcomed. The aforementioned definitions are based on federal laws, and states may have additional criteria in accordance with state labor code. Employers can be held liable for harassment and hostile work environments if they did not take reasonable and proper steps to prevent the treatment from occurring. This is where the district HR office can be useful in providing the necessary policies and protocols in place to help protect employees from illegal treatment.

Discussion Questions: Research has suggested that teachers of color often disproportionately receive lower ratings and this phenomenon is also reflected in your school (see e.g. Kraft & Gilmour, 2017). As a result, your assistant principal tends to inflate the ratings of underperforming teachers of color. Is this ethical? Why or why not? If not, how would you handle the situation?

PRINCIPAL EVALUATION

While the research base for principal evaluation is more limited than for teacher evaluation, there is overlap in the key findings. For example, as for teachers, student and principal demographics have been correlated to principal ratings (Grissom et al., 2018; Herrmann & Ross, 2016). Because the influence of principals on student learning is largely indirect, disentangling the contextual factors from the principal's performance is particularly complex, yet critical, in principal evaluations.

As with teachers, principals need to trust both the evaluation process and their evaluator if they are to accept their evaluation feedback. Relatedly, not all principals modify their work in accordance with their evaluation feedback, and this affects improvement efforts post-evaluation (Emstad, 2011). Effective two-way communication between the principal and the evaluator can be helpful, not only with building trust but with establishing common views and perspectives about the role of the principal and the purpose of evaluation given that principals and superintendents often have differing perspectives on the matter (Sun & Youngs, 2009). As echoed throughout this book, developing and sustaining a strong partnership between school and district leadership can yield more productive outcomes for school improvement.

CONCLUSION

While performance evaluations can serve the dual purposes of accountability and professional growth, one often takes precedence over the other. Weighting the focus of evaluation systems more heavily on collaboration for professional growth is consistent with a Talent-Centered Education Leadership approach to strategic talent management and has the potential to pay dividends in terms of increased teacher buy-in and acceptance/utility of performance feedback. This is especially beneficial because the performance of teachers who work at schools that promote collaboration and support improves more over time than of teachers who lack that supportive structure (Kraft & Papay, 2014).

Principals should understand that the evaluation process is a means to an end, not the end itself. Especially from a developmental perspective, the ultimate goal of the process should be to improve student learning. As demonstrated from past research findings (Steinberg & Sartain, 2015; Taylor & Tyler, 2012), teacher evaluations can be a tool to help improve teacher performance. However, to have the desired impact, the evaluations themselves have to be useful and trusted by those being evaluated.

Summary of Key Points

- If used strategically, evaluation can provide an opportunity for the school or district to develop a clear shared definition of good teaching and provide guidance to help teachers achieve that vision.
- The teacher evaluation system has historically not achieved effective accountability or promoted professional growth in the classroom. In many schools, evaluation was sporadic for many teachers.
- The best evaluation systems rely on multiple methods for assessing teacher performance. Three common methods are value-added models (based on student test scores), teacher observations, and student learning objectives.
- Many employees respond poorly to performance feedback; researchers suggest that performance feedback should be framed from a strengths-based perspective.
- Performance evaluations and employee conversations about performance should be well-documented. When an employee's performance is so poor that it cannot be remedied, the documentation should include clear indication that due process has been followed before progressing with the release of the employee from the district.

NOTE

1 *ESSA* is the reauthorization of *the Elementary and Secondary Education* Act.

REFERENCES

Adnot, M., Dee, T., Katz, V., & Wyckoff, J. (2017). Teacher turnover, teacher quality, and student achievement in DCPS. *Educational Evaluation and Policy Analysis, 39*(1), 54–76.

Aguinis, H., Gottfredson, R. K., & Joo, H. (2012). Delivering effective performance feedback: The strengths-based approach. *Business Horizons, 55*(2), 105–111.

American Statistical Association. (2014). *ASA statement on using value-added models for educational assessment.* http://www.amstat.org/policy/pdfs/ASA_VAM_Statement.pdf

Baker, E. L., Barton, P. E., Darling-Hammond, L., Haertel, E., Ladd, H. F., Linn, R. L., Ravitch, D., Rothstein, R., Shavelson, R., & Shepard, L. A. (2010). *Problems with the use of student test scores to evaluate teachers* (EPI Briefing Paper# 278). Economic Policy Institute.

Board on Testing and Assessment, Division of Behavioral and Social Sciences and Education, National Academy of Sciences (BOTA) (2009). *Letter report to the U.S. Department of Education on the Race to the Top Fund.* Retrieved August 4, 2019 from http://books.nap.edu/openbook.php?record_id=12780&page=1

Bryk, A., & Schneider, B. (2002). *Trust in schools: A core resource for improvement.* Russell Sage Foundation.

Campbell, S. L., & Ronfeldt, M. (2018). Observational evaluation of teachers: Measuring more than we bargained for? *American Educational Research Journal, 55*(6), 1233–1267.

Cantor, D. (2018a). Investigation: New records reveal what it takes to be one of the 75 NYC teachers fired for misconduct or incompetence between 2015 and 2016. *The 74.* www.the74million.org/article/investigation-nyc-tried-to-fire-154-teachers-for-incompetence-or-misconduct-75-were/

Cantor, D. (2018b). Investigation: Overshadowed by shocking abuse and misconduct cases, teacher incompetence often harms New York City's poorest students. *The 74.* www.the74million.org/article/investigation-teacher-incompetence-often-harms-new-york-city-poorest-students/

Chetty, R., Friedman, J. N., & Rockoff, J. E. (2014). Measuring the impacts of teachers II: Teacher value-added and student outcomes in adulthood. *American Economic Review, 104*(9), 2633–2679.

Danielson, C. (2007). *Enhancing professional practice: A framework for teaching.* ASCD.

Dee, T. S., & Wyckoff, J. (2015). Incentives, selection, and teacher performance: Evidence from IMPACT. *Journal of Policy Analysis and Management, 34*(2), 267–297.

Derrington, M. L., & Campbell, J. W. (2018). Teacher evaluation policy tools: Principals' selective use in instructional leadership. *Leadership and Policy in Schools, 17*(4), 568–590.

Doherty, K. M., & Jacobs, S. (2015). State of the states 2015: Evaluating teaching, leading and learning. *National Council on Teacher Quality.* www.nctq.org/dmsView/StateofStates2015

Donaldson, M. L., & Woulfin, S. (2018). From tinkering to going "rogue": How principals use agency when enacting new teacher evaluation systems. *Educational Evaluation and Policy Analysis, 40*(4), 531–556.

Education Next. (2018). *2018 EdNext poll interactive.* www.educationnext.org/2018-ednext-poll-interactive/

Emstad, A. B. (2011). The principal's role in the post-evaluation process. How does the principal engage in the work carried out after the schools self-evaluation? *Educational Assessment, Evaluation and Accountability, 23*(4), 271–288.

Ford, T. G., Urick, A., & Wilson, A. S. (2018). Exploring the effect of supportive teacher evaluation experiences on US teachers' job satisfaction. *Education Policy Analysis Archives, 26*, 59.

Gallagher, H. A. (2004). Vaughn elementary's innovative teacher evaluation system: Are teacher evaluation scores related to growth in student achievement? *Peabody Journal of Education, 79*(4), 79–107.

Griffith, D., & McDougald, V. (2016). *Undue process: Why bad teachers in twenty-five diverse districts rarely get fired*. Thomas B. Fordham Institute.

Grissom, J. A., & Bartanen, B. (2019). Strategic retention: Principal effectiveness and teacher turnover in multiple-measure teacher evaluation systems. *American Educational Research Journal, 56*(2), 514–555.

Grissom, J. A., Blissett, R. S., & Mitani, H. (2018). Evaluating school principals: Supervisor ratings of principal practice and principal job performance. *Educational Evaluation and Policy Analysis, 40*(3), 446–472.

Grissom, J. A., & Loeb, S. (2017). Assessing principals' assessments: Subjective evaluations of teacher effectiveness in low-and high-stakes environments. *Education Finance and Policy, 12*(3), 369–395.

Halverson, R., Kelley, C., & Kimball, S. (2004). Implementing teacher evaluation systems: How principals make sense of complex artifacts to shape local instructional practice. In W. K. Hoy & C. G. Miskel (Eds.), *Educational administration, policy, and reform: Research and measurement* (pp. 153–188). Information Age Publishing.

Hazi, H. M. (2017). VAM under scrutiny: Teacher evaluation litigation in the states. *The Clearing House: A Journal of Educational Strategies, Issues and Ideas, 90*(5–6), 184–190.

Herrmann, M., & Ross, C. (2016). *Measuring principals' effectiveness: Results from New Jersey's first year of statewide principal evaluation* (No. 5f9c12f1d7404636aaf2e98e5abfaf6f). Mathematica Policy Research.

Jackson, C. K., & Bruegmann, E. (2009). Teaching students and teaching each other: The importance of peer learning for teachers. *American Economic Journal: Applied Economics, 1*(4), 85–108.

Jacob, B. A., & Lefgren, L. (2008). Can principals identify effective teachers? Evidence on subjective performance evaluation in education. *Journal of Labor Economics, 26*(1), 101–136.

Kelley, C. (1999). National board for professional teaching standards: Accomplished teaching through national board certification. *Teaching and Change, 6*(4), 339–345.

Kelley, C. (2000). *Douglas County Colorado performance pay plan*. Consortium for Policy Research in Education, Wisconsin Center for Education Research, University of Wisconsin, Madison.

Kluger, A. N., & DeNisi, A. (1998). Feedback interventions: Toward the understanding of a double-edged sword. *Current Directions in Psychological Science, 7*(3), 67–72.

Koedel, C., Li, J., Springer, M. G., & Tan, L. (2017). The impact of performance ratings on job satisfaction for public school teachers. *American Educational Research Journal, 54*(2), 241–278.

Kraft, M. A., & Gilmour, A. F. (2017). Revisiting the widget effect: Teacher evaluation reforms and the distribution of teacher effectiveness. *Educational Researcher, 46*(5), 234–249.

Kraft, M. A., & Papay, J. P. (2014). Can professional environments in schools promote teacher development? Explaining heterogeneity in returns to teaching experience. *Educational Evaluation and Policy Analysis, 36*(4), 476–500.

Leis, M., & Rimm-Kaufman, S. E. (2015). Principal actions related to increases in teacher-principal trust. *Journal of School Public Relations, 36*(3).

Looney, J. (2014). *Personnel administrators academy.* Association of California School Administrators.

Marsh, J. A., Bush-Mecenas, S., Strunk, K. O., Lincove, J. A., & Huguet, A. (2017). Evaluating teachers in the big easy: How organizational context shapes policy responses in New Orleans. *Educational Evaluation and Policy Analysis, 39,* 539–570.

Maslow, V. J., & Kelley, C. J. (2012). Does evaluation advance teaching practice? The effects of performance evaluation on teaching quality and system change in large diverse high schools. *Journal of School Leadership, 22*(3), 600–632.

Meyer, R. H. (1997). Value-added indicators of school performance: A primer. *Economics of Education Review, 16*(3), 283–301.

Milanowski, A. (2004). The relationship between teacher performance evaluation scores and student achievement: Evidence from Cincinnati. *Peabody Journal of Education, 79*(4), 33–53.

Milanowski, A. (2017). Lower performance evaluation practice ratings for teachers of disadvantaged students: Bias or reflection of reality? *AERA Open, 3*(1).

National Council on Teacher Quality. (2019). Teacher & principal evaluation policy. *National Council on Teacher Quality. State of the States 2019.* www.nctq.org/pages/State-of-the-States-2019:-Teacher-and-Principal-Evaluation-Policy

Nelson, B. S., & Sassi, A. (2000). Shifting approaches to supervision: The case of mathematics supervision. *Educational Administration Quarterly, 36*(4), 553–584.

Neumerski, C. M., Grissom, J. A., Goldring, E., Rubin, M., Cannata, M., Schuermann, P., & Drake, T. A. (2018). Restructuring instructional leadership: How multiple-measure teacher evaluation systems are redefining the role of the school principal. *The Elementary School Journal, 119*(2), 270–297.

Papay, J. P., Murnane, R. J., & Willett, J. B. (2016). The impact of test score labels on human-capital investment decisions. *Journal of Human Resources, 51*(2), 357–388.

Pressley, T., Roehrig, A. D., & Turner, J. E. (2018). Elementary teachers' perceptions of a reformed teacher-evaluation system. *The Teacher Educator, 53*(1), 21–43.

Reid, D. B. (2018). How schools train principals to use new teacher evaluation systems: A comparative case study of charter school and traditional public school principals. *Journal of School Choice, 12*(2), 237–253.

Reinhorn, S. K., & Johnson, S. M. (2014). *Can evaluation provide both accountability and development for teachers? Evidence from six high-poverty schools.* Project on the Next Generation of Teachers, Harvard University. Retrieved March 3, 2017, from https://projectngt.gse.harvard.edu/

Rockoff, J. E., Staiger, D. O., Kane, T. J., & Taylor, E. S. (2012). Information and employee evaluation: Evidence from a randomized intervention in public schools. *American Economic Review, 102*(7), 3184–3213.

Sartain, L., & Steinberg, M. P. (2016). Teachers' labor market responses to performance evaluation reform: Experimental evidence from Chicago public schools. *Journal of Human Resources, 51*(3), 615–655.

Sartain, L., Stoelinga, S. R., Brown, E. R., Matsko, K. K., Miller, F. K., Durwood, C. E., & Glazer, D. (2011). Rethinking teacher evaluation in Chicago. *Chicago: Consortium on Chicago School Research.* http://evaluation.ccsd59.org/D59_Evaluation_Page/Resources_for_the_Plan_files/Rethinking%20Teacher%20Evaluation%20in%20Chicago.pdf

Schochet, P. Z., & Chiang, H. S. (2010). *Error rates in measuring teacher and school performance based on student test score gains* (NCEE 2010–4004). National Center for Education Evaluation and Regional Assistance.

Shields, P. M., Humphrey, D. C., Wechsler, M. E., Riel, L. M., Tiffany-Morales, J., & Woodworth, K. (2001). *The status of the teaching profession.* CA Center for the Future of Teaching and Learning.

Steinberg, M. P., & Garrett, R. (2016). Classroom composition and measured teacher performance: What do teacher observation scores really measure? *Educational Evaluation and Policy Analysis, 38*(2), 293–317.

Steinberg, M. P., & Sartain, L. (2015). Does better observation make better teachers: New evidence from a teacher evaluation pilot in Chicago. *Education Next, 15*(1), 71–77.

Sun, M., & Youngs, P. (2009). How does district principal evaluation affect learning-centered principal leadership? Evidence from Michigan school districts. *Leadership and Policy in Schools, 8*(4), 411–445.

Taylor, E. S., & Tyler, J. H. (2012). Can teacher evaluation improve teaching. *Education Next, 12*(4), 78–84.

Tran, H., & Bon, S. C. (2015). Assessing multiple stakeholders' perceptions of an effective principal evaluation system. *Education Leadership Review, 16*(2), 1–18.

Tschannen-Moran, M., & Gareis, C. R. (2015). Faculty trust in the principal: An essential ingredient in high-performing schools. *Journal of Educational Administration, 53*(1), 66–92.

U.S. Equal Employment Opportunity Commission. (n.d.). *Harassment.* www.eeoc.gov/laws/types/harassment.cfm

Walsh, K., Joseph, N., Lakis, K., & Lubell, S. (2017). *Running in place: How new teacher evaluations fail to live up to promises.* National Council on Teacher Quality.

Weisberg, D., Sexton, S., Mulhern, J., Keeling, D., Schunck, J., Palcisco, A., & Morgan, K. (2009). *The widget effect: Our national failure to acknowledge and act on differences in teacher effectiveness.* New Teacher Project.

Williamson, A. (2018). NYC opt out wants students to say 'no!' to state exams. State exam opponents are concerned that standardized tests do not adequately gauge student performance and are used to penalize under-performing schools. *BKReader.* www.bkreader.com/2018/11/16/nyc-opt-out-wants-students-to-say-no-to-state-exams/

Young, I. P. (2008). *The human resource function in educational administration* (9th ed.). Pearson Merrill/Prentice Hall.

CHAPTER 10

Teacher Leadership Development

Chapter Summary

This chapter highlights the importance of the leadership development of teachers. Teaching is the core technology of schools, and the expertise of teachers needs to be developed, respected, and leveraged to support instructional improvement and school-level decision-making. Opportunities for teacher leadership promote engagement and job satisfaction throughout the teaching career, but these opportunities need to be supported by professional development and structured time to complete the leadership tasks. This chapter examines the role of the principal in supporting the growth and development of teacher leaders and in leveraging teacher expertise to support school-level decision-making. The chapter draws on research, practice, and theory to illuminate the important role that principal leadership practices play in supporting teacher leadership. The chapter also provides a case study and discussion questions for readers to consider.

> *Effective leaders develop the capacity, opportunities, and support for teacher leadership and leadership from other members of the school community.*
>
> (PSEL Standard 6g)

INTRODUCTION

Teacher leadership is a hallmark of Talent-Centered Education Leadership because it involves recognizing and building on the talents of individual teachers

DOI: 10.4324/9781003457060-13

to promote the success of the school. In a comprehensive review of the research literature on teacher leadership, Wenner and Campbell (2017) define teacher leaders as "*teachers who maintain K–12 classroom-based teaching responsibilities, while also taking on leadership responsibilities outside of the classroom*" (p. 140, emphasis in original). Consistent with distributed leadership theory (Spillane et al., 2004; Spillane, 2012), teacher leaders may occupy formal leadership positions (e.g., instructional coach, mentor, department chair, or team lead), or they may act as informal leaders, carrying out leadership tasks that advance the mission of the school or district without the formal recognition of a title.

Teacher leadership can promote organizational effectiveness and can also be an important motivational tool to enhance teacher engagement and reduce turnover, as it provides opportunities for professional growth throughout the teaching career. Evidence of its importance can be seen in the growing number of master's degree programs targeted towards strengthening the leadership of classroom teachers; in the development and adoption of state teacher leadership standards (Diffey & Aragon, 2018); in state teacher evaluation models, the Danielson Framework for Teaching, the National Board for Professional Teaching Standards, and the National Education Association's Teacher Leadership Institute, to name a few (Berry, 2019; Wenner & Campbell, 2017).

Teacher leadership has been shown to have impacts on the teacher leader, their colleagues, and students (Ingersoll et al., 2018). Positive impacts include psychological benefits, such as the sense of empowerment that comes with better understanding and contributing to decisions that affect the whole school, and the growth and learning of teachers themselves that can result in improvements in their instructional practice. Further, teacher leadership is an important resource for teacher collaboration, as teacher leaders are needed to guide and facilitate conversations about practice among teachers. However, leadership roles can sometimes upset the power balance between teachers, resulting in conflict or tension between teachers and teacher leaders. The principal can play an important role in mitigating this conflict by clearly establishing and defining roles and expectations and by working to create a culture in which teacher leadership is recognized and embraced (Kelley & Salisbury, 2013; Printy & Marks, 2006; Wenner & Campbell, 2017; York-Barr & Duke, 2004). Teacher leadership has been shown to increase the rate of teacher learning, strengthen instructional practice among teachers in the school, and strengthen teacher empowerment and collective responsibility for students (Wenner & Campbell, 2017; York-Barr & Duke, 2004). In addition, high levels of instructional leadership from teachers have been found to be correlated with higher math and English language arts test scores compared to comparable schools with lower levels of teacher leadership (Ingersoll et al., 2017). The focus of teacher leadership matters as well. For example, teacher participation in decision-making about discipline and school improvement planning has the strongest relationship to improved student achievement, but few schools leverage teacher leadership for decision-making around these areas (Ingersoll et al., 2018).

From a succession-planning perspective, teacher leadership has also historically been an important source of training to provide a pipeline for future administrators (Gordon, 2020). Leadership in teacher unions, mentoring, curriculum development, and facilitation of colleague conversations, for example, provide an important training ground for principals, assistant principals, and district office leaders. In sum, teacher leadership yields many potential benefits to the organization and its stakeholders.

DISTRIBUTED LEADERSHIP THEORY

Distributed leadership provides a useful theoretical lens to view teacher leadership. In a distributed leadership model, leadership is spread across many individuals in a school organization. Teacher leadership matters because it is carried out by many actors across the school. As subject-matter experts and individuals who have direct contact with administrators, students, and parents, teachers have a wealth of knowledge and connections that make them uniquely situated to provide leadership in their interactions with others throughout the school organization.

The distributed leadership perspective defines leadership as a product of the interaction between leaders, followers, and their situation. Activity theory is foundational to distributed leadership theory in that the important measure of leadership is practices that emerge from interactions between leaders and followers. Using a lens of leadership as practice, rather than leadership as a formal role, sheds light on a broad array of leadership practices carried out by actors across the school who provide leadership to help move the school forward (Harris & Spillane, 2008; Spillane, 2005, 2012; Spillane et al., 2004).

Through tools, routines, and structures, leadership is enacted to help moderate action. Spillane (2005) explains:

> Tools include everything from student assessment data to protocols for evaluating teachers. . . . Structures include routines such as grade-level meetings and the scheduling of teachers' prep periods. From a distributed perspective, these routines, tools, and structures define leadership practice; the situation both enables and constrains leadership practice.
>
> (p. 147)

Thinking about leadership this way frees you from having to think of leadership as simply vested in formal leadership roles. It enables attention to the teacher who steps up and offers to lead professional development around a new math curriculum. It enables attention to the staff member who works with colleagues to redesign the attendance system so teachers can keep better track of student attendance and the department chair who uses the resulting attendance data to propose a system for addressing chronic student absences. And it highlights the contributions of teacher teams who build communities of practice to improve teaching and learning in the school. The principal's role, then, becomes one of working with teachers and staff to build a shared direction for the school, defining and supporting critical leadership practices, and developing and supporting the use of tools, routines, and structures that facilitate leadership practice and help the school move forward. It also involves encouraging and building the leadership capacity of teachers, staff, and students so they can draw on these skills as the need arises (Halverson & Kelley, 2017).

THE PRINCIPAL'S ROLE IN DEVELOPING TEACHER LEADERSHIP

The principal plays an important role in fostering teacher leadership and establishing the conditions for teacher leaders to succeed (Wenner & Campbell, 2017). Some aspects of the principal's role include:

- *Building a shared vision for the school*: Distributed leadership theory posits that leadership is stretched across the organization, and teachers, like others, can emerge as leaders by carrying out the tasks of leadership that are essential to the effective functioning of the school. Because distributed leadership establishes leadership as highly decentralized and shared across many actors, the principal needs to ensure that the many actors working to support the school's direction are working together in a unified direction. In this way, the principal acts as the conductor of the symphony, who helps to build a shared vision and works to align individual actors to produce harmony in a shared direction (Halverson & Kelley, 2017; Muijs & Harris, 2006; Wenner & Campbell, 2017).
- *Establishing structures that support teacher collaboration*: An important aspect of teacher leadership is the teacher leader's ability to facilitate meaningful conversations about practice among teachers. The principal plays an important role in establishing a culture that supports such shared work by providing time (e.g., course release) and space for teachers to meet and work together (Halverson & Kelley, 2017; Wenner & Campbell, 2017).
- *Defining leadership expectations*: Principals lead efforts to clearly define teacher leadership roles and build a shared understanding of the expectations for teacher leaders and their collaborators in the school. The role definition needs to include a clear statement about what leadership tasks the teacher will take on and what tasks will be eliminated to enable teachers to take on these new tasks (Kelley & Salisbury, 2013; Wenner & Campbell, 2017).
- *Selecting leaders*: For more formal leadership roles, the principal also needs to carefully select teachers who are respected by their colleagues, have strong instructional expertise, and are willing to take on the leadership role (Kelley & Salisbury, 2013).

- *Promoting a supportive culture*: Finally, the principal needs to work to promote a culture of trust and support, in which teachers are willing to share problems of practice and work collaboratively to solve them (Muijs & Harris, 2006).

TEACHER LEADERSHIP AND TEACHER UNIONS

Active participation and leadership in the teacher union can provide an important training ground for teachers in building leadership skills. Both of the major national teachers unions recognize the importance of teacher leadership to well-functioning schools and the profession, and they provide training opportunities to support the development of teacher leaders (National Education Association, National Board for Professional Teaching Standards, and the Center for Teaching Quality, 2018; Vitucci & Brown, 2019).

Teacher union contracts may have provisions relating to compensation for leadership and the allocation of time to leadership activities, so principals should be aware of contract provisions in establishing opportunities for teacher leadership roles.

THE ROLE OF DEPARTMENT CHAIR AS INSTRUCTIONAL LEADER

The department chair role is a particularly interesting focus for leadership development as part of a strategic human resources management strategy. Department chairs are subject experts situated between the principal and classroom teachers. They have the potential to provide an important source of support for ongoing professional growth for themselves and their colleagues, and they provide an important perspective that needs to be represented in school-level decision-making. Furthermore, the leadership role of department chair is an important training ground for administrative positions.

Despite these strategic advantages, the department chair role is typically vaguely defined and underutilized, and department chairs rarely receive training for their roles. They serve both administrators and teachers, in a mix of administrative and human relations functions (Weller, 2001). Research on department chairs has shown that when they focus on instruction and learning, the result is improved classroom instruction and achievement in their departments (Harris, 2003). But research by Weller (2001) found that typical chair roles do not focus on instructional leadership but instead involve channeling information, scheduling classes, completing routine reports, coordinating programs, and enforcing rules. A challenge to shifting the chair's role towards instructional leadership is determining what other activities will be taken off the chair's plate or how the chair will be given time to perform the additional instructional leadership roles.

As part of its work to develop a pipeline to the principalship, the Wallace Foundation supported an initiative to strengthen the role of department chairs as instructional leaders in high schools (see Bredeson, 2013; Kelley & Salisbury, 2013; Klar, 2012). The case study in Box 10.1 explores how one of these high schools redesigned its department chair role to be an instructional leader.

BOX 10.1: CASE EXAMPLE: THE PRINCIPAL'S ROLE IN REFRAMING THE DEPARTMENT CHAIR AS INSTRUCTIONAL LEADER

Juan Garcia was in his second year as principal of Pennant Hills, a diverse urban high school with approximately 2,000 students. Garcia agreed to participate in a research/practice partnership focused on building the instructional leadership capacity of urban high schools as a possible pipeline for the high school principalship. The Pennant Hills culture had evolved to have power centralized in the principalship, with teachers working in silos, largely independent from one another. Subject-area department chairs were appointed based on seniority and served in an administrative function: passing communication on from the principal to the teachers in their department, coordinating class schedules, managing their department's budget, and, as needed, serving as the subject-matter liaison to district curriculum initiatives. However, the chairs were not viewed as instructional leaders, and other than their administrative roles and sometimes their longer history with the school, colleagues viewed them as peers.

As a result of a grant competition that the district had applied for and won, Garcia agreed to undertake a year-long process of transitioning the department chairs from a managerial role (e.g., coordinating teaching schedules, approving departmental purchases, relaying communications from the principal) to an instructional leadership role (e.g., facilitating discussions about student work, planning curriculum, analyzing student learning data, supporting instructional improvement). The school would get a small amount of funds that they used to pay for two department chair retreats and to update a meeting room that they planned to use for the team meetings.

Through the course of the year, the principal designed monthly department chair meetings to build the capacity of the leadership team and to redefine the role of the department chair as an instructional leader. Key strategies included careful crafting of meeting agendas to build trust, modeling effective leadership behaviors, establishing shared goals for student learning, building a personal vision and a shared vision for the school, formally redefining the department chair role to be an instructional leader, and providing opportunities for the chairs to practice instructional leadership skills with one another. These activities were designed in skill development loops, with open communication with the chairs to capture their concerns about skills they would need to be successful, revisiting areas needing further development, commitment, understanding, and experience.

Garcia felt a critical element of the plan was the individual meetings he held with each department chair in early January to confirm their understanding of the newly defined role and to confirm their commitment to taking on the new role. Garcia talked through the changes with each chair, asked them to make sure they wanted to take on the new role, and gave them a commitment sheet to sign after they thought it over. All but one department chair agreed that they wanted to continue as chair and serve in the newly revised role.

A challenge planned for early in the second year was to share the redefined role of department chair with the full staff, with an effort to make sure that the whole school understood the redefined role. Providing this support to back the chairs as they made the role transition was critical to them being accepted in the new role.

The journey from department chair as manager to department chair as instructional leader was transformational. It would be difficult to fully capture the difference between the energy and engagement of the chairs at the beginning and end of the year, but some key differences were the level of trust and community among the chairs; their willingness to turn to one another to solve problems; and their commitment to practicing effective instructional leadership behaviors.

Source: Adapted from Kelley and Salisbury (2013)

Discussion Questions: How are department chairs selected in your school? In what ways do the activities described scaffold the change process for department chairs to re-vision their role as instructional leaders? What challenges do you foresee? How would you work to overcome those challenges? Please rationalize and justify your response based on ethical, legal, professional, and/or leadership frameworks.

Learning Activities

Discussion Questions:

1. Who exercises leadership in your school? When is teacher leadership exercised, and what is the focus of the leadership? Is that the right mix? What should teacher leadership focus on?
2. How can a principal support the exercise of teacher leadership? What kinds of training do teachers need to take on leadership roles? What other supports are important?

3. One of the concerns that some teachers express is that they don't have time to take on additional leadership responsibility. How can the principal help to mitigate this challenge to teacher leadership efforts?
4. Teacher leadership provides an opportunity to empower a broader diversity of voices in leadership. Why is this diversity important, and how can the diversity in leadership be broadened?

CONCLUSION

Teacher leadership development is an important Talent-Centered Education Leadership practice, and principals need to recognize and develop the talents of their teachers and staff as a core strategy in promoting the success of their schools. Teacher leadership provides important psychological benefits for the teacher including teacher empowerment, contributes to better decision-making for the school by incorporating teacher perspectives, and promotes collective responsibility for students. Building teacher leadership skills strengthens leadership capacity and school effectiveness in a distributed leadership system. Returning to the themes of earlier chapters, teacher leadership can increase teacher satisfaction and reduce turnover; it can enhance teacher collaboration and professional learning communities, and it provides an important training ground for the development of future administrators.

Summary of Key Points

- Teacher leaders are teachers who take on leadership responsibilities outside the classroom while retaining their classroom teacher role.
- Teacher leadership can conflict with norms of equality among teachers if there is not a clear shared understanding that teacher leaders are expected to perform a leadership role; the principal can provide substantial leadership support to build shared understanding and support for teachers taking on leadership roles.
- Distributed leadership can be a useful lens for considering teacher leadership, as it focuses on leadership practices that are carried out by many different individuals rather than focusing on formal administrative or leadership roles.
- The department chair is one of the most underutilized leadership roles in schools; redefining the department chair as instructional leader can leverage the significant experience and subject expertise of chairs to support school improvement.
- Because distributed leadership involves many actors across the school, it is even more important for the principal to work with the school community to build shared language, common understandings, and a shared vision for the future so that many actors carrying out leadership practices can continue to support the school moving forward in the same direction together.

REFERENCES

Berry, B. (2019). Teacher leadership: Prospects and promises. *Phi Delta Kappan*, 49–55. https://journals.sagepub.com/doi/pdf/10.1177/0031721719841339

Bredeson, P. V. (2013). Distributed instructional leadership in urban high schools: Transforming the work of principals and department chairs through professional development. *Journal of School Leadership, 23*(2), 362–388.

Diffey, L., & Aragon, S. (2018). *50-state comparison: Teacher leadership and licensure advancement*. Education Commission of the States.

Gordon, S. P. (2020). The principal development pipeline: A call for collaboration. *NASSP Bulletin, 104*(2), 61–84.

Halverson, R., & Kelley, C. (2017). *Mapping leadership: The tasks that matter for improving teaching and learning in schools*. Jossey-Bass.

Harris, A. (2003). Teacher leadership as distributed leadership: Heresy, fantasy or possibility? *School Leadership & Management, 23*(3), 313–324.

Harris, A., & Spillane, J. (2008). Distributed leadership through the looking glass. *Management in Education, 22*(1), 31–34.

Ingersoll, R., Sirinides, P., & Doughtery, R. (2017). *School leadership: Teachers' roles in school decision-making, and student achievement*. Consortium for Policy Research in Education.

Ingersoll, R., Sirinides, P., & Doughtery, R. (2018). Leadership matters: Teachers' roles in school decision making and school performance. *American Educator*, 13–17, 39.

Kelley, C., & Salisbury, J. (2013). Defining and activating the role of department chair as instructional leader. *Journal of School Leadership, 23*(2), 287–323.

Klar, H. W. (2012). Fostering department chair instructional leadership capacity: Laying the groundwork for distributed instructional leadership. *International Journal of Leadership in Education, 15*(2), 175–197.

Muijs, D., & Harris, A. (2006). Teacher led school improvement: Teacher leadership in the UK. *Teaching and Teacher Education, 22*(8), 961–972.

National Education Association, National Board for Professional Teaching Standards, and the Center for Teaching Quality. (2018). *The teacher leadership competencies*. National Education Association.

Printy, S. M., & Marks, H. M. (2006). Shared leadership for teacher and student learning. *Theory into Practice, 45*(2), 125–132.

Spillane, J. P. (2005, June). Distributed leadership. In *The educational forum* (Vol. 69, No. 2, pp. 143–150). Taylor & Francis Group.

Spillane, J. P. (2012). *Distributed leadership* (Vol. 4). John Wiley & Sons.

Spillane, J., Halverson, R., & Diamond, J. (2004). Towards a theory of leadership practice: A distributed perspective. *Journal of Curriculum Studies, 36*(1), 3–34.

Vitucci, R., & Brown, M. (2019). Cultivating teacher leaders: A union-led effort connects classroom practice to education policy. *American Educator* (Spring), 4–11.

Weller Jr, L. D. (2001). Department heads: The most underutilized leadership position. *NASSP Bulletin, 85*(625), 73–81.

Wenner, J. A., & Campbell, T. (2017). The theoretical and empirical basis of teacher leadership: A review of the literature. *Review of Educational Research, 87*(1), 134–171.

York-Barr, J., & Duke, K. (2004). What do we know about teacher leadership? Findings from two decades of scholarship. *Review of Educational Research, 74*(3), 255–316.

Index